# Virginia's Diary

*Based on a true story*

Suzanne Peyton

Tree House Books

This body of work is based on a true story. Some of the names and locations have been changed to protect the innocent.

Revised Edition 2019

Copyright@2015 by Jacquelyn Suzanne Peyton
Cover design: Suzanne Peyton and Jodi Breckenridge
Back cover photograph by Susie Malloy

ISBN: 978-0-578-49341-1


PRINTED IN THE UNITED STATES OF AMERICA

When I was four-years old, my cat, *Blackie,* ran in front of a car and I thought he had been hit, even though he was still able to run under our house. In trying to console me, my Father told me not to worry; cats had nine lives. I will never forget the look on his face when I asked, "How many lives do people have?" Thank you, Daddy, for simply walking away, and not trying to come up with an answer for your always inquisitive, young daughter. This book is dedicated to you.

Matthew 17:10-13 (NIV)

The disciples asked Him, "Why then do the teachers of the law say that Elijah must come first?"
Jesus replied, "To be sure, Elijah comes and will restore all things. But I tell you, Elijah has already come, and *they did not recognize him,* (Italics mine) but have done to him everything they wished. In the same way the Son of Man is going to suffer at their hands.

Then the disciples understood that he was talking to them about John the Baptist.

# Acknowledgements

The journey that produced this body of work all began with what seemed like a short, but very detailed dream. I thank God for revealing to me that it was so much more than that. I, along with others, would witness things that were nothing short of a miracle, as He led me to uncover the truth of what really happened so many years ago.

My sister was the first person I told after awakening from the dream and she walked that early path with me and I will be forever grateful for her belief in what we were discovering.

As things progressed, my children and grandchildren, encouraged me to continue on even when the path twisted and turned in ways I would never expect. I love you all immensely.

Time moved on and two witnesses showed up; Cindy Ford and Jan Ragland. The shock I saw on their faces as we discovered the *'buried truth'* mirrored my own. Then God began to bring people onboard that supported me in so many ways. Judy Covey, Sue Lewis, Patti Christmas, Jan Quinn, Pam Fisher, Judy Denny, Grace Christmas, Marchele Maranto, Laura Shurtleff, and our guy Jim Williams, just to name a few. So many came with such big hearts and shared my belief that what we were witnessing could not be orchestrated by anyone but God.

All of you allowed me to stand on your shoulders so that I never lost sight of the goal of getting this story out there. I thank you from the bottom of my heart.

# *Virginia's Diary*

# Chapter 1

*They will come back, come back again, as long as the red earth rolls. He never wasted a leaf or tree.  Do you think He would squander souls?*
*-Rudyard Kipling*

*Virginia*
*1958*

The doctor told me this morning that it won't be long now.  He knows I demand honesty.  I told him the day they admitted me, I would not tolerate hand-holding lies about my condition or the time I have left.  I had been diagnosed with cancer of the uterus before I left California, and the doctor there told me, at best, I had a year left.  It was ironic; the very organ that had given me the children who hated me would be the part of my body to kill me.  Maybe it was meant to be this way; the final payment for my sins.  But, it was still the lies I couldn't or wouldn't tolerate now.  They have ruined my life.

At the age of twenty-one, I was sent to Texas to meet my parents.  Well, not so much meet them, I had vague memories of them when we had all lived with my grandparent's in New Orleans. I had only been four-years old the last time I had seen their faces.  My aging Grandparent's believed it was in my best interest, since they were getting up in age, to reacquaint myself with them.   So, when the request came from my parents wanting me to come for my younger sister's funeral, Grandmother Abby saw it as good a reason as any to send me to Texas.

My grandmother knew her other daughters, my mother's sisters, had always envied me. They believed since I was the baby of the household, I received preferential treatment.   Because of their feeling towards me, Grandmother Abby thought it best if I had other alternatives. She had no idea what laid in wait for me in Texas, none of us could have.  By the time she found out what they had done to me, it was too late.  She, nor I, would ever get over it and both of us would take it to our graves.

Even though I had not seen my mother or father in seventeen years, my vile father felt he had the right to arrange my marriage. Andrew wasn't Catholic, but that was the least of it. I had never known such repulsiveness then or since, but my voice didn't matter. Grandfather refused to attend the wedding, so Grandmother Abby came alone. Andrew knew I couldn't or wouldn't lie to her, so he did it for me. I stood beside him and listened as he weaved the web of deception so tightly around all of us, trapping me forever with his words. I wanted to scream as I listened to him promise her that he would take care of me. I desperately wanted to tell her not to listen, that it was all lies, and beg her to take me back home with her to New Orleans, the only home I had ever known. Besides, would she have believed that her own daughter, my mother, could be a party to this?

I stood beside Andrew and listened as the lies flowed so smoothly from his lips. How long had he and my father rehearsed this scene? I admit, it never occurred to me then that someone that could be that seasoned at telling falsehoods must have done so all their life to be as accomplished in his craft as he was. By the time he was through with me, he would have taken everything that meant anything away from me by the same means.

I had only gone back to that God forsaken place to try to make peace with the only ones who were left, and the only ones that mattered; my children. My late husband, Walt, had tried to tell me it would be a mistake, but I wouldn't listen. He said all the lies were truth to them and that I needed to let it go, but I couldn't. I knew Walt could never fully understand because I had never told him the whole truth. After he died, and I was diagnosed with cancer, I settled the estate in San Francisco and boarded a train for the last time. I was going back to do what I had tried to do for the better part of the last fifty years; set my children straight and set myself free from the guilt and pain. The guilt has been my constant companion. I only wanted the chance to tell my children the truth about what really happened so many years ago. I stayed away until I was sure Andrew was dead, but even then, they were still loyal to him and his sisters. All my letters came back; unopened.

So, now here I am dying, surrounded by strangers in a mental hospital. It isn't dying I dread, in fact, it will be a relief to just put an end to the nightmares that haunt my sleep and the grief that accompanies my every breath. To stop a memory from replaying the faces of my children that never aged from the last time I saw them. To just put a stop to all the pain; that is my prayer now.

I'm not sure, but the best I can figure is I have been here about eight months now. My only friend has been my nurse, Hazel. She is a petite woman and always carries the scent of lavender soap. Her hair is auburn, and she has the deepest brown eyes I have ever seen. She appears to be in her fifties, younger than my daughter. I always find myself comparing everyone I meet with my children. I suppose in an effort to get an idea of how they must look now. But even after all this time, the only picture my mind will conjure up is that of a three-year old girl in a white dress with a blue bow holding back her thick blonde hair. Beside her stands a cotton-topped toddler. Both were squinting their eyes from the bright sun, when they looked up as I tapped on the window of the attic where I was kept. I think that memory stayed with me through the years because I knew if my plan worked, there might be a possibility that it might be a while before I could see them again. Knowing Andrew as I did, I don't know why it never occurred to me that I might never see them again. My mind won't hold that memory very long anymore, and for that, I am grateful. Pain does not always go away with time as some people say.

Hazel and I became close from the start. She was the nurse who took me to my room when he left me here that first day. She held my hand when we walked past patients who stood talking to themselves or lunged at me as if they knew me. I'm fairly certain she knew from the beginning that I didn't belong here. But, this is what becomes of eccentric relatives with tales to tell.

The lines on Hazel's face tell me she has always smiled at life's ups and downs, and I am nothing special, just one of the lucky ones who gets to share her company. I trust her and that is something odd and rare for me. There has only been one other woman that I completely trusted and that was Grandmother Abby.

When I first came here and Hazel realized I never had any visitors, she started spending more time with me than some of the other patients. I wasn't shocked when I heard myself sharing the secret details of my life with her, even though I could count on one hand and have fingers left, the people I have told my tale to in my eighty years. Sometimes the stories I would tell her would bring her to tears and I would feel terrible for upsetting her. I would tell her I wasn't going to tell her anymore, but she always insisted I tell her all that I wanted. I think she knew I just needed to tell someone. A confessional of sorts I suppose. She has never asked questions; she just listens and I respect her deeply for that.

In time Hazel and I became so close that even on her days off she would come to the hospital to see me; many times, bringing a plate of whatever she had prepared for her own family. She has truly been the highlight of my days since I have been here. One morning she came in and had a young black girl with her. She told me her name was Lizzie and she had come to work as a helper at the hospital. She didn't look to be a day over twelve, and I told her so. She quickly corrected me and said she was fourteen and that she had to go to work to help her Momma with the bills because her Daddy was sick. I wondered if what she was doing now would be the mark she would leave on this earth with no more education than what she must have. Then, I realized being raised in the finest parochial school in New Orleans had not guaranteed my happiness in life. Maybe she would do better with her lot in life than I had with mine. Once again, the realization of dying with so much unfinished business hit me. I try daily to remind myself people can only do so much to correct the errors of their ways, and then, it is simply out of their hands. I only wish I had another chance to live my life over. I would not make the same mistakes I made in this lifetime. No, I would fight for my children and nothing else. No one would come between us, especially a man, even if that man was their father.

Lizzie and I became friends over time, and I can still remember the look on her face the day she asked me if I had children. Forgetting for a moment who I was talking to, I began to describe them the way I always have, as children, not as the grown woman and man they surely are today. I knew immediately by the look on her young face, that I had made yet another mistake. I had been forced for so many years to lie and say the children and their father had died in a terrible house fire that I just couldn't do it anymore. Days later, while they thought I was sleeping, I heard Hazel defending me when Lizzie suggested Hazel was wrong and I really did belong in this place since I thought my children were still babies. I knew what was coming next; I had grown accustomed to what people thought and said about me. The ones who believed the tale about the fire thought I had grieved myself into a state of insanity. The others who had heard Andrew's story, that I had run off and deserted my children and him, thought I was plain sorry. It never occurred to any of them that neither story was right. They formed their own opinion, and that was that. The truth didn't matter then, and it doesn't matter now. They were both judge and jury. I used to believe when I got old it wouldn't matter anymore, but I was wrong. I don't care if I die tomorrow or even today, but I hate dying knowing my children will never know the truth.

I turned eighty this past October, and I probably wouldn't have even remembered if Hazel hadn't come into my room that day singing her rendition of Happy Birthday to me. I knew she had to have gone through my file to know it was my birthday, but it didn't bother me. She wouldn't find anything there; I had made sure of it. I didn't want to burden my children with any guilt at my death they had not harbored during my life. I knew where all of my money had gone and who paid the monthly payments for me to be kept here, and that is enough. No one else needed to know. I knew it was the boy they say I sent back, alone on the train, when he was only three years old. They said I pinned a note to his shirt that read, *'Andrew, if you don't want him, put him in a home.'* It didn't matter that in reality it had never happened, growing up in his world being told the lies, it had. He told the people at the mental hospital I had showed up on his porch in Marshall clearly out of my mind and telling outlandish tales. He told them there was no one to tend to me and he wouldn't. His revenge had been sweet. He would put me in a home because no one wanted me. It was justified in his mind. He only paid back what he thought had been done to him, by me, so many years ago.

All the answers Hazel hoped to find in my file were long ago buried with the ones who made torturing me their lifelong goal. Their lies had lived on without them, like something born and raised to take care of itself in their absence.

After discovering it was my birthday, Hazel insisted I tell her what she could get me. I reminded her it was against the rules for her to buy me anything, but she still insisted. She laughed and said if I didn't tell her what she could get for me that she would buy me a sexy nightgown. We both howled with laughter. Before meeting Hazel, I couldn't tell you the last time I had laughed and looked so forward to seeing someone. With much reluctance, I finally told her she could bring me more stationary and stamps as I was almost out of both. She was thrilled to do this for me. She knew how important the letters I wrote weekly were to me, even though they always came back; unopened. Touched just long enough to write *Return to Sender* across the front.

I had just finished eating a rather awful dinner when I heard Hazel's familiar tap on the door. She pushed the door all the way open and I saw she was pushing a wheelchair. I raised myself up in my bed and just stared at the contraption.

"Now don't you go fussing, Ms. Virginia. I know you don't really need this thing, but it's just going to make it easier for me to take you where I want us to go."

She brought the wheelchair over close to the bed and eased my aged and worn out body down into it. Clad in a plain hospital issue dress, she helped me adjust in the seat until I was comfortable. She had a beautiful knitted throw with her that she draped across my shoulders and over my lap.

After she positioned my feet on the silver footpads, I said something I had not said since I was a young girl in New Orleans. "Okay driver, let's go." I had forgotten those long-ago memories of living in luxury riding in my Grandfather's carriage. I had not thought of my beloved Grandfather and the beautiful Garden District, where I had been raised, in so very long.

Hazel wheeled me out of my door and down the hall. We went through the dining room and out the double doors into the courtyard. She could have stopped right there and I would have been thrilled beyond measure. I had not been outside the walls of the mental hospital since I was admitted.

The sun had just begun to set, and the sky had taken on hues of yellow, lavender, and pink. Colors I have rarely seen an artist truly capture. Within minutes the tree frogs and crickets began their evening symphony and I felt like I was a patron in the finest opera house.

It was still warm, even though it was the end of October. Texas could be like that, no respect for seasons. Hazel continued to push the wheelchair down the sidewalk to a sitting area with a bench and light post under an old oak tree. The lights around the grounds began to flicker on just as she turned the wheelchair around so I could face the bench. She locked the wheels, as if I might take off in the contraption, and came and sat down on the bench in front of me.

"Okay, Ms. Virginia, here you go." She handed me a box wrapped in paper with yellow butterflies all over it. She knew I loved them, and it touched me deeply she had gone to the trouble. I took my time opening it. I wanted to savor every moment and I wanted to save the paper, for what or whom, I didn't know. Inside, just as I had requested, were the stationary and stamps, and she had added a beautiful gold ink pen. Then, I opened the card she handed me with my gift. As I read the words, I felt the tears brimming in my eyes. I couldn't remember the last time I had cried from actual joy instead of pain. I guess I believed the well from which all tears flowed had dried up in me years ago. But, here I was, eighty years old, and they streamed down my wrinkled face as if they were the first. A friend that would go to such extremes was rare, and I knew it.

"Hazel," I said as I put the card back into the envelope and swiped at the tears with my hand, "I don't know what to say, a simple thank you seems gravely insufficient." I put the stationary, stamps, pen and card back into the box and when I looked up at her, that's when I saw the tears streaming down her cheeks as well. She just shook her head and then she did something she hasn't done since I've known her, she reached over and hugged me.

"I meant what I said in the card," she said as she pulled back from me and wiped her tears with a handkerchief. "You miss your children, and I miss my own mother. I think this is just God's way of helping us both."

We were both wiping tears then, and we began to laugh at the sight of each other. We sat a little longer and enjoyed the evening and each other's company before I told her to take me back inside because I was getting tired. I knew I was keeping her from her family. The truth of the matter was I would have stayed right there, just Hazel and me, and slept under the stars if they would have let me. God has truly blessed me; these being what I know will be my last days, with someone like her. There were those that were sure I would die alone and forgotten, left here to serve penance for my sins. They never dreamed there would be someone like Hazel, but of course, I never dared to hope or dream of such a person either. I'm quite sure I don't deserve her.

As Hazel wheeled me back down the sidewalk to the building, I drew in as much of the sweet-smelling evening air as my lungs would hold. We went back through the double doors and she wheeled me back down the desolate hallway to my room. Most of the patients had been given their nighttime medicine and were no longer screaming or hysterical, but finally asleep and free in their dreams, hidden from the madness of their minds.

She opened the door and pushed the wheelchair back into my room. She helped me get up and sat me on the side of my bed while she pulled a fresh nightgown from my bureau. She waited until I had changed into it and then she helped me into bed, pulling the covers over my weary body. She then bent down and kissed my forehead. The sensation made a memory dance through my mind of when Grandmother Abby had done the same thing all my days as a child in New Orleans. It's amazing to me how the love of just one person can soothe the soul of another so easily. I blew Hazel a kiss as she left and pulled the door closed behind her. I suddenly realized I would not be alone in death, something I had genuinely feared. I felt a peace I hadn't expected to feel.

I propped myself up in the bed and turned on the bedside lamp to once again write to my daughter. It almost seemed a shame to ruin this night with the slightest hint of sadness, but I knew my time was running out. I only prayed, before I left this earth, just one letter would not come back, unopened; untouched. If she would only give me a chance to set things right with her. A chance to tell her my side of the story, not her father's or her aunt's version. The opportunity to tell her that leaving her and her younger brother was never what I had wanted, but I wasn't given a choice. Would she believe me even if she read my letters? I've been writing them for years with no response, but I can't give up, not now; not yet.

Hazel has promised to keep the letters and my diary that I keep in my keepsake box under the bed. The letters, journal and a few business papers are all that is left of eighty years of living. The box I keep them in was a gift from Grandmother Abby on the occasion of my twelfth birthday. It is a beautiful wooden box with a mirror inside, and etchings cut in the glass in all four corners. Grandmother always said mirrors were important to not only see who we are now, but more importantly, they could be used to see behind us and where we had been. She said I was to never forget, no matter where I might roam, that my home would always be with her and Grandfather, in New Orleans. The box is all I have to remind me of that life now, it's all I felt I deserved to keep for not fighting Andrew harder for my children. It took so long for me to accept I couldn't fight him, his family and an entire town that believed every word he said. He had me beat at every corner.

When Grandmother gave me the box, she said I could store all my precious treasures in it. I'm glad she is no longer here to see what I store in that box now. She left this world with nothing but regret for putting me on the train that day. Such a legacy of lies and pain, one I desperately had hoped would end with my life. So no, I can't give up on my daughter; I keep writing the letters with the hope that she will open just one of them and finally know the truth.

After I finished writing the letter and sealed my hopes and dreams in the envelope with it, I put it on the side table so Hazel could mail it for me. I slid out of my bed and made it over to my potty-chair before I laid my body down for the night. When I stood back up off the chair, I found myself staring into the mirror on the wall. Hazel must have moved my potty-chair to be able to bring the wheelchair in earlier, because I had purposely positioned everything in the room to avoid seeing my reflection in the mirror. I didn't need to be reminded of what time had done to me. The hair that Grandmother Abby had said was the color of chestnuts that flowed down my back was now replaced with gray that was pulled into a loose bun on top of my head. The wrinkles hid the skin that my young friends in New Orleans had envied. But the eyes; they remained the same. The sorrow that had entered them when I realized my fate, would remain there the rest of my days. Even when I finally allowed myself to be loved again when I met Walt in my late fifties, it was too late for him to change the sorrow of my soul. The damage was long done and his kind words could not unlock the prison my memories kept me in. The lies were the warden and they held the key.

I finally turned my back on the mirror and my memories, and made my way back to my bed. I leaned into the mattress in total exhaustion. It was if going back in time and remembering had taken what little bit of strength I had left away from me.

As the weeks passed I found myself in yet another year. Deep inside of me something significant had changed. One night after eating dinner, I knew what I had to do. I couldn't face another day of the pain; both physical and mental. I had to make my body let go of my soul. My doctor, once he truly realized I wasn't crazy, just condemned, allowed me to keep a bottle of pain pills in my room; hidden of course. But now as I pulled the bottle from the back of the drawer in the nightstand beside the bed, I no longer saw them as something to ease the pain, but something to end it, once and for all. I reached for my stationary and pen and wrote a letter to Hazel. Then I took the top off the bottle and poured the pills into my hand. I took them, one after the other until they were gone. Sleep gently took me. Then, from somewhere outside of myself, I heard the familiar voice of Grandmother Abby as she whispered, "I've missed you my darling Virginia."

# Chapter 2

*Suzanne*
*January 3, 1999*

I sat straight up in the bed. It was still dark out as I turned and looked at the digital clock on my nightstand. It read *4:44.* I suddenly felt a chill in the room. My breathing was erratic and my chest hurt. "What's wrong?" Tony's voice made me jump. He then rolled over and faced me. "What's the matter with you?" My husband's attitude that he had brought to bed with him was still present. His words dripped with sarcasm.

I wouldn't face him. "I had the strangest dream," I said and yet it sounded like someone else talking. "Mamaw was there, but she didn't look like she did when she was alive."

"What the hell are you talking about?" He raised up on one elbow.

"Nothing," I said as I pulled the covers back and grabbed my yellow chenille robe from the foot of the bed and put it on. "Go back to sleep."

I made my way to the bathroom and closed the door and leaned against it. I stared into the mirror above the sink and was relieved to see my own forty-year old reflection, not the face I had seen in the mirror in my dream. I pulled my hair up in a loose pony-tail, washed my face and brushed my teeth. I somehow knew what I had just experienced was not a dream at all; it felt too real. I gently turned the bathroom door handle and crept quietly by the bed and made my way downstairs.

I flipped the switch on the kitchen wall and was comforted by the light that surrounded me. I went over to the stove and got the teakettle and filled it with water and put it on the grate. I turned the knob and watched the blue flame dance around the bottom of it. I pulled a mug down from the cabinet and put a tea bag in it and glanced at the black and white checkered board clock above the stove. Still too early to call my sister, Gina. I walked over and pulled back the curtain from the window in the breakfast nook. I looked out into the nothingness of the morning. Fog surrounded the streetlight on the corner. My mind replayed every moment of the dream like it was on automatic replay. I jumped when the teakettle began to whistle and rushed over to remove it from the fire. I poured the hot water into the cup and was bobbing the tea bag up and down when I heard a noise behind me. Startled I turned to see Tony standing in the doorway in just his pajama bottoms.

"Why are you so jumpy? You must have something to hide?" He made his way over to the coffee pot and turned it on.

A deep sigh escaped me. "I don't have anything to hide, Tony." I went over to the small kitchen table and sat down.

He leaned against the counter and stared at me. "So, I guess this means we're staying up."

I closed my eyes. "You can always go back to bed."

"I'm already awake now. So, what was the dream about?"

"I told you, my dead grandmother."

"That doesn't tell me what it was about, that tells me who was in it." He reached into the cabinet and retrieved a mug and filled it with coffee and came over and sat down across from me.

I got up from my chair and went over to the refrigerator and pulled out a package of bacon. "Do you want breakfast?"

"So, you're not going to answer me. That's fine!" He got up from the table shoving his chair back. "I'm going to get the paper."

I put four slices of bacon into the skillet and went back and sat down at the table. I could see him through the kitchen window as he searched the yard for the newspaper. Right on cue, Mrs. Miller, our neighbor from across the street, pulled back her curtain and watched him as well. Tony always said she spied on him every time he went outside. He said it reminded him of the nosy neighbor, *Mrs. Kravitz* from the television show *Bewitched*. I thought it was funny and had to hide my face when he finally came back into the kitchen. He sat back down across from me and pulled the newspaper from the cellophane sheath and the water from last night's rain splattered me in the face.

"Thanks a lot!" I said as I wiped my face with a napkin.

"That's what you get for waking me up so early on a Saturday morning."

I just shook my head and rolled my eyes and got up to tend to the bacon on the stove. "What do you want with the bacon?"

He had pulled the sports section from the paper and his face was hidden from me but I heard him mumble something.

I was really getting put out with him now. "What did you say?"

He looked over the paper at me. "Did you forget to put your hearing aids in? I *said* I want a bagel with my bacon."

I opened the package of bagels and jerked one out and separated it and put it in the toaster. I knew he was digging for a fight and I refused to give it to him. All I had to do was get through breakfast and then I knew he was going to play racquetball with his friend, Mark. I glanced at the clock again; it was almost six. The toaster popped and I slathered cream cheese on the bagel and put it on the plate with the bacon. I took the plate over to the table and sat it down in front of him. He never uttered a word, he just kept reading the paper. I turned and went back to the counter and poured more hot water over the tea bag in my mug. Then I watched him. In his own sweet time, he folded the newspaper and put it aside and began to eat. I despised him on mornings like this following his drunken nights and his verbal abuse.

When had it happened? When did our marriage go down the tubes? Had it been so gradual that neither of us noticed and worse yet, did nothing to stop it? He and I had known *of* each other before friends had introduced us one night when a group of us had met up in a bar in Dallas' West End district. My best friend, Kate, had been with me. Tony was good looking but he had that 'bad boy' persona that I had sworn off of. But as the alcohol flowed that night, my defenses cratered. We started seeing each other daily. Months passed and he asked me to marry him on Valentine's Day five years ago. I said yes and friends started putting up their bets on how long we would last. They all knew he was a womanizer and I was fiercely independent; not a good match. He had never been married and I had two failed marriages on my resume with three kids to his none. I had no idea that he drank the way he does until we had been married about a year and he quit trying to hide it. He was very jealous of my relationships with my sister Gina, my friend Kate but especially of how close I am to my kids.

"I'm going to take a shower."

His voice startled me again. "Okay," I managed as I moved to pick up his plate and throw the newspaper into the recycling bin.

"What the hell is up with you?"

"Nothing," I said as I turned my back to him and started wiping down the stove and the sink and putting the plate in the dishwasher.

"You do remember I'm playing racquetball with Mark, right?"

"Yes, of course," I said turning to face him.

"You're having lunch with Kate?"

"Yes." Then I saw the look cross his face and he grinned. "No, Tony. She's already said she will not go out with Mark. He's not her type."

"So? We weren't each other's type either."

"I rest my case."

"Don't be an ass, Suzanne! Just ask her. He really likes her." With that he turned and headed upstairs and again, I looked at the clock on the wall. Six-thirty. Gina was going to kill me for waking her up, but I had to talk to her. I walked past the staircase and heard the shower running upstairs. I went into the den and picked up the cordless phone and punched in my sister's number.

The phone rang twice before a groggy Gina answered.

"Hello," she mumbled.

"Gina, it's me," I said just above a whisper.

"What? Suzanne, what's wrong?"

I could see her sitting straight up in her bed and pushing back her sleep mask.

"Nothing's wrong; well not exactly. I had this really bizarre dream and I…"

"You're calling me at six-thirty in the morning because you had a bad dream? What are we little kids again?"

"Gina!" I said louder than I intended. "I need you to call Mother and see if anybody died the year I was born."

"What?"

I sat down on the sofa and lit a cigarette. "Okay, just listen. I was back in Marshall and I was driving to the bank to make a deposit. There was a green bank bag bulging with money on the passenger seat. I got to the bank, but it was already closed. I pulled onto the street behind it and made a U-turn. I pulled up to the stop sign and I saw this woman standing across the street and she was waving at me to pull over to where she was. Gina," I hesitated. "It was Mamaw, but she looked nothing like she did when she was alive."

"Mamaw? Mama's Mother?"

"Yes."

"What do you mean she didn't look like she did when she was alive?"

"She just looked different," I sighed. "This woman was tall and thin; sophisticated looking. She had gray hair pulled up in a French twist on the back of her head. She had on khaki colored slacks and a white blouse."

"Wow, okay I get she looked nothing like Mamaw, go ahead."

"Anyway, I pulled my car over to the curb where she was standing and I rolled down the passenger side window. She leaned down and said, *'Park your car and follow me, I'm having an Estate Sale and I think I have something you are going to want.'* So, I turned the car off and got out and followed her. She went down the sidewalk across the street and then went into a house in the middle of the next block. When we got inside it was dimly lit, but I saw Aunt Margie at the back of the house. She looked like she did when she was in her thirties. Then I turned back to this woman that had brought me there and I said, *'But you're Mamaw.'* She just nodded her head and said, *'Ah, yes, I used to be your grandmother.'* Then she went behind this table. She bent down to pick something up and when she did, I saw a huge clock hanging on the wall, but Gina, the hands were slowly turning backwards. When she raised back up, she had this wooden box in her hands, and it had a mirrored lid. She set it on the table between us. I stepped closer and she took the lid off the box. I looked inside and there was another box just like it. She takes the lid off that one and there is another box just like the one before. I have to lean over to see down into the box and I expect to see my reflection in the mirror of the fourth box, but it's not me! It's a young woman, but the picture looks old, like the ones you see in an antique store. I jerked my head up and was about to ask Mamaw what all of it meant, when a woman I didn't see speaks from behind me and asks, *'Who died the year you were born?'* And then I woke up. What do you think it means?" There was silence on the line. "Gina, are you there?"

"Did you and Tony go out drinking last night?"

"No! And you know I haven't drank in years!"

"Okay, okay. But you do have to admit that is one crazy dream!"

"I do admit it, but it wasn't like a dream at all! Will you please just call Mother? She's been doing all that genealogy stuff for years, she'll know."

"Oh yeah, all that family tree business that you have told her repeatedly you want nothing to do with."

"I still don't care anything about all of that! Come on, Gina you know how it is between us! I can't call her!"

She let out a loud sigh. "Alright. Let me get up and get some coffee

14

in me and I'll call her. You owe me big!"

"Oh, thank you! Call me as soon as you talk to her."

"I will."

I hung up the phone and turned and was almost face to face with Tony.

"So, you'll tell your sister your dark little dreams, but not your husband?"

"Dammit, Tony! I can't even have a private conversation?"

I stormed from the den into the kitchen with Tony following. Max, my sixteen-year old son came into the kitchen behind us. "What is everybody doing up so early on a Saturday?"

"Your mother had a dream about dead people," Tony said with a laugh. "Anyway, I'm late." He went out the kitchen door into the garage.

I turned and watched out the window as his car sped away down the street. I turned back to my son and smiled. "Sorry we woke you up."

He walked over to the refrigerator and pulled out a can of Coke, popped the top and without saying another word went back upstairs to his room. I sat down at the kitchen bar feeling totally exhausted. The phone rang then and I picked up the cordless and answered it.

"Hey, it's me," Gina said. "I called Mother and got her answering machine. I forgot that she's gone out of town with a friend. She's supposed to be back late Sunday night, so it might be sometime Monday before I can talk to her."

"Oh." A deep sigh escaped me.

"You're really bugged by this dream, aren't you?"

"Yes, and I had no intentions of telling Tony about it, but he was eves-dropping when you and I were talking earlier."

"Where is the ass now?"

"He's gone to play racquetball with Mark supposedly."

"*Supposedly?* You don't believe him?

"I don't believe anything he says these days."

"So, things are worse between the two of you then?

"Yes," I admitted. "Well listen, I'm having brunch with Kate so I'll call you later.

"How is Kate doing?"

"She's fine. Tony is still dogging me to get her to go out with Mark."

Gina laughed. "That's never going to happen."

"Yeah, I know and you know, but Tony and Mark's egos can't accept any woman turning them down."

"Oh, I get it; it just makes him want her that much more."

"I'm sure."

"I can't stand that chauvinistic pig!"

"Which one," I asked with a laugh.

"Either of them!"

"Join the club. Okay, well I've got to run so I'll call you in a bit."

"Okay talk to you then."

I hit the end button on the phone and rushed up the stairs to take a shower. Max met me in the hallway. "Are you going out?"

"Yes, I'm having brunch with Kate, you want anything?"

"Yeah, bring me back a cheeseburger."

"Sure, okay." I went into my bedroom and closed the door and the phone beside the bed rang. I rushed to pick it up thinking Gina forgot something. "Hello?" There was sound coming from the background, but no one said anything. "Hello?" I repeated; still no response. "I can't hear you. You'll have to call back." I hung up the phone but I had a pretty good idea what that call was all about. But, I decided, rather quickly, not to let it ruin my day.

I was running late as I pulled into the parking lot of the restaurant where Kate and I had agreed to meet. It had started sprinkling rain as I got out and rushed inside. She waved me over to a corner booth where she sat.

"I'm really sorry," I said as I slid in across from her. "Have you been waiting long?"

"No, you're fine," she said with a smile. "I just got here myself. I ordered us both iced tea, I hope that's okay."

"That's fine," I said as I took my coat off and draped it across the back of the booth.

The waitress came with our drinks and we placed our food order. I waited until she walked away and then turned back to Kate.

"So, what's new?" She asked before taking a drink of tea.

"Tony is being a real pain and just so I can say I asked...."

"Oh no," she said rolling her eyes. "Not the Mark thing again!"

"I'm afraid so," I said with a smirk.

"No, no and forever no. Do they not understand the part about hell freezing over?"

"Apparently not. Okay, so on to something else. Tell me about your *blind date* last night."

She hung her head. "Let's just say I wish I had been blind and deaf wouldn't have hurt either."

"Ouch, that bad huh?"

"It was terrible," she said looking back up at me. I'm thinking of becoming a nun, did I tell you already?"

I almost spit tea everywhere. "Sure you are, and you've discovered a way to regain your virginity I assume."

"Oh yeah, that could be a problem huh?"

We both busted out laughing. I love Kate. We met when we were in our twenties, but I feel like I have known her forever. We have been through thick and thin together. I have to admit since she never married or had kids, it's usually me that needs a shoulder to cry on more than her. But we know all of each other's secrets, so I couldn't wait to see what she thought about the dream. As I told the story again, for the second time since having it, I was surprised at how vividly I could still see it in my mind.

"Have you ever had a dream like that?" I asked as the waitress brought our food and sat the plates in front of us and walked away.

"No. I mean it's really weird that your grandmother didn't look anything like she did when she was alive! That's just strange!"

"I know! And, that question, 'Who died the year you were born?'

"But Gina's getting in touch with your Mom to see if anybody died that year, right?"

"Yeah, but Mother's out of town. It's probably going to be sometime Monday before I can find out anything."

"I can't wait to see what she says," Kate said as she speared a fry with her fork. "But what happens if somebody did die the year you were born? Then what?"

I shrugged my shoulders. "I don't know. I guess I won't know that until I find out."

"Yeah, I guess you're right," she said nodding her head.

We ate the rest of our meal just catching up with the latest gossip we had heard through mutual friends. When we finished I pulled my coat from the back of the booth and put it on. "I need to drop off a cheeseburger for Max at home and then I was thinking about going to the mall; I need to get a few things. Are you up for it?"

"Oh good," she said grabbing her purse. "Retail therapy; I'm all in."

"Okay, just follow me to the house and we'll leave your car there and we'll ride together."

We reached the house and Kate pulled up in front while I pulled into the driveway and got out and went inside to give Max his burger. Kate came in behind me and she and Max almost ran into each other in the kitchen doorway.

"Maximillian! I can't believe how tall you are!" They hugged and I laughed to see Max's head towering at least a foot above Kate's.

"Well, if you would come over more often," he said with a smile.

"*And*," he continued with a grin, you know that's not my *real* name, right?"

"It is as far as I'm concerned." She laughed. "And you know," she said glancing over at me, "I would come over more often except I can't stand that *ass* of a step-father of yours."

"Oh, now wait a minute," he laughed. "That's Mom's husband, he's no relation to me at all."

"Alright you two," I said as I swatted Max on the bottom. I reached and pulled a package of meat from the freezer and put it in the sink to thaw. "While we're at the mall I want to find some new curtains for the kitchen. What do you think Kate?"

"Oh, I don't know," she said turning to look at them. "I kind of always thought these checkered ones went with the Tudor style of the house."

"What?" I asked with a laugh.

"You of all people know I am challenged in the decorating area! Now if you need a new pair of jeans, I'm your girl!"

I put my arm around her shoulder. "Well, as a matter of fact, I do need a new pair, so let's hit the mall!"

"Right behind you," Kate said as she followed me to the front door. "Bye Max!"

"Bye, Aunt Kate," Max shouted as he went back up the stairs to his room.

We spent the better part of the afternoon hitting almost every store in the mall. I regretted it when it came time to lug all the bags back to the car. The drizzling rain that we ran through earlier when we arrived, had picked up and was now, a full-fledged cold rain. I told Kate to wait at the front exit and I would make a run for the car and bring it to the door so that everything we had just bought didn't get soaked.

I was drenched when I pulled back to the front of the mall. I popped the trunk and jumped out to help her load our bags in the back. When we got back in the car we were both soaking wet.

"Let's go back to the house, I'm sure I have something you can change into so you don't have to drive all the way back to your house like that," I said pointing to her jeans, that now clung to her legs.

"I thought you said Mark was with Tony," she said as she pulled the seatbelt around her and latched it.

"He is," I said as I pulled out of the driveway of the mall. "They're playing racquetball."

"Not unless the racquetball court is now in the mall."

"What are you talking about?" I asked glancing over at her.

"I just saw Mark come into the mall."

I slammed on the brakes. "What? You saw Mark?"

"Yeah, while I was waiting on you. He came running up from the parking lot."

"Are you sure it was him?"

Kate rolled her eyes. "Of course I'm sure it was him. I've been dodging him long enough that I can spot him a mile off."

"He didn't see you?"

"No, I don't think so. I pulled the hood of my jacket down over my face and turned my back to him."

I turned the car around and started going slowly through the parking lot.

"Look! You're right! There's his truck! If he's here, where the hell is Tony?"

"I'm sure there's a logical explanation," Kate tried to sound upbeat.

"Did he have on gym clothes?"

"Well no, but.."

"No," I said holding up a finger to her. "You and I both know I just caught Tony in a lie and we both know he wouldn't lie unless he was hiding something!"

I pulled the car out of the parking lot and drove slowly home. As the windshield wipers slapped back and forth a thousand things went through my mind, but one thing was for sure. I couldn't *'un-see'* the proof of my husband's deception. I knew he had been drinking a lot more lately than usual and I couldn't remember the last time we had been intimate with each other. I had told myself, repeatedly, that he wasn't cheating and chose to believe him when he told me it was stress from work. And then at that very moment I remembered the *'mysterious phone call'* that had come in right after he left this morning. "Dammit!"

"I'm sure he's already home." I could hear the regret of telling me what she had seen in Kate's voice.

We got back to my house and by then the rain had stopped, and there was no sign of Tony. We brought the packages inside and Kate and I went upstairs to find something to change into. When we came back down, Tony and Mark were in the den.

"What are you doing back so early?" I asked looking straight at Tony.

"Well hey, Kate," Mark said as he grinned and winked.

Tony went over to the bar and poured himself a drink. "You want one Mark?"

"So, you're just going to ignore my question?" I put my hands on

19

my hips.

"What the hell?" Tony spun around with a glass of whiskey in his hand. He downed it all in one gulp and slammed the glass back down on the bar. "See what I mean?" He said looking over at Mark.

"Oh, no," Mark said laughing. "Don't get me caught up in y'alls argument. Huh Kate? We're just innocent by-standers."

Kate shot him a look. "*We're* not anything." She picked up her purse and headed for the door. "Call me later, Suzanne," and she was gone.

I turned and looked back at Tony and Mark quickly headed for the door as well.

"I'll touch base with you later man," Mark said as he followed Kate out the front door.

Tony just stood there staring at me. "What the hell is wrong with you?" He turned back to the bar and refilled his glass.

"How was racquetball, Tony?"

"It was fine, Suzanne. It was great." He slammed the glass down and stormed past me as I stood frozen in the doorway.

# Chapter 3

*Virginia*
*New Orleans – 1877*

The Fontenot home bustled with excitement as Caroline lay upstairs in labor in the same bedroom where she had been born. The stately Victorian estate took up an entire block on Napoleon Avenue in the Garden District of New Orleans.

Henry Fontenot was the man of the house; period. Caroline had followed in her sister, Katherine's footsteps, and married against her father's wishes and by his standards *'beneath'* them. Katherine had buckled and her father had paid for the divorce and she had turned the only child that had resulted from the marriage over to her other sister, Mary Margaret and her husband. The young boy now lived with them and their children in Jefferson, Texas. Caroline's younger brothers, Theo and Georgie, along with Theo's twin sister Anna Beth, were away at boarding school. Then of course there was Harry, the oldest son that had married and moved across town. Henry Fontenot had held such high hopes for him, but not unlike the girls, he too had disappointed his father in a myriad of ways.

Caroline had met Jonah Barrister when he and his father had been hired by Henry Fontenot to build the wrought iron fence around the estate to restrict the unwanted from venturing in, but it had failed in keeping the two apart. They had run off in the middle of the night and took a steamboat to Jefferson and were married in the Catholic Church. Shortly afterwards Caroline had become pregnant. When Jonah couldn't find work and they had overstayed their welcome with Mary Margaret and her husband, they went back to New Orleans and begged for mercy from Caroline's father. But, she knew she would never give up her child the way Katherine had.

Abbigail, Caroline's mother, was an advocate for her own sons and the men her daughters had chosen. She tried desperately to keep the peace between everyone, but at times it was all in vain. She hadn't been able to stop her oldest daughter from following her husband to Texas. She had tried to warn her of the dangers of traveling into what she considered uncivilized, not to mention unsettled territory. Mary Margaret hadn't listened, and Abbigail had lost a young grandson to her daughter's stubbornness. He had contracted Scarlett fever on the boat and never recovered. Abbigail viewed every child born into the family since then as a gift from God to help heal her broken heart. Now, with Caroline upstairs in the full throes of hard labor, there would be another child to love.

Cissy, the black servant who had been with the Fontenot family since Caroline and the other children were mere babies themselves, was downstairs in the kitchen boiling water over the open fireplace and shouting orders to the rest of the help. When the water finally reached a boiling point, she took towels and grabbed the handle of the cast-iron pot and slowly poured the water into smaller buckets. She heaved the buckets and her heavy body up the stairs to Caroline's room. Cissy could tell when she entered the room the birthing was progressing rapidly.

"Cissy," Abbigail said as she took the buckets from her. "Send for the men. It won't be long now."

"Yes 'em, Miz Abbigail." Cissy grinned from ear to ear, her white teeth in sharp contrast to her dark skin.

Cissy walked out of the room and stopped at the top of staircase and yelled down to her nephew that stood ready at the front door. "Go git da men. It be time."

The young boy jerked the front door open and ran out. He raced down the steps and down the sidewalk and pushed open the wrought-iron gate and ran down the street towards the newspaper office Henry Fontenot owned and Jonah, Caroline's husband, worked as an apprentice.

Cissy went downstairs to tell the rest of the staff that the baby and the men of the house were on their way. It was just after mid-day when she saw the carriage pull up close to the stables at the back of the estate. She hurried to the foot of the staircase, "Miz Abbigail, they be here!"

Abbigail came out of Caroline's room and stood on the landing at the top of the stairs. She was still a beautiful woman. Time had been kind to her delicate features. She was a tall, slender woman with dark, deep-set eyes. She had her dark hair, that now had traces of gray in it, pulled into a bun on top of her head. Strands hung down loosely now, showing signs of the ordeal she had just been through with Caroline.

"Cissy, send them right up when they get in. We have a beautiful baby girl."

"Glory be to God, Miz Abbigail. I sho nuff send Missa Jonah up, but you know Missa Henry ain't goin' nowhere near where there be a new baby," she said with a chuckle.

"Ah yes," Abbigail smiled. "Of course, Cissy, you're correct. Just send the proud father then."

"Yes 'em. I already got my William settin' up bourbon and a cigar for Missa Henry in his study."

"Very well, will you tell him I will join him shortly?"

"Yes 'em, sho will."

Jonah came running through the house then and almost ran over Cissy. He grabbed her and spun her in a circle and ran up the stairs to his wife.

"Hello son," Abbigail whispered to him as he came into the bedroom. She patted his back as he passed her and went to his wife and child lying in the bed. He stared at his new daughter as she lay nestled in her mother's arms.

"Isn't she beautiful?" Caroline whispered.

"She is at that." Jonah glanced back over his shoulder. "With all that dark hair, she looks like you, Mother Abbigail."

Tears welled in Abbigail's eyes, and she couldn't respond for fear of crying in front of them. All she could manage was a smile. When she finally brought her emotions under control, she moved around the bed and stood next to Jonah. "What will you name this precious child?"

"You haven't told her?" Jonah's mouth gaped open and his eyes grew wide as he faced his wife. "I can't believe you actually kept the secret for so long," he said with a laugh. "Why, Mother Abby," he said as he turned to face her. "We decided months ago that if this child were a girl, we would name her after you. That is if you approve," he said with a chuckle.

Before she could respond, Caroline reached and touched her Mother's hand. "Here, Mother. Hold your namesake."

Abbigail took the baby from her mother's arms and walked over to the window overlooking the fall foliage in the garden below. "Virginia Abbigail Barrister," she said just above a whisper. "You are my granddaughter, and grand you shall be." She held the infant's cheek to her own and felt her tears run down both of their faces. She held the baby for a moment longer and then turned and handed her to Jonah. "I'll leave you two alone now to get acquainted with this angel you have been given." She leaned down and kissed Caroline on the forehead and quietly left the room, pulling the door shut behind her. She walked to the staircase and stopped for a moment to relish what had just occurred.

"You alright, Miz Abbigail?" Cissy called from the foot of the staircase.

Abbigail swiped at the tears on her face. "Oh yes, I'm quite fine," she said as she started down the stairs.

"I swear you be shinin' like one of the Good Lord's own angels!"

"I suppose I am," she said as she stepped off the last step. She patted Cissy on the arm. "They have named the little girl after me." She walked away slowly towards her husband's study.

"Well Lordy be," Cissy called out after her. "That be fittin', Miz Abbigail, it sho nuff be!"

Abbigail continued down the hall. As she approached her husband's study she could see the flicker of the gas lamps through the small opening in the pocket doors. She smelled the scent of her husband's cigar as she pushed one of the pocket doors into the wall. Henry stood with his back to her, looking out the window towards his beloved horse stables. She appreciated the distinguished look age had given him. His suit and vest, with his gold pocket watch tucked inside, spoke authority to most, but not to her. There was a gentleness that came over him when they were alone that spoke of the intimacy they still shared. Abbigail, lost in her thoughts, stood with one arm crossed at her waist while the other toyed with the brooch at the neck of her dress.

"Abby?" Henry summoned her attention as he held out a glass of wine to her.

She made her way over to him and took the glass. "Henry," she said just above a whisper. "They have a beautiful baby girl. She is the most beautiful baby I have ever seen." She walked over to the window where her husband had been standing.

"Should I command the militia to come and guard our home now that we have this precious cargo upstairs?"

"Henry," she said turning to face him. "I'm quite serious. There is something special about this child."

"Ah yes, I would think a child that is to be your namesake would indeed be special." He smiled coyly at her.

"You knew they planned on naming her after me and you said nothing?"

"What, and spoil this moment?" His laughter boomed into the quiet of the room. He filled his glass with more bourbon and sat the crystal decanter back on the table. He walked slowly over to her. "This calls for a toast," he said holding up his glass to her. "To Miss Virginia Abbigail Barrister. May she bring some lad as much happiness as her grandmother has brought me."

Abbigail smiled at him through teary eyes as their glasses chimed together. Henry leaned down and kissed her gently on the cheek.

A ruckus in the foyer brought them back from their moment of bliss. They could hear the voices of Cissy and their four-year old grandson, Ralston, getting louder. They both set their glasses down and went to inquire as to what was going on.

"You gonna' get tanned if you be disturbin' that new baby sister of yo'rs!" Cissy made another grab at the boy as he flung himself towards the stairs.

"Ralston!"

The child's blue eyes grew wide when he heard the tone of his grandfather's voice. Even he knew such shenanigans weren't tolerated in the house. "You behave this instant!"

He immediately grew still in Cissy's arms and mumbled, "Yes, Grandfather."

"Now, young man," Henry said as he pulled Ralston from Cissy's arms. "your grandmother will take you to see your new baby sister if you think you can behave like a gentleman."

He nodded and his blonde curls danced all over his head. Henry and Jonah had both insisted the boy be raised without a lot of coddling from the women of the house, but it was Henry who gave in more than the others, but only when no one was around to witness it.

Ralston's limitless supply of energy abounded as Abbigail escorted the boy up the stairs to his parent's bedroom. It seemed the only part of his body not moving with excitement was the hand his grandmother held firmly in her own.

Abbigail tapped on the bedroom door and heard Jonah answer quietly for them to come in. As soon as the door opened, Ralston pulled free from his grandmother's clutches and ran to his father's side.

"Ah, Ralston my boy," Jonah greeted him as he stooped to face his young son. "So, you have come to pay your new sister a visit, have you?" The boy never answered, he was on his tip-toes getting his first look at Virginia as she lay in the crib against the wall.

"Father," he whispered. "She's much too little to play with me." He spoke with such disillusion in his voice that Jonah burst out laughing. The two women quickly hushed him as he picked up his young son and hugged him.

"Yes, Ralston," he whispered. "She's much too small now, but someday soon she will grow and the two of you will be wonderful playmates." He eased his barefoot son, still clad in his white nightgown from his afternoon nap, back to the floor. "Now you go with Grandmother Abby and let Cissy dress you and I'll see you at dinner."

"Yes, Father." Ralston reluctantly took his grandmother's hand again and Abbigail led him to the side of the bed and he leaned and kissed his mother, Caroline, on the cheek and they quietly left the room.

That day seemed to get away from them all, as they found themselves six weeks later at the christening for baby Virginia. Abbigail watched as Caroline held the baby and Jonah announced to the world her given name, *Virginia Abbigail Barrister.* At that very moment Grandmother Abby knew this child would forever hold a special place in her heart.

The months following the christening quickly turned into years, and Virginia was constantly underfoot. She had beautiful dark, wavy hair that draped down her back, and thick black eyelashes that guarded the smoky blue eyes that would make even strangers stop and stare. She was a joy to be around as well. She had the most delightful disposition of any child they had ever seen, and she was rarely at odds with anyone for very long. Her whimsical laughter was constantly heard around the Fontenot home.

However, Ralston never gained the playmate his father had promised the day she had been born. Being all boy, he was just too rough with her. Soon enough he grew tired of the reprimands from everyone to be 'gentle' with her and went back to tagging behind the men in the house.

The New Orleans Telegraph, the newspaper that Henry Fontenot founded and ran himself, flourished. Now with the public showing such a keen interest in poetry, he decided to publish a few books of the more prominent authors as well. Jonah hoped it would mean a promotion for him.

Henry became acquainted with a man from New York when they printed a small book of poetry the man's sister, that lived in New Orleans, had written. The man met with Henry and convinced him to bring him in as a partner, and in return, he would help him learn the latest techniques in printing. After many meetings behind closed doors, the deal was made.

Early in the Spring of the following year, Richard Rhineheart arrived in New Orleans. The two shook hands at the front door of the newspaper and then went into Henry's office and closed the door. The meeting lasted until late in the day. When the two emerged, they were laughing gaily and shook hands again before Mr. Rhineheart left the building.

Unbeknownst to Henry, Jonah had been watching. Hidden behind a door that led to a storage closet, he had heard their parting remarks. He could feel his heart pounding as his father-in-law offered him up to the new man as an assistant. Jonah waited until Henry went back into his office and then he stormed in.

"Did you bring this man here for the reason I think you have?" Jonah all but yelled the words.

Henry's age appeared in the deep-set wrinkles now etched around his eyes and extended past the rims of his spectacles. He slowly lowered himself into the chair behind his desk. He knew what was about to happen; it had happened before, with another son-in-law, his oldest daughter's husband, years earlier.

"Why have you brought someone else in when you know I have waited patiently for this promotion?"

Henry leaned back in his chair. "Close the door, Jonah."

"I will not!" He shouted.

"Very well," Henry said calmly as he fought to control his temper. "Simply put, Jonah, you are not ready for the position I have hired Mr. Rhineheart to fill."

"How can you say that? If I am not prepared, it is no fault of my own!" Jonah was yelling now where anyone in the office could hear him.

Henry became fed up with his rhetoric. "I have said all I intend to on the subject. Now, kindly, go back to your station and return to your work so that I may do the same."

"Don't you dare dismiss me like I am nothing more than some hired hand you took off the streets of New Orleans. I've given myself completely to you for the past seven years! I will not allow you to deal with me in this manner!"

Henry let out a sigh but never raised his voice. "I will know when you are ready. At that time, I will see to it that you are promoted to an area of your expertise."

"I know this business inside and out, and you know it!" Jonah's temper flared out of control. "You're only keeping me in my current position with my current pay so I will continue to live in your house with my wife and children! You fear if my station in life improves that I will move my wife and children out from underneath your control!"

Henry jumped up, pushing his chair into the wall behind his desk. It was as if his anger surged through his body making it impossible to remain seated. "You ingrate!" He took his glasses off and slung them on his desk.

Through clenched teeth he continued. "The only reason I allow you to live in my house is because you could not support my daughter and her children in the proper fashion to which she is accustomed and deserves! I tried to stop her from marrying *'your kind'*, but she was as stubborn as her sister and wouldn't listen! You had nothing! Your family had nothing! Everything you have today is strictly due to my generosity, including your job!"

Jonah planted both of his hands firmly on Henry's desk as he leaned across it to face the old man. "I came from a long line of hard working men! Men who didn't mind getting their hands dirty to make a living for their families. That wrought iron fence that surrounds that *'mansion'* of yours displays my father's skills and talents!"

"Oh yes and that fence did little to keep the likes of you out! If you think you can support my daughter and her children by doing what your father died trying to do for your own mother, go to it!" Henry knew the minute the words left his mouth he had made yet another mistake. He had played right into Jonah's impulsiveness and said the very words he had fought for years to keep suppressed. He had already lost one daughter and grandchild to just such a fight as this. It was his pride that had kept him from correcting the situation then, and it would be the same vice that would prevent him now from asking Jonah to stay.

Jonah took his hands from Henry's desk and stood up straight; the gauntlet had been thrown down. Without saying another word, Jonah pulled his work apron over his head, wadded it into a ball and threw it on the desk between them. He turned and went into the work area and retrieved his coat and hat and walked out of the newspaper office slamming the door behind him. Henry dropped into his desk chair and shook his head.

Jonah knew he had to walk out and leave all of it behind or he would be selling himself, lock, stock and barrel to his father-in-law. He walked slowly down the sidewalk in the Garden District, passing other homes of the wealthy and suddenly despised them all. He had only one option now. Caroline's sister and her husband lived in Jefferson, Texas and were doing well. They had invited them numerous times to come for a visit. Jonah only hoped now that they would offer them a place to live while he looked for work. He knew he had to leave New Orleans.

When he got to the Fontenot home he entered through the servant's entrance; it felt more fitting now. He realized the house had never been a home to him. When he came into the kitchen Cissy was preparing dinner. She spun around to face him.

"Missa Jonah, what you be doin' comin' in this house through that door?" Before he could answer her, she wiped her hands on her apron and came and put her big brown hand to his forehead. "Lordy, you be sick?"

"No, Cissy," he said as he took her hand from his face and gently squeezed it. "I'm not sick. Well, not in the way you mean. I'm afraid it's worse than that."

"It be you and Missa Henry again, ain't it? Now Missa Jonah, I know he beez rough on you sometimes, but I don't really think he means it. It be alright, you see." She started to turn to get back to her cooking when Jonah gently grabbed her arm.

"Not this time, Cissy. We're leaving." He was as shocked as she was to hear the words spoken out loud. She spun her big body around to face him. Her eyes wide with fear.

"Now, Missa Jonah, you don't mean that. You kill Miss Abbigail if you go takin' them babies from her; and me too." Tears streamed down her face.

Without saying a word, Jonah let go of her arm and turned and quietly left the kitchen. He made his way to the foyer and up the staircase, dreading his next move. He needed to find Caroline and tell her the news.

Over the next three days, they packed everything they owned with Abbigail and Cissy's cries reverberating in their ears. The night before their scheduled departure, Henry summoned Jonah to his study. Jonah pulled the pocket doors open and walked into the dimly lit room.

"Close the door, Jonah." Henry stood in a corner of the room drinking bourbon and staring out the window into the nothingness of the night. He turned then to face Jonah.

"Care to join me for a drink?"

"No," Jonah answered flatly. He sat down in the chair in front of Henry's desk.

Henry made his way over to the desk and sat down across from him. "I respect your decision to leave Jonah, but certain considerations need to be discussed."

"Such as?" Jonah's words dripped with resentment.

"The children. Jonah. You need to consider the children."

"I am considering my children and my wife, but I won't stay here under your roof another day. We're leaving in the morning."

"Listen to reason. We have already lost one grandchild to the irresponsibility of the parents. I don't want to lose another."

"And what do you suggest to prevent it from happening again?" He assumed Henry was going to offer him the promotion now, just to get him to stay.

"Ralston is old enough to survive such a trip; it's Virginia I am concerned with. She's young, and she has suffered several ailments already. Nothing major, I realize, but that's not to say that with being exposed to all of the diseases and without adequate doctors...."

"Are you suggesting I leave my daughter here with you?" Jonah was incredulous.

"Yes, but only until you are settled in Texas, then you can send for her and I will personally escort her back to you and Caroline."

Jonah stood and looked at his father-in-law and just shook his head. He walked to the pocket doors and pushed them open and walked out of Henry's study without another word spoken between them. He went upstairs to his and Caroline's bedroom, slamming the door behind him. He sat down on the bench at the end of the bed and ran his hands through his hair. Caroline came in and he turned to face her. He could tell she had been crying again.

"Did you talk to Father?"

"Yes, I did and you won't believe what he suggested. He wants us to leave Virginia here with them until we are settled in Texas! Can you believe it?"

"Jonah, Father says the railroad will be finished early next year and..." Caroline broke down into sobs.

"He spoke to you about this?" Jonah yelled.

"I know you want to leave, but I don't want to lose my child the way my sister lost hers."

Jonah jumped to his feet and rushed to her and grabbed her arms. "It won't happen. Do you hear me? It won't happen."

"I'm not willing to risk her life, Jonah! I'm leaving her here with Mother and Father until we are settled and he can bring her by train. It will be safer!" She pulled away from him. "Otherwise you can go alone and come back for all of us."

Jonah turned and walked out of the room. He couldn't believe the sudden turn of events now forcing him to either leave his young daughter or his entire family behind. Later that night, before he finally fell asleep, he knew who he would be waving good-bye to from the boat the next morning. What he couldn't have known was that he would become a bent and bitter man, with his life almost spent, before he would lay eyes on her again.

# Chapter 4

*Suzanne*
*Texas -1999*

I awoke this morning with still no word from Gina. I usually hate Mondays, but I've lived for this one all weekend. I hoped Mother might have returned early from her trip and Gina would have called with an answer by now. Patience is not my strong suit and curiosity is now inching closer and closer to anxiety. I haven't slept well in the past few nights. The dream is haunting me.

I woke up before daylight and since Max is still out of school for the holidays, I decided to go into work early. Besides, I didn't want to see Tony, so I left a note on the bar telling them I had to be at the bookstore early. I've grown smarter over the years. When you catch a husband in a lie, you don't show your cards until you're ready, and well, I'm not ready; not just yet.

I got to work just as daylight began to lighten the gray and rumbling sky. I have always relished the quiet before the customers come rushing in for cappuccino, coffee, and their morning newspapers. As I went around the room, turning on the banker's lamps with their shades of emerald and amber, my thoughts suddenly went back to when I took this job and left the corporate world behind. I felt myself smile for the first time in days.

I remember it like it was yesterday, even though I've been here four years now. I was going through something back then and I wanted; no, I needed to visit a familiar place. After marrying Tony, while our love was still new, he had seen how burnt out I was with my job. He told me to take some time off and explore other avenues. I had jumped at the chance, but then reality set in and I realized I had no idea what I wanted to do with my life. I found myself seeking solace and got dressed one day and drove to the last place that I had really felt peace; Drexel's Bookstore.

It was the memory of finding that haven the first time that had stuck with me. I had always loved Brookfield with its tree lined sidewalks that led you in front of unique shops that were housed in the old buildings that had once been department stores of the sixties. The town square looked like something from a Norman Rockwell painting.

I pulled my car into a space right in front of the store. There wasn't a parking garage in sight. I got out and felt my body exhale as if I had been holding my breath. When I opened the paned glass door and heard the tinkling of the all too familiar bell that hung from the top of it, a smile crossed my face and I felt it travel all the way through to my soul. I suddenly felt at home. I hadn't been back in so long; I was shocked and relieved to see that very little had changed. There were people from all walks of life milling around the shelves and at the counter of the coffee area. I was so happy to see the store had survived and was thriving. I knew people were genuinely drawn to a place like this. Not just for books and magazines, but for the nostalgia of days gone by. I was lost in my memories when a woman's voice brought me back to the moment.

"May I help you?"

I turned to see an attractive middle-aged woman smiling at me. "Hi, yes, does Mrs. Drexel still own this store?"

"Yes, she does. She should be in at any moment if you would care to wait."

I was shocked. "She still comes in?"

"Well, not as often, but she is this week for the interviews."

I felt one of those 'God' nudges in my spirit. "What is she interviewing for?"

"I'm sorry, I thought you might be one of the applicants. We're interviewing for a manager. We lost our last one a few weeks back."

"Oh, I see. Well, I worked here when I was in my twenties. I just wanted to come by and visit."

"Oh, okay. Well, can I get you a cup of coffee while you're waiting?"

"No thanks, I'm fine. I think I will hang around and wait for Mrs. Drexel though."

The woman smiled and nodded her head. "Well, if you need anything just let me know."

She turned then and I watched her make her way back up to the counter. I stood still with the woman's word's running through my mind; they were looking for a manager. Granted, it was a world away from the kind of work I had been doing for the past twenty years, but I couldn't help thinking how nice it would be to come to this oasis every day. I felt that smile come across my face again. I turned and went over to one of the displays and picked up a book and was thumbing through it when I heard the bell above the door and turned and saw her come in. I put the book back on the display and walked over to her.

"Mrs. Drexel?"

She turned around and looked over the top of her glasses. "Suzanne?"

"Yes," I said smiling at her. "How are you?" My voice was muffled, as she dropped the mail she was carrying to the floor and pulled me into a strong embrace.

"Let me look at you," she said as she held me at arm's length. "You haven't changed a bit young lady." She cupped my face in her wrinkled hands. I could feel myself blush. "What brings this unexpected, but delightful surprise into my life today?" She asked as she bent down to pick up the mail.

"Actually," I said as I stooped down to help her, "I think I just needed to visit an old familiar place. You know what I mean?"

"Oh yes dear." She stood back up. "Well, come along then, and let's go into my office where we can visit."

I followed her, stopping briefly at the counter so she could introduce me to the woman that had greeted me earlier.

"Suzanne, this is my daughter-in-law, Carol. She's helping me out until I find a replacement for my manager. I lost the last one to a large store over in the city." Her brow furrowed at the mention of such a place. "Carol, this is my dear friend, Suzanne."

"It's nice to meet you," Carol said as she shook my hand. She nodded her head towards Mrs. Drexel, "She still refuses to call the big chain store a bookstore."

"That's right, because it's not." She turned to face me again. "Here, take my things," she said as she handed me the mail and her purse. "Go on in to my office and make yourself comfortable and I'll get us some coffee." She then stopped and turned back to face me. "Wait, If I remember correctly, you don't like coffee. How about some hot tea?"

I was stunned that she would remember. "Yes, you're right. Hot tea please." I looked at Carol after she was out of earshot. "I can't believe she would remember."

"Oh," Carol nodded her head and smiled. "Her mind is a steel trap. She doesn't forget a thing."

I laughed and made my way behind the counter and opened the door to her office and went inside. I laid her things on her desk and sat down in the chair across from it. I was looking at the pictures that were framed on the table behind her desk. There were pictures of numerous authors that I recognized that had come there to do book signings. Then my eyes stopped on one photograph that surprised me. I got up and went over and picked it up. It was a photograph of Mrs. Drexel with one arm draped over my then twenty-year old shoulder, when I had worked there before.

"We looked pretty good back then, didn't we?" She said as she came back into the office carrying two mugs. She held one out to me and I took it and sat the picture back on the table. "That's a new blend of tea we're carrying. I hope you like it."

"Oh, I'm sure I will. Thank you. I can't believe you still have that picture."

"Suzanne, you've always been special to me." She motioned towards the chair. "Have a seat. So, how are things with you? The children and your husband, they're alright?"

I came back around the desk and sat down in the chair in front of her desk. "Oh, yeah, everybody's doing great, well, except I don't have the same husband I used to have. Actually, I'm on number three." I winced at the admission of my failures.

"Well, that's nothing to be ashamed of my dear. I was married four times." She tilted her head, made a face, and then smiled. "Sometimes it's just an indicator that you can't pick well and that's all."

"I had no idea. I thought your husband was dead."

"They are in my eyes," she said with a chuckle. "I say kick them to the curb if they aren't treating you right. Life's too short; you know?"

I laughed and shook my head suddenly remembering how funny she had always been. I took a sip of my tea. "Well, I seem to be going through some sort of mid-life crisis or something. I've taken a leave of absence from my job."

"Mid-life crisis huh?" She laughed. "Are you still in accounting?"

"Yes, but I'm beginning to think that wasn't such a good decision. I mean it has paid the bills, but it's just not what I thought it would be in the long run."

"Few things are my dear. I often wondered how you would cope with being locked up in an office all day. You were always so good with people."

"It wasn't easy," I said as a heavy sigh followed my words. "I've felt like a prisoner more than an employee to the company where I've worked."

"Well, you heard me say I'm looking for a manager, right?" She sipped her coffee.

"Yes, I did. I'm sorry you lost your last one."

She waved her hand. "I knew she wouldn't last. But what about you?"

"Me?" I laughed. "I don't have any experience in management." I took a sip of my tea. "I will admit though, the thought of being here every day again does sound enticing."

"Then you should take the job. It would be great for you."

"You're kidding; right?"

"Not at all." She leaned forward and crossed her arms on the desk. "You were great with the customers when you worked here before, and I trust you. Do you know how hard it is to find a person you can trust your business to these days? I don't cherish the thought of coming down here every day trying to weed out the bad ones to find a 'maybe' person. I'm getting older you know."

I smiled. "I'm flattered, truly I am, but I have absolutely no experience in management. I wouldn't know where to begin."

"It's not hard for a smart girl like you. I would train you myself. What do you say? You'd be putting me out of the misery of interviewing one more person."

I sat for a moment and imagined what it would be like to come back to this place every day. It would hardly be considered work; not to me anyway. "Well, if you think I can do it."

It surprised me how fast Mrs. Drexel moved around the desk to hug me before I could even get out of my chair. Then it hit me. I had just quit the job I had for the past ten years. I would be venturing into something I had never done before. The thought sent a thrill through me. It was exhilarating and frightening at the same time. Apparently, it was just what I needed because I suddenly felt a joy flood me that I had not felt in a very long time.

Mrs. Drexel went to the office door and jerked it open. "Carol! Come in here!"

Carol came rushing in the door. "What's all the commotion?"

"No more interviews! We have our girl. Suzanne has agreed to accept the position." She turned around and hugged me again.

"Fantastic!" Carol smiled, as she stepped further into the office and shook my hand. "Welcome aboard!" She then turned and faced her mother-in-law. "Does this mean I can go home now?" she asked pleadingly.

"Soon, soon." Mrs. Drexel said with a smile. "My son has spoiled her. She'd rather be out and about with her friends."

"Guilty as charged," she said with a laugh.

"She'll train quickly, I assure you. Then you can be on your way."

I was still smiling from the memory when the tinkling of the bell above the door brought me back to the reality of the moment. I turned to see Hank, my newspaper and magazine delivery man, at the door.

"Mornin' Ms. Suzanne. Looks like it's going to be a nasty one today, but what can we expect from January?" He stomped his boots on the sidewalk before coming all the way inside.

"Good morning Hank. I think you're probably right, but that usually means good business for us."

"Ah, that coffee sure smells good. How long before I could get a cup?"

"It will be ready by the time you come back up this way."

"Great, let me unload your order and then I'll go and fill up the newspaper machine in front of the bank. I'll run back in and get a cup."

"You got it," I said smiling at him.

Tracy, my young assistant that has been with me since day one came in the front door. "It's starting to rain," she said as she stood in the open doorway. She lowered her umbrella and shook the rain from it before coming back to the counter.

"You're here early, how was your weekend?"

I turned and smiled at her. "You think you know me so well, don't you?" I put the last of the money in the cash drawer and closed it.

"Well, yeah," she said with a laugh. "I know you love this place, but I also know you usually don't get here this early. So?"

"Okay," I said with a grin. "Something interesting happened."

"Oh! Tell me everything," she said as she hopped up on the stool behind the counter.

"Let me ask you a question first."

"Shoot." She arched an eyebrow.

"Do you dream much? I mean do you remember your dreams?"

"I guess," she said as she tilted her head. "I don't always remember very much about them, but yeah, I dream pretty often. Why?"

"Well," I shook my head, "I don't dream very often, but I had a doozy of one Saturday night. My dead grandmother came to me in the dream."

"Well, that's just creepy."

"It wasn't really creepy; bizarre maybe since she didn't look the way she did when she was alive." I felt her staring at me.

"What do you mean she didn't look the way she did? How did you know it was her then?"

I turned then and went over to one of the bookshelves and began to straighten books and she jumped off the stool and followed me. "I can't explain how I knew it was her, I just knew."

The bell above the door rang as Hank came back in. "I'm back for my coffee."

Tracy eyed me and grinned. "Hey Hank. You ever dream about dead people?"

Hank smirked. "Yeah, my ex-wife."

I looked at him. "Wait a minute. I thought you told me you took the part-time job of newspaper and magazine delivery to be able to pay alimony to your ex-wife."

"Right," he said rolling his eyes. "You ask me if I ever dream of dead people. Well, I dream she's dead all the time."

"Oh Hank," I said with a chuckle. "You do not!"

"Well maybe not all the time, but at least once a month when I write the check."

"You're terrible," I said with a scowl on my face.

"You telling me you never wished one of your exes was dead?'

"Does current count?" I whispered.

"What was that?" Hank asked with a laugh.

"Nothing. Now get out of here, we have work to do."

"Yeah, yeah," he said as he headed for the door.

"Be careful out there," Tracy called after him.

He threw a hand up as he went out the door.

Mrs. Murphy, one of the local first grade school teachers came through the door as Hank went out. "Good morning Suzanne. I need to place an order for a book I want to give to all my kids to read during Spring break. I know it's a little early, but I thought I would get a jump on planning. You think you can get me a deal?"

"I'm sure we can fix you right up. Come on back." She followed me to the counter.

"But I want to hear the rest of your dream," Tracy protested.

"Later, I promise."

The day took off and we were busier than I had anticipated. A lot of our customers that day were people from nearby offices. Some were teachers still on vacation for the holidays, and then there were my regulars. Retirees that found the bookstore a place to go in the morning when they were still on their *'work'* clocks and got up early with no place to go.

It was almost noon when I glanced at my watch. Somehow, I had temporarily forgotten all my troubles when the phone rang. I picked up the cordless from the shelf behind the counter. "Drexel's bookstore, may I help you?"

"Suzanne, it's Gina. Is Tracy there with you?" My heart leapt into my throat.

"Yeah, why?"

"Get her to watch the front. You're going to want to take this call in your office." She sounded winded.

"Okay," I said trying to calm the beating of my heart. "Hold on." I motioned for Tracy to come and take over and took the cordless into my office. I sat down at my desk and took a deep breath. "Alright, I'm in my office now. What did you find out?"

"Are you sitting down?"

"Stop it Gina! Just tell me what you found out!"

"Okay." I heard her take a deep breath. "Grandma Avery died the year you were born!" She almost yelled the words.

"Who?" I had never heard anyone in our family by that name.

"Grandma Avery. Virginia Avery was Mama's grandmother on her mother's side."

"So that would make this woman our great-grandmother and I've never heard her name. Have you?"

"Nope, and there is a very good reason for that."

"And what would that be?"

"Well, according to Mama, Virginia was a horrible woman. She had three children; Mamaw and two younger boys. She abandoned her husband and the kids in Marshall when they were all little. She initially took the youngest boy with her, but then she sent him back on a train with a note pinned to his shirt that said, *'Andrew if you don't want him, put him in a home.'* Mama has the whole twisted story in her family tree book."

I hadn't noticed that I had begun to shake until I pulled a cigarette from the pack and tried to light it. I paced the floor with the phone in one hand and the cigarette in the other. I took several puffs from it. "That's a lie," I heard myself say.

"What? How do you know?" Gina asked. "Are you smoking? I thought you quit!"

"Mother's wrong; it's not true!"

"You do know you're making no sense right now, right?" Gina laughed.

"It's not funny Gina!"

"Well, I don't know what you're talking about or how you think you would know if it was true or not, but there is one more thing."

"What's that?" I asked as I put the cigarette out in the ashtray on my desk.

"When did you say you had the dream?"

"Well, I guess it was actually Saturday morning, because I woke up and looked at the clock and it was four-forty-four."

"Okay, well Saturday was January third."

"Yeah, so?"

"Suzanne that's the date she died."

"No way!" I sat back down in my chair and flipped my desk calendar back to Saturday and stared at the date.

"I know! It's really weird. But…"

"Gina I'll call you back."

I hit the end button on the phone and could still feel the hairs on the back of my neck standing up. Tracy tapped on the door and told me a customer needed to talk to me and I was suddenly grateful for the interruption. I followed her to the counter and went through the motions of helping the customer as if I was on automatic pilot. When the woman walked away Tracy was staring at me.

"Are you alright?"

"No," I sighed. "I've suddenly got a splitting headache. I think I'm going to leave early. Do you think you can handle things here?"

"I'm sure I can, but are you sure you're okay to drive?"

"Oh, it's not that bad." I smiled and went to my office and grabbed my purse and came back out and stopped again at the counter. "If you need anything call me at home. I'll see you tomorrow."

"Okay," Tracy called out behind me. "I hope you get to feeling better."

I walked to my car in a stupor. It had stopped raining, and once on the highway, I was relieved to find myself stuck in traffic. All I could think about were Gina's words. I had to come to some kind of understanding, if there were such a thing, that would help my mind make sense of it all. I knew in my heart if I tried to just forget the dream, it would haunt me for the rest of my life. And why had there been such a strong urge to defend the woman when Gina told me what Mother had said about Virginia abandoning her kids?

*'I never knew the woman',* I yelled into the emptiness of the car. Suddenly a car passed me on the highway. The driver was honking and

yelling at me. How long had I just been sitting there? Traffic had moved on and I was just sitting there in the middle of the highway? What was happening to me? I turned the radio on and turned it up to drown out the thoughts in my mind.

When I finally reached my driveway, I had to pull up short. Max and some of his friends were in a heated game of basketball. I sat in the car staring at my teenage son. He was sixteen and almost fully grown, yet I could easily remember when he had been a baby lying in the baby bed in the nursery. The memories continued and I could see him riding his tricycle down the sidewalk. I couldn't imagine any woman just leaving her children, especially putting one on a train alone and so young.

I almost jumped out of my skin as Max tapped on the car window. "Hey Mom, what are you doing?"

"I'm fine," I said as I opened the car door and got out.

He laughed. "I didn't ask how you were, I asked what you were doing? You still spooked about that dream?" He asked with a chuckle.

"Maybe I am," I answered with a sarcastic tone. "Is Tony home?"

"He called and said he would be late. Maggie's in the kitchen fixing soup or something. Can I order pizza for me and the guys?"

"That's fine," I said over my shoulder as I went up the front steps and opened the front door and went inside. I stopped by the foyer table and gathered the mail and followed a tantalizing scent to the kitchen. Maggie, our housekeeper and cook, but also my friend, was standing in front of the stove stirring the pot of whatever smelled so good.

"Hey, welcome back," I said as I dropped my purse and the mail on the bar and made my way over to her. I put an arm around her shoulder. "Whatever you're cooking smells heavenly. What is it?"

"Never mind missy," she said with a smile. "It's one of my sister's secret recipes." She laid the big spoon down on the spoon rest and turned the fire down under the pot. She wiped her hands on the big white apron she was wearing and looked at me suspiciously.

"So," she said raising her eyebrows. "What's been going on around here while I was gone?" She picked up the tea kettle from the stovetop and went over to the sink and filled it with water. She took it back over to the stove and put it on a burner and turned it on.

I could see her standing there with her hands on her hips, staring at me. "How is your sister?" I turned and sat down on one of the barstools at the bar.

"She's fine, and don't try to change the subject."

"You've been talking to Tony; haven't you? What did he tell you?"

She came over and sat down across from me. "I haven't talked to Tony, but Gina called a little while ago. She said she had tried you at the bookstore but you had already left. You might as well go ahead and tell me what's going on; you know I'll get it out of you eventually."

I looked at her and sighed. 'Okay. Something really strange happened while you were gone, but let me run upstairs and change while you get us a cup of tea."

I ran upstairs and found my favorite pair of jeans and a long sleeve t-shirt and changed into them and went back down to the kitchen. Maggie had just placed two mugs full of steaming hot tea on the bar. I sat back down on the bar stool and pulled the mug to me and bobbed the tea bag up and down in it before taking it out and putting it on the saucer between us. I poured sugar and creamer in and stirred before I made eye contact with her again. "Okay look," I said hesitantly. "I know what I'm about to tell you is strange, but I just don't want you to think I'm crazy for making something out of it. Okay?"

She cocked her head and looked at me while she stirred sugar and cream into her own mug. "This must be a doozy. Let's hear it."

"I had this really weird dream early Saturday morning." Over the next few minutes I shared all the sordid details with her and what Gina had found out from my mother. When I finished, she sat quietly for a few minutes just looking at me.

"Well say something!" I nervously reached into my purse and pulled out a pack of cigarettes and lit one.

"Wait just a minute! When did you pick up that nasty habit again?" She was clearly upset remembering what a bear I had been when I had quit over a year earlier.

"Oh Maggie, I've been smoking again for weeks. I've just been hiding it from everybody. But please, no lectures; not right now."

"Very well, but we will discuss this little matter later," she said with a scowl on her face.

"Thank you. Now tell me what you think about the dream and what Mother said!"

She sighed. "Let me see if I've got all this. You had a dream where your dead grandmother came to you, but she looked nothing like she did when she was living. She takes you to a house in the town where you grew up and your dead aunt was there."

I nod my head.

"And your grandmother gives you a keepsake box that has a mirrored lid and when you look in the mirror, it's not your face you see. Then some woman, you don't see, asks, *"Who died the year you were born?"*

"Yes," I say as I take a drag from my cigarette and exhale the smoke away from her.

"Then your mother tells Gina that this woman, *Virginia,* was your grandmother's mother that abandoned her in Marshall and never came back, and she is the only death the year you were born in 1958?"

I took a sip of tea. "Yes, that's it. And she died on the same day I had the dream; January third."

Maggie got up from the barstool and went over and stirred the soup on the stove. "And this *Virginia* woman took your grandmother's youngest brother with her when she left but then sent him back on a train; alone, and she had pinned a note to him to his father instructing him to put him in a home if he didn't want him?"

"Yes," I frowned. "That's what Mother said."

Maggie came back over and sat down across from me. She waved smoke from her face. "Either smoke that awful thing or put it out!"

"Sorry," I said as I snubbed the cigarette out in the ashtray and fanned the smoke away again.

"Here's what I think," she said as she took a sip of tea. "Your mother's opinion is obviously tainted if all of her information came from her mother, one of the children that was abandoned. So, I guess you need to find out if what she was told was the truth."

"How am I supposed to do that?"

"Well, I think you were definitely given the dream for a reason."

"What do you mean?"

"What I *mean* is, I think that was more than just a dream. It was more of a message of sorts."

I sighed. "Yeah, I was afraid that's what you would say." I started rubbing my temples trying to ward off the headache that was gaining strength.

"Well, you did ask for my opinion." She got up and went back to the stove and turned off the fire under the soup pot. You know you're going to have to start with your mother to figure all of this out." Maggie glanced over at me and frowned. "I know you two aren't close, but I don't see where you have a choice. She's the only one left out of her family that's still living, isn't she?"

"Yeah," I sighed. "She's the only one, and she does all that genealogy stuff."

"Well then, there's your answer."

"I dread it. Plus, the woman has been dead forty years. I'm not sure how much information Mother has on her."

Maggie walked into the foyer and I followed her. She took her coat and purse from the closet. I helped her into her coat. "Suzanne, your grandmother came to you in that dream for a reason. I believe she's trying to tell you something."

"Really? You believe that?"

"I certainly do," she said as she turned around to face me. "Look, sometimes things happen to people that devastate them so much they find a way to communicate the truth to us; even after they die."

"Maybe, but why me? I wasn't any closer to my grandmother than I am to my mother."

She patted me on the shoulder before opening the front door. "Just call your sister, I promised her you would. I'll see you in the morning."

I watched her as she went down the front steps and made her way to her car in the driveway. She turned and waved and I went back inside. I closed the front door and went into the den and picked up the cordless phone. I sat down on the couch and called Gina. She answered right away.

"What took you so long?" She yelled and before I could say another word, she was yelling again. "Suzanne, she's buried here in Marshall, in an unmarked grave in the Catholic Cemetery!"

"What?" My body sprang up from the couch like a jack in the box. I began pacing the floor. "I thought Mother said Virginia left Marshall when she abandoned her kids."

"She did, but something about all of this was just bugging me. I had to return some books to the library, so I just thought I would ask the librarian if they had old obituaries from the paper, and they did. It took just a little looking and I found the write-up."

"What did it say?" I lit a cigarette and watched as the smoke snaked its way into the room.

"Hang on, I have it right here, I'll just read it to you. It says Virginia Avery died on January 3, 1958. It says she lived in the Oakland-San Francisco Bay area for fourteen years before returning to Marshall. She is survived by three children, Elisabeth, Jonathon and Addison. Wright's Funeral Home handled the funeral and she is buried in the Catholic Cemetery."

"That's it?"

"What do you mean *is that it?* It's a lot more than you had five minutes ago!"

"No, I didn't mean it that way. I just meant it's not a lot of information." The pounding in my temples increased. "Wait. You said she's in an unmarked grave? How do you know that?"

"After I got the obituary, I went to the Catholic Cemetery to see if I could find her grave. When I couldn't find it, I came back home and called the Catholic Church office. The woman that answered the phone told me about the fire."

"What fire?" I hated it when Gina talked in riddles like she was doing now.

"Back in 1958, the secretary for the church had taken the record books home to do some work in them, and her house caught fire and the record books were destroyed. But, the woman I talked to today said they have a master copy and she would look into it and see if she could find the record of which plot in the cemetery is Virginia's. She's going to call me back when she finds it."

"Hey, let me call you back."

"Alright, but don't forget."

I hung up the phone and went back into the kitchen and sat down at the bar. My mind was reeling. Could this have really just happened? Over the next few hours I did everything I could to keep my mind occupied, but nothing was working. My thoughts continually went back to Virginia. Finally, I decided what I needed to do. I picked up the phone and called Gina back.

"Okay, I'm coming to Marshall tomorrow. We will go together to the Catholic Church and see if they have any other information about her. They might know more than Mother does."

"Great! I'll be ready when you get her."

"Thanks Gina."

I pushed the end button on the phone and then punched in Maggie's number.

"Maggie, I spoke with Gina and she's found some things concerning Virginia. I want to take off and go to Marshall tomorrow. Can you stay over and hold down the fort with Max?"

"Goodness, she must have found a great deal for you to be taking off to go there. How do you think Tony will handle you going?"

"Not well, of that I'm sure, but I feel like I need to do this. You don't think I'm over reacting, do you?"

"No, I don't. I think if it was me, I would want to find out what I could."

"Okay then, you'll stay tomorrow night?"

"Of course I will. You have certainly peaked my curiosity. You'll have to call and tell me what you find out. I won't be able to wait until you get back."

"I will Maggie and thanks."

## Virginia's Diary

I hung up the phone and went upstairs to take a shower. Tony still wasn't home when I came back downstairs to fix myself a bowl of the soup Maggie had cooked and left on the stove. I called Tony's office but it went straight to his answering machine. Max came in and we visited before he went upstairs to his room. I straightened up the kitchen and went into the den. I grabbed a book I had been reading from the coffee table and curled up on the couch with it. After just a few minutes I laid it back on the table. You would think my thoughts would be consumed with where my husband was, but that wasn't the case. I could not stop thinking about the woman that lay buried in an unmarked grave, in a town she left so many years before, and why she was coming to me to help her.

# Chapter 5

*Suzanne*

I hate to tell a lie, even the little white ones that we almost all tell; it weighs me down with guilt. I told Mrs. Drexel and Tony that I had to go to Marshall to be with Gina. I told them she was sick and might need surgery. I added the surgery part just in case one day wasn't enough time to find what I was looking for, whatever that might be, so I would already have an excuse if I needed to stay longer. The whole thing was starting to worry me. I had never been one to obsess about anything, and yet that's precisely what this felt like; an obsession. I kept telling myself that I was too old to be acting foolish over a dream, but my mind just wouldn't let it go. Somewhere, deep inside of me, I know there is something to all of this. I just know. I wish I could find the words to really explain how I felt when I woke up from the dream. I couldn't seem to find the right words when I tried to describe it to Maggie or Gina. I'm not sure we have the *'right'* words in the human language to describe certain *'feelings'*. At least not this time.

How was I going to tell either of them that after waking at 4:44 that morning that I now saw those same numbers all the time. Every time I looked at the clock lately it seemed to be the same time, although in the afternoon, not the wee hours of the morning. I saw them on license plates on cars. I got a bill in the mail for repairs to the back-walk way at the house and the invoice read $444.00!

I had gone to bed early, even though Tony wasn't home yet, but I couldn't fall asleep. But, I pretended to be sleeping when I heard him come into the bedroom just before midnight. This morning, I slipped quietly from the bed and pulled on a jogging suit I had laid across the bench at the foot of the bed. I put my shoes on and pulled my hair up into a pony tail without going into the bathroom to brush it. I didn't want to make any unnecessary noise. I pulled the overnight bag that I had packed from the closet and slipped downstairs. I wrote a note and left it on the bar in the kitchen.

It was still dark when I pulled onto the freeway. I had never seen it so empty of cars. I pulled into the driveway of my childhood home, that is now Gina's house, a little over two hours later. I saw a look of surprise on her face when she came out onto the porch. Then she laughed when I got out of the car. I knew I had to look a mess.

"Well, well. If it isn't Sherlock Holmes all decked out in her finest." She reached and hugged me as I stepped up onto the porch. "You sure got here early."

"I snuck out of the house before anybody was up," I said hugging her.

"Aw, I see. Up to your old teenage tricks, huh?"

"Ha. Ha."

"Glad you didn't have car trouble looking like that," she said as she pulled away from me and looked me up and down.

"Yeah, well I love that worn-out robe you're sporting too."

"Touché," she said as she opened the front door. "Well, come on in and I'll put the tea kettle on."

I stepped into the foyer of the house and felt a calmness wash over me I hadn't felt in a long time. "I love coming back here," I said as I turned and took everything in. "I'm so glad you bought the place when it came up for sale."

"I just had to have it. I never really got over it when Mama and Daddy sold it when they got the divorce."

"Me either," I said as I closed the front door.

"Well, go on upstairs and put your things away. I've got everything set up for you in your old bedroom."

"Oh Gina, that's great. Thank you. I'll be back down in a minute."

I slowly climbed the same staircase I had climbed until I was ten years old. A thousand memories flooded my mind as I gripped the banister I had once slid down as a kid. I could almost hear the old familiar laughter coming from the comedies playing on the television in the den downstairs.

I finally reached my old room and slowly turned the door knob. I stepped inside and was almost moved to tears. Gina had painted the room the same shade of buttery yellow that I had loved as a child. I dropped my bag and purse on an upholstered chair in the corner of the room. There was an iron bed against one wall that was painted robin's egg blue. It had a fluffy white comforter that draped over it and fell to the sides that overlapped the white eyelet bed skirt that went to the floor. I couldn't help myself, I went over and just fell back onto the bed. I felt the tension I hadn't realized was gripping me, slip away. I lay there with my eyes closed and remembered lying there as a child with a flashlight under the covers, reading *Nancy Drew Mysteries.* I wanted those days back. I wanted the freedom I had taken for granted back then to return. Unexpected tears welled in my eyes and escaped down my cheeks. I slowly raised from the bed and wiped my face and that's when I saw it. Through the white laced curtains, I could see the branches of the old oak tree that still stood outside my window. As a child, I had always thought it was big, but it was massive now.

I walked over to the window and pulled the curtain back to have a closer look at my favorite tree. That's when it hit me. I glanced past the barren limbs and saw the Catholic Cemetery in the distance and memories flooded my mind once again. I had climbed out my window many times as a child; out onto the limbs of that old tree, with my binoculars hanging around my neck to watch the funerals as they were taking place. I suddenly remembered one particular day.

I must have been all of six-years old when Daddy had caught me high up in the tree with my binoculars to my face.

"Suzanne! What are you doing up in that tree?" He had startled me. I thought he was still out back in his shop.

"Daddy, look." I said as I pointed towards the cemetery. "Who are those women in the black dresses with the capes on their heads?"

Daddy turned to look and then motioned for me to come down out of the tree. "Be quiet and get down out of that tree!"

I shimmied down to the lowest limb and he reached up and pulled me into his arms and then stood me on the ground in front of him. "Listen darlin'," he said getting close to my face. "I know you can't hear everybody else real well, but we can hear you just fine. Those *women* are nuns and they are having a funeral over there and you need to show some respect and pipe down!"

"Oh Daddy, I have to be a nun!"

He stood up straight in front of me and shook his head. "You can't be a nun! Hell girl, we're barely Baptists! Now go and play and stay out of trouble."

"Suzanne?" Gina called from downstairs, jerking me back from the memory that seemed to have happened only yesterday.

"Coming," I yelled as I left the window and grabbed my cigarette case from my purse and left my childhood behind. I reached the kitchen just as Gina sat mugs of hot tea and biscuits on the table.

"Do you remember when I was obsessed with being a nun?" I asked as I sat down at the table.

"Oh Lord," she busted out laughing. "I had forgotten about that. Mama threatened to beat you if you didn't quit crossing yourself every time she said a cuss word."

"Yeah and do you remember I would dress up in Daddy's black suit jacket and wear that black toboggan with the white handkerchief around my neck?"

Gina and I were rolling in laughter at the memory. "What in the world made you think of that?" She asked as she sat down across from me at the table.

"I was just looking out the window upstairs at the Catholic Cemetery and remembered telling Daddy I wanted to be a nun."

"Yeah, you were definitely a strange little girl."

"I was not," I said as I bobbed the tea bag up and down in my cup. "But hey, wait a minute. Didn't you say Virginia's in an unmarked grave in the Catholic Cemetery?"

"Oh yeah!"

"Is that the only Catholic Cemetery in town?"

"I'm sure it is," she said nodding her head. "So that means she was in the ground over there the whole time you were watching those nuns at the funerals."

"That's just weird." I pulled a cigarette from the package and lit it and went over to the counter and picked up an ashtray and came back and sat down. I pulled the tea bag out of the cup and put sugar and cream in it and slowly stirred while my mind drifted elsewhere.

"Okay, you're too quiet. You want to tell me what you're thinking?"

"Well," I said as I took a drag off the cigarette. "It's just weird. To realize I spent so many days of my childhood staring through binoculars at the very place she's buried."

"We don't know where her plot is yet, but yeah, she's out there somewhere." She sighed. "I've got to tell you, that dream of yours has to be the strangest dream I've ever heard. There were so many things in it that I think are symbolic."

"I think so too." I took another drag from the cigarette. "Oh, and by the way, I love what you did with the bedroom. It looks so much like it did when I was a kid."

"It will always be *your* room any time you want to come and stay." She reached across the table and patted my hand.

It felt good to be back in this house again. I felt protected somehow with my big sister sitting across the table from me. I hadn't slowed down long enough in a very long time to realize how much I had missed her. It's funny, when we're young we can't wait to grow up and move away to start our lives. But, when we have hard times or hit unfamiliar ground, we want the comfort of an old house and a big sister.

"How is Doug these days?" I put the cigarette out in the ashtray and slid it to the side of the table.

"Same as always. He's a good husband." She sipped her tea.

"You hit the jackpot with that man. Too bad I didn't luck out like that. I just turned forty and I've got two failed marriages under my belt and one on the way."

"I didn't want to ask." She frowned. "So, things haven't improved."

"Nope." I shook my head. "I caught him in a lie just the other day. He said he and Mark were going to play racquetball, but Kate saw Mark while we were at the mall. If I hadn't been going after the car, I would have run into him too."

"I guess all hell broke loose."

"He doesn't know I saw him. I haven't said anything yet."

"Ah, saving it for a rainy day," she said with a laugh.

"Something like that," I said with a smirk.

"I'm surprised he didn't throw a fit when you told him you were coming here."

"Well, he probably would have, but I left him a note saying you were sick and might need surgery, and you needed me to come stay with you a few days."

"What? Geez Suzanne!" She rolled her eyes. "Now why did you have to go and tell him that? Why didn't you just tell him the truth?"

"Well for starters he's already giving me a hard time about making anything out of the dream, and besides it wouldn't have mattered why I wanted to come, he would have found a reason for me not to."

We both heard a car pull up outside and then a car door shut. Gina got up and looked out the window. "Oh no." She looked back over her shoulder at me. "Mama's here."

"What?" I jumped up and looked out the window just in time to see my mother coming up the sidewalk. "Did you tell her I was coming?"

"Of course not!"

The front door flew open and Olivia Duffey came barreling in. "Yoo-hoo Gina! It's just me."

Gina looked at me and made a face. "Batten down the hatches-incoming!" She covered her head with her hands and grinned.

"No kidding," I mumbled. I sat back down at the table and braced myself.

Olivia stopped dead in her tracks as she came into the kitchen and saw me sitting there. "Well, well. Look what the cat's drug in. I wondered whose car that was in the driveway."

I couldn't help but notice she still looked good. I guess slathering her face with night cream all those years had paid off. "Good to see you too, Mother." The distance between us wasn't just geographical. Vinegar and water, Daddy used to say.

"I was going to let you know she was here," Gina tried to defend herself.

"When?" Mother glared at her. "When she was gone?"

"She came in earlier than I expected. You want some hot tea or a muffin?"

"No, I can't stay. I just wanted to drop these papers off to you."

"What papers?" Gina asked as Olivia held out a brown envelope.

"It's the information you were wanting on Virginia Avery."

I dropped my head and then looked back up at her. "Actually Mother, it was me that wanted the information."

"You?" She spun around to face me. "Now why would you want information on her or anybody else in my family? You've always made it quite clear you weren't interested in any of my family's genealogy." She plopped down in the chair across from me, clearly changing her mind about not staying.

"I had a really weird dream and this woman in my dream asked me *'Who died the year you were born?'*

"And you somehow thought it had something to do with my side of the family? Why not your Daddy's? You were certainly closer to him than you were to anybody else."

"Well, your mother and sister were in the dream, so I thought it might have something to do with your side of the family."

Mother reached and took the envelope back from Gina's hands. "Well, she was the only one that died in my family the same year you were born, but none of us ever knew her; including your Mamaw. I guess your sister told you she abandoned her husband and children. She just ran off. She took the youngest boy, my uncle Addison, with her at first, but then she sent him back on a train alone. She had penned a note to him that said, *'Andrew, if you don't want him, put him in a home.'* She untied the string around the clasp of the envelope and pulled the papers out and laid them on the table in front of me. A picture slid out of the envelope and fluttered down on top of the papers. A gasp caught in my throat. The picture was of a young woman; the same woman I had seen in the mirror in my dream.

"Fix me some iced tea Gina," she said without taking her eyes off me. "So, tell me about this *dream* you had." She crossed her arms and leaned back in her chair.

I felt like I was under interrogation. "It's like I said. Mamaw came to me in a dream and it ended with another woman asking me, *'Who died the year you were born?'*"

My mother looked away just long enough to stare Gina down. "So, you never thought to tell me it was Suzanne that wanted the information?"

"What difference does it make *who* wanted the information Mother?" Gina was clearly getting put out with her now.

She then turned back to me. "So, all this sudden interest in your family roots, which you never gave two hoots about, has all been brought on by a dream?"

"Yes Mother!" I crossed my arms mirroring her posture. "That's right."

"Fine. Virginia Avery was a horrible woman!" She let out a sigh. Then just above a whisper she said, "they thought I looked like her." I almost didn't catch the meaning behind what she was saying, then it hit me. She didn't want to look like the woman who had abandoned her mother. I knew something about that. After my parent's divorce my mother had made no bones about her hatred for me since I looked like my father. I suddenly felt my mother's pain and felt sorry for her, but then just as fast as my sympathy had come, it was gone. She came right back with venom dripping from her words concerning Virginia; a woman she never knew. "She was a sorry excuse for a mother!"

I was about to defend Virginia when Gina shoved a muffin into my mouth. I took the cue and didn't respond to her remark. The old black and white photo lying on the table in front of me showed an attractive woman, probably in her twenties. I had only seen her face in the mirror in my dream, but this picture showed her sitting in a chair, holding a baby in her lap. There was a young girl that looked to be three-years old or so, standing next to the chair. The girl had placed her hand over her mother's. This was not a picture of a horrible woman that didn't love her children. But, the faint smile on Virginia's face looked as if it were somehow forced. My heart ached. But why?

"It was just awful to be compared to her." My mother's words brought me back to the moment. I saw the far-off look in her eyes and I knew she was remembering the pain of being ostracized for something you had no hand in. Again, I knew her pain as my own.

"Who hated her?" Gina asked.

"My grandfather and his sisters, that's who."

"Just tell me what they said to you," I prodded as gently as I could.

She turned sideways in her chair and crossed her legs. "The story they told me was..."

"Wait," Gina said. "Why did *they* tell you the story and not Mamaw?"

"Mama never talked to me about Virginia. And I knew not to ask after what Aunt Esther and Aunt Mattie had told me."

Gina looked over at me, her eyes wide, and shook her head. "Okay Mama," Gina said. "Go ahead."

"They said Virginia ran off with some man and left them all behind. Like I said, she originally took the youngest, my Uncle Addison, with her, but later she sent him back alone on a train with that note pinned to him that said, *'Andrew, if you don't want him, put him in a home.'* Poor little boy. Who would do such a thing?"

"But how do you know that's really what happened?" I asked.

"And just what do you mean by that?"

"What I mean is, Mamaw was just a child. Her father and his sisters must have been the ones to tell her what happened. What if there was more to the story?"

Olivia jumped up from the chair she had been sitting in. "Now you wait just a minute!"

"Mama, I'm not trying to make you mad," I said trying to keep my wits about me and not respond with yelling of my own. "I'm just asking you to consider the possibility that maybe they didn't tell Mamaw everything."

"Mama, please just sit back down and tell us the rest," Gina pleaded.

"There's nothing left to say! My grandfather and his sisters raised my mother and her two little brothers. He didn't remarry until they were grown."

"So, Virginia and your grandfather were divorced then?"

"No, aren't you listening?"

I had to bite my tongue. I had heard those words so many times as a child as she spewed them at me. She knew I couldn't hear well, but she never knew how well I could read lips.

"Yes Mother, I'm listening! I'm just asking you to consider what they told Mamaw would have been obviously tainted where Virginia was concerned and she wasn't there to defend herself."

"You're absolutely right! She wasn't there! That's the whole point, isn't it?"

I dropped my head and took a deep breath. "So, that's all you know?"

My mother dropped back down into her chair. "Well, no, not exactly. I guess I must have been around thirteen-years old."

"What happened then?" Gina asked with a gentleness to her voice. I knew she was feeling the same thing I was. My grandmother and my mother had been caught up in this saga for most of their lives. A legacy of lies that had trickled down through several generations.

"A letter came," My mother began slowly. "If I remember correctly, the return address was Carrollton. That's up close to you, isn't it?" She asked as she looked over at me.

"Yes, it is," I nodded. "Who was the letter from?"

"I didn't know at first. It just had an address in the top left corner; no name. I took it in to my mother and she opened it. I watched as she read it and her face turned red and she began to shake. She folded the letter back up and shoved it back into the envelope and taped it shut. She wrote 'return to sender' across the front and handed it back to me and told me to put it back in the mailbox." A deep sigh escaped my mother then. "I had never seen her so mad. The next time we went to see Aunt Esther, I told her about the letter and they made me leave the room. I tried to listen in from the other room, but they were whispering. When we left, my Mother told me not to ever tell Aunt Esther or Aunt Mattie any of 'her business' again. I never could get that day out of my mind. After I got older, I guess I just assumed the letter must have been from Virginia, but I never knew for sure. So, eventually, I talked to Aunt Esther and Aunt Mattie about it, and they told me everything."

"So, did any more letters come after that one?" Gina asked.

"Oh yes, occasionally another would show up, but I didn't dare take them into Mother. I would just do what I had seen her do, and write 'return to sender' on the front and put them back into the mailbox."

"You never told Mamaw that more letters came then?"

"No Suzanne I didn't! Why would I purposely upset her? Unlike you, I never wanted to hurt my mother!"

I jumped up from the table. "Good Lord, I have never purposely hurt you Mother! What about how you treated me? I've lived underneath this wrath of yours for most of my life! What is it? What did I ever do to you?"

"Okay, that's enough!" Gina said getting up from her chair.

"It sure is," Olivia said as she got up from her chair and shoved it back to the table. "You've never had a problem going against me. You were always defying me as a child and now just look, you're doing it again! You have never passed up an opportunity to upset me. Just like when you were a child, always running to your precious *Daddy!*"

"He's dead now Mother," I yelled. "Do you think you could at least let him rest in peace? He certainly never knew peace where you were concerned!"

"Okay, y'all need to stop!" Gina stepped between us. "This isn't doing anybody any good!"

"You're absolutely right Gina." Olivia grabbed her purse from the table.

"Here." I gathered the papers up and noticed there were a few more pictures of Virginia underneath. I picked them up as well and offered them to her.

"No." My mother stepped back from me. "You keep them." She stormed from the room slamming the front door behind her as she left.

Gina plopped down in a chair at the table. "Well, that went well."

"I know you don't believe me, but I really don't want to fight with her. She knows just exactly which buttons to push to get me riled up. I know you didn't see it that much when we were little kids, but Gina it was terrible. When you went off to school and Daddy went to work, she made my life hell. Do you know that she has never told me she loves me?" I choked back tears. "She talks about how awful Virginia was, but she *knows* how badly she treated me. Does she think I don't remember? The way I see it, I wish she had abandoned me! Living with anybody would have been better than being raised by her! I don't think she has ever hugged me. But she must have, right?" The tears I had fought so hard now betrayed me and ran down my face.

Gina came over and put her arms around me. "Why do you let her do this to you? Listen to me. At least maybe now we may know why she is like she is."

I pushed away from her. "Don't make excuses for her," I said as I swiped the tears from my face.

"I'm not really, just listen a minute. You just heard her say that Mamaw and the rest of her family hated Virginia and they all thought Mama looked like her."

"So?" I rolled my eyes. "Her defense is that since she was mistreated, she should mistreat me because I looked and acted like Daddy; somebody she hated."

55

"Oh Suzanne, some people never get over what is done to them in childhood. Be grateful, you did. You're a great Mom to your kids and you've always hugged and kissed them and they know you love them. So, see? The curse stopped with you. That's something to be proud of. Surely you can look at Mama and Mamaw now and know the apple didn't fall far from the tree and be grateful you're not like them."

"I guess you're right," I sighed.

"But seriously, you and Mama need to find some common ground."

"Well, I don't know where that would be." I walked over to the kitchen window. "By the way," I said as I turned and picked up the picture of Virginia from the table and handed it to her. "That's the woman I saw in the mirror in my dream."

"What? You're sure?"

"Positive."

Gina looked at the picture again and then shook her head. She handed the picture back to me. "I don't know how you're handling all of this. I mean if you hadn't had the dream, I'm not sure we would have ever known this story about Mamaw and Virginia. Oh, hang on." She went over to the counter and pulled a piece of paper from her purse. "It's Virginia's obituary. I thought you might want it."

I took it from her and read it. "That's just so weird," I said shaking my head.

"What?"

"The other day when you read it to me over the phone, something struck me. Do you remember that business trip I took to San Francisco?"

"Vaguely," she said tilting her head. "Why?"

"Don't you remember? I called you that night crying." I could tell by the look on her face that she didn't. "I checked into the hotel and that night I walked alone to the steak house and ate. I told you something about the building seemed so familiar. But then, the next morning I got up and had breakfast at that place across the street. It looked like an old German café and then when I finished I took the bus to the subway station, and there were a bunch of trains sitting there and I just got on one and it took me downtown. Then I got off and got on a trolley and went shopping until it was time for my meeting over in Oakland. Then Aunt Dot and Uncle Lehman picked me up after the meeting and took me way up into the hills above San Francisco and showed me the house Daddy had designed for them."

"Okay," she nodded her head. "I'm beginning to remember now. They took you out to eat and when y'all left the restaurant, Uncle Lehman couldn't remember how to get back on the bridge and you gave him directions and it was right. When you got back to the hotel you called me crying. It scared you that had traveled all over the city and then you were able to give them directions, when they've lived out there their whole life. That was weird! What made you think of that?"

"I guess just reading that Virginia had spent the last fourteen years of her life in the San Francisco-Oakland area."

"Hmm," she nodded her head. "What a coincidence."

"Yeah," I said with a sigh, "quite the *coincidence*". I picked up the envelope and put the papers and the picture of Virginia back in it and put it in my purse. "Let's get dressed. We've got work to do." I headed for the staircase and she followed. At the top of the landing, I headed for my bedroom and she went the opposite way down the hall.

I went in and closed the door behind me. I sat down in the chair and pulled my shoes off and dropped them to the floor. What I really wanted to do was crawl into the bed and pull the covers over my head and pretend I was a child again. A child with no responsibilities in life other than deciding what I wanted to eat for lunch or what game I wanted to play with my girlfriend down the street. I wanted to walk to the library on a warm summer day, check out a stack of books and come back home and escape. It had been such a reprieve to me when I was young. I wanted to be free from the cares of worrying about another failing marriage or hope I was raising my last child with enough love. *'I have to snap out of this'* I said aloud.

I went into the bathroom and stripped down and got in the shower. I stood underneath the hot water until it began to turn warm and knew I wanted to get out before the cold water shocked me. I got out and dried my hair and made a feeble attempt at putting on make-up. I got dressed and grabbed my purse. I went out my bedroom door, shutting it behind me. When I turned around, I was surprised to see Gina coming out of her bedroom, as well.

"Wow, I thought I'd have to wait for you to get ready," I said with a chuckle.

"Oh, I can get it together pretty quick when need be. Where are we going?"

"I want to go to the Catholic Church." I pulled my car keys from my purse. "I feel like there is some kind of urgency about all of this. It feels like I'm working with a time line of sorts."

Driving down the streets of Marshall, I realized not much had changed in the twenty plus years since I had moved away. Within ten minutes I pulled my car into the parking lot of the Catholic Church. I got out and craned my neck to see the cross at the top of the steeple. The sun glistened against the stained-glass windows that portrayed the Virgin Mary holding baby Jesus. I reached into my purse and pulled out the paper and picture of Virginia my mother had left behind.

"It says Virginia was born in New Orleans and her maiden name was Barrister," I said as I stopped to read.

"Well, that's a start."

We walked up the sidewalk that ran between the church and an adjacent building. I saw a door that had a plaque on it that read *'Office'*. I turned the doorknob but it was locked. "Oh no." I said turning to face Gina. "Now what are we going to do? I guess we should have called first."

Suddenly a man came from around the back of the church. He was wearing a Hawaiian shirt and khaki pants. "Hello. I'm Father Frank. Can I help you ladies with something?"

"You're a priest?"

"Yes," he smiled. "Not what you expected, huh?"

"I'm sorry Father," Gina shot me a look that I fully recognized from childhood. It was that *big sister* look.

"It's quite alright," he said with a wink. "I get that a lot."

Gina stepped forward and extended her hand. "My name is Gina and this is my sister, Suzanne." They shook hands and then he extended his hand to me. "We are trying to get some information about our great grandmother. I called the other day and your secretary said she thought she might be able to help. My sister is visiting from out of town, so we thought we would just come by, but I see she's not here?"

"She's out to lunch, but she should be back any time. You're welcome to come inside and wait on her if you would like."

"That would be great." I smiled.

"Well then, follow me." He went back to the office door and pulled a key from his pocket and unlocked it and we followed him inside. "Can I get either of you something to drink?"

"Oh no, we're fine." Gina started to close the door behind her when a woman put her hand up and held the door. "Oh, I'm sorry, I didn't see you there."

"There she is," Father Frank said with a smile. "Ladies this is Amy, my secretary."

"Hello," she said as she passed us and sat her purse on her desk.

"This is Gina and Suzanne," Father Frank said as he pointed to each of us. "I believe Gina spoke with you about some family research?"

"Oh yes," Amy stepped forward and shook our hands. "I remember speaking with you."

"I know I said I would call," Gina said with a smile, "but my sister is in town so we thought we would just come by. I hope that's alright."

"Oh yes, that's fine. Let me find my notes," she said as she went behind her desk. She put her things away, and pulled a book from her desk drawer and flipped through the pages. "Ah, here we are. You were wanting me to look in the master log for a plot number on your great-grandmother's grave; Virginia Avery, right?"

"Yes," Gina said with a smile. "That's right."

"Well ladies, I'm going to leave you with Amy and finish up with my work outside," Father Frank said as he headed for the door.

"Thank you, Father," Gina and I said in unison and I had to stifle a laugh. Here I had been so obsessed with the Catholics as a child and had finally spoken words they would speak.

"Well, you ladies just follow me," Amy said as she went into another room and pulled a large book down from the shelf. She had marked a page with a piece of yellow paper. "I looked up your information the other day when you called and I have found a few things for you." She ran her finger down the paper as she read. "Virginia Avery is in plot A-4. She actually died in Terrell, Texas. Wright's funeral home picked her up and brought her back here for burial."

"Do you have anything else on her?" I asked as I jotted down the information on the back of the paper mother had given me. I saw the surprised look on her face. I knew she thought we should know about our own great-grandmother.

"What other type of information are you looking for?"

I sighed. "You see, Virginia was estranged from our grandmother, so we never heard much about her."

"I see," Amy said with a frown.

"Maybe school records, or information on her parents?"

Amy nodded. "We can sure look." She closed the book she had pulled from the shelf and replaced it and pulled another down. Gina and I inched closer when she opened it. "Do you know her maiden name?"

"Barrister," I said as I flipped the paper in my hand back over and read my Mother's familiar handwriting.

Amy flipped the book open to the 'B's" and ran her finger down the page. "Well, what do you know? She got married here at our church."

"Really?" I stepped closer to see what she was looking at.

"Yes, her parent's names were Caroline and Jonah Barrister. Oh, wait," she said as she reached and pulled down the same book she had just put away. "I think I recognize those names." She opened the book back to where she had discovered Virginia's plot. "Yes! See!" She turned the book around to us. "That's Caroline and Jonah Barrister's plots that are next to Virginia."

"Oh wow," Gina said as she looked over at me and smiled.

"Well, we know we are dealing with the right people now, so let's go back and see what else we can find." She went back to the other book and looked at us and made a face. "Oh my, this may take a little longer. There is a reference under Jonah and Caroline's name concerning our children's school. We will have to go through each year," she said pointing towards a group of smaller books that lined several shelves.

I hooked the strap of my purse over the back of a chair and sat down. "We'll be glad to help go through them. Right Gina?"

"Absolutely," she said as she pulled out the chair next to me and sat down.

The three of us sat for a long time pouring over the records. Amy finally found a school record for Ralston and Francesca Barrister, but no record for Virginia. Francesca's record showed she had died in an accident at the age of twelve.

"That's so sad," Gina commented as she looked over Amy's shoulder at the entry. "I wonder what she died from."

"It has a note here," she pointed towards the bottom of the page. "It says she was killed by runaway cattle."

I shook my head. "That is awful, but I don't understand why her brother and sister would be listed as attending your school, but no mention of Virginia."

The priest came back through the door. Amy turned in her chair to face him. "Do you have any idea why we would have school records for two children from one family, but the third child, which was in between the ages of these two, isn't listed as having gone to our school?

"Hmm," he said as he stroked his chin. "That is strange, but I assure you there isn't a mistake on the school's part. Our records are so accurate, that over the years they have been used numerous times for proof of this or that, even in court."

"Oh no," I spoke up. "I'm not saying your records are wrong, I'm just trying to figure out where Virginia might have been while the rest of her family was in Marshall."

"Amy, is there any information on her burial form?" Father Frank asked.

"Well, some. It says she was born in New Orleans."

"Then that is where I would look. Maybe she was living with

relatives. It happened a lot back then. But, I will tell you this. Most Catholic Churches in Louisiana are stricter than we are, you will probably have to go down there and prove you're related before they will give you the information."

"Alright," I said with a sigh. "Well, thank you for all your help." I stood up from my chair. "You did say you found a marriage license?"

"Yes," she said as she stood up. "I'll get a copy for you."

Gina rose from her chair and she and I began putting the school record books back on the shelf. Amy came back into the room a few minutes later with a copy of the marriage certificate. "It says she married someone named Andrew Lipton and he was from here, in Marshall. He must have died at some point and she married again to someone by the last name *'Avery'*. That may help down the road."

I glanced over at Gina and I could tell she was thinking the same thing. If the Church knew the story that had been handed down, there was no way she would be in their cemetery. I took the paper and thanked her for all her help and Gina and I started to leave.

"Wait," she said picking up a piece of paper from her desk. "Don't forget this." She handed me the map of the cemetery with an 'X' drawn to mark the spot of Virginia's plot. "I guess since she died just a few days ago, you're wanting to put flowers on her grave?"

"Uh, of course." I answered as I glanced over at Gina. "Thank you so much for all of your help."

"My pleasure," she said with a smile. "If I can do anything more, just let me know."

Gina and I walked slowly to the car and got in. I sat staring out the windshield with a thousand things running through my mind. "Okay," I finally said out loud; as much to myself as to Gina. "There is no way the Catholic Church would have handled her funeral if she had done everything Mother said she did. And why did she live in Terrell, Texas?"

"Maybe she wanted to be near her kids?"

"That's not really close. Terrell is almost two hours away and in the fifties, the roads couldn't have been that great."

"That's true."

"I'd say it's time to find out. Is Wright's Funeral Home still in business?"

"Right where it's always been," Gina said as I cranked the car.

"Okay, but first I need to find a florist and pick up some flowers so I can go and put them on her grave. At least nobody can accuse me of standing in a church office and telling a lie. Anyway, I think it's high time somebody visited her grave."

# Chapter 6

*Virginia*
*New Orleans – 1899*

*Dearest Diary,*

*Today is my birthday, and I know I should be happy, but to the contrary, I find myself quite sad. Grandmother and Grandfather arranged a grand party for me, and I had a lovely time, but it was later that I became grief stricken.*

*I had turned in for the night and was beginning to read the novel my dear friend Elisabeth had given me earlier at my party, when I heard Grandmother's familiar tap at my door. She came in and sat on the side of my bed, and I could see by the light of the oil lamp that she had been crying. Before I could inquire as to what had upset her, she put an envelope in my hand, hugged me and quietly left my room.*

*I slowly opened the envelope, and I immediately recognized the contents. It was a train ticket to Texas. It was when I pulled the ticket from the envelope that I saw the note flutter to the floor. From the bed, I saw my mother's signature on the bottom of it. I reached down and picked it up and read the news of my younger sister's demise, and learned of my father's all but fatal injury as well. All due to runaway cattle and I shudder at the thought of such things.*

*My mother was requesting I come for my sister's burial. I knew the ticket was from my grandmother, and the presence of it in the envelope told me she agreed with the request my mother was making of me. That was the thing that grieved me. The letter had been dated a week ago. I can only assume Grandmother and Grandfather didn't want to spoil my birthday with such terrible news. I know they must have already buried my sister, but Grandmother must still think I need to go to Texas, although I cannot imagine her reasoning.*

*I do not know these people nor the siblings they say I have. I have seen photographs of them from a time when they still lived here with us. Few have been sent since their trip to Texas. I wonder if the memories my mind recalls are real, or if in fact, they are simply memories of the photographs themselves. I was only four when they left me here, and took my older brother Ralston with them. Aunt Mary had lost a baby on the same journey, and that had been the reasoning behind them leaving and sending for me later, when I was older, but that day never came. At times, I think I remember them, especially my brother Ralston, as he is only three years older, but still, at times, I think it is just my imagination.*

*Even before the receipt of this dreadful news, Grandmother has been telling me, for the past few years, that I need to go to Texas to see my family. I know she believes it would be in my best interest, as she and Grandfather are getting up in age now. She simply cannot understand I think of them and the servants here as family and no one else. I hold no ill will towards my mother and father for being left here. I have read the letters from my mother, and I know of the hardships they have encountered there, and I have no desire to join them in that lifestyle. I do not consider myself prudish, as Grandmother has suggested. I simply do not understand people that choose a hard life for themselves. Grandmother doesn't like it when I speak of such things, but I remind her that I am grown now, and it is simply my opinion. Although, as I sit and write these words, I do not feel grown at all., I feel very much the scared little girl of earlier days. I confess a part of me wants to know who they are, but somehow going alone on such a journey frightens me. Not the journey itself, but of meeting people that are supposed to be my family, yet I do not know the sound of their voices.*

*Tonight, after reading the letter and knowing what lies ahead of me, I walked through the darkness of this place that has always been home to me. I slid my hand along the banister of the staircase as I crept downstairs. I remember the days when I was younger and I would slide down the banister into Grandfather's strong arms and he would toss me into the air amidst my childish laughter. I went into Grandmother's parlor and all the memories of the tea parties came back to me. Then, I slipped quietly into Grandfather's study and could still hear the stories he would tell me while I snuggled in his lap and inhaled the scent of cigars on his clothing. I found myself weeping by the time I reached the kitchen to get a glass of warm milk. I know my Grandparents only want what is best for me, but I have been quite content living here and teaching from time to time at the orphanage. I have no reason to go to Texas to grieve for a young girl I never knew, even though she was my sister. But, I will go all the same. I will not disappoint Grandmother Abby.*

*I know it will be William, Cissy's husband that will take me in the carriage to the train station tomorrow. I will travel to what I have been told is an uncivilized area, and I do so with much fear in my heart. My mind is made up. My stay will be brief. I will see my mother and father and brother through their tragedy, and I will come back home to New Orleans to the people that are my true family.*

*Well, goodnight dearest diary. We shall count the days together until I return and write of happier times.*

*Dearest Diary,*

*Morning came sooner than I wanted or expected. Somehow, I had hoped the darkness of the night would swallow us all for a time and protect us from the request Texas has once again made on this family. I awoke to Cissy packing my trunk to make certain I had all the necessary items I would need for my mission. Grandfather came in only briefly and told me to expect to be on the train for two days before reaching my destination. He spoke as if I were only making another leisurely trip to visit friends, even though I have never had to travel overnight in the past. He instructed me to find another woman that was traveling alone and stick closely with her. He then kissed me gently on the forehead and whispered good-bye. After he left me, his words began to sink in. Two days on the train! The thought of sleeping among strangers is a horror I cannot even begin to bring myself to think about or I will change my mind altogether. I simply will not sleep until I arrive in Texas. I have never been given to tantrums of any sort, but the child that still lives inside of me wants to collapse at my grandparent's feet and beg them to reconsider. What possible good can a total stranger be to my mother in her time of need? I want to scream the words at them, until I consider their sad eyes and see the pain that already exists, and I simply cannot hurt them further and add to their grief.*

*Cissy prepared a wonderful breakfast for me this morning and never voiced a word of objection when I couldn't bring myself to partake of it. She too must have known this day would come. I keep wondering why we must do this thing if it clearly is against the will of us all. But, I do not question my grandparent's authority, I never have.*

*I have heard the story many times of why I was left behind in New Orleans. Cissy told me that Jonah, my father, didn't want to leave me. My mother only insisted because she feared for my life. Grandfather had never meant for things to turn out the way they had. None of them could have known that the once prosperous Jefferson, Texas would become all but a coffin for its inhabitants once the river ceased to flow beside it. The river had provided a way for a man to become rich, and when it's waters stopped flowing, the very blood of the people stopped as well. Picking up and moving to Marshall, the nearest town, and trying to find work had not been easy nor as rewarding as they had hoped. The stability Grandfather insisted upon and would warrant me being delivered back to them, never came to pass. Grandfather has never discussed any of it with me. Cissy has said she believes it is still too hard for him. He blames himself for my station in life and yet I would have it no other way.*

*As the time neared for me to depart, I lied and said I had forgotten something and ran back upstairs to my room. I closed the door and cried. I do not know why this is affecting me this way. It will only be a short time before I return, and yet I cannot understand this nagging in my soul. I will not be held hostage by Texas the way the ones that have gone before me have. I will be back!*

*I dried my tears and left my room and saw Grandmother and Cissy waiting for me at the foot of the stairs. I stopped and stared at them for a moment as I tried to create a mental picture of them in my mind. Grandfather wasn't with them as he had gone to his office at the newspaper earlier than usual. I suddenly longed for the days of my childhood when Grandmother would take me down to see him at his office. He would take me by the hand and lead me through the building and let me watch as the men worked. I had once entertained the idea of doing the same with my days when I became older, but he had said it was not work for one so fair. Grandmother had made the arrangements with the nuns to allow me to indulge in my other passion and teach at the orphanage. There were so many orphans due to plagues brought over on the ships sailing from foreign lands, and I felt a sort of kinship to them. Even though I have ever so much love in my life, I know there are other children that do not. I felt it my duty to share mine with them. I love my work with the children. I hope to have children of my own someday, but I haven't found a beau that I fancy enough to marry. Grandfather says I mustn't wait too long. He fears I will become a spinster. However, they have provided well for me, and I have a substantial dowry that will accompany me when I do decide to become some gentlemen's* bride.

 *I finally made myself join them downstairs. It was when they escorted me out the front door and I saw Cissy's husband, William, waiting beside the carriage that I broke down and sobbed like a small child. Cissy grabbed me and hugged me and told me to promise her I would take care of myself. It frightened me. It occurred to me she was acting as though she did not believe she would ever see me again. Grandmother reached and took me from Cissy's arms and cried with me. I finally let go of her and William helped me climb into the carriage. I clutched the keepsake box Grandmother gave me so many years before and held it close to my body. William gently tapped the reins against the horse's backs and we gently pulled away. I turned and looked back and saw the two women that have raised me go arm in arm back into the house. I felt like I was viewing a funeral procession and I can only hope it wasn't my own.*

 *We reached the train station and William stayed with me until the train pulled in. I boarded and did as Grandfather had instructed and sat down next to a woman that appeared to be traveling alone as well. I looked out the window as I felt the train begin to pull away and saw William waving goodbye with his worn-out hat.*

 *I must close now dear diary as my heart is simply too heavy to bear.*


*Dearest Diary,*

*I jerked awake as the train pulled alongside the depot in Shreveport. I had tried desperately to stay awake, but Mrs. Tulley, the woman I chose to sit with, has made me quite comfortable and put my fears at ease. I have taken note of how well I am being treated by the employees on the train and know Grandfather's influence is responsible and I am grateful. Mrs. Tully informed me she will be on the train with me for the entire trip as she is going on further west. I feel very fortunate to have someone like her to converse with. She is probably my mother's age, and she has told me she is going to visit her daughter on the occasion of the birth of another grandchild. I have told her the circumstances for which I am making my journey and she seems very compassionate to my plight. We talked quite some time before we shared the biscuits Cissy had packed and sent with me and then I must have fallen asleep again.*

 *It was early morning when we pulled into Marshall, Texas. The town was all a bustle with activity. I must say I am greatly surprised by the size of the town. The first building I saw was the Ginocchio Hotel, the very place where Grandfather has arranged for me to stay while I am here. He said he had no doubt there would be no room at my parent's house. I don't know if he meant that in the sense that he didn't believe they had the money to provide a large enough home or not, but I did not object to staying alone in a room at the hotel. Sleeping amongst strangers on the train has been enough, but to do so with these people in their home would be unthinkable for me. As I climbed down the steps from the train, I noticed the vast buildings in the train yard that surrounded the depot. I could not see the end of the buildings where I assume they must work on train cars and such.*

*As I entered the hotel, a strong longing for New Orleans swept over me. The lobby reminded me very much of Grandfather's study. The ornate woodwork is exceptionally beautiful. The staircase that led to my room had a landing midway, and I turned and looked back as the train pulled out of the station. The finality of my situation burdened me to tears. There's no turning back now. I assumed my mother would be here to meet me, but I saw no one that looked like the woman in the photographs we have at home, nor did anyone else accost me as I entered the hotel.*

*Well dear diary, I will close for now. I fear they will be here soon enough.*

# Chapter 7

*Suzanne*

I leaned down and laid the flowers on the ground in front of us. Except for the tombstones of Virginia's relatives that surrounded the barren patch, you would never know anyone lay beneath the cold ground where we now stood.

"It's so sad," Gina said breaking the silence that felt heavy against my body.

I couldn't say anything at first, I just stood there with a cold wind blowing in my face. "I just can't make the pieces of this puzzle fit. If the church hadn't told us, we still wouldn't know where to look for her. It's almost like somebody was trying to hide the grave."

"Yeah, I know, but who?"

"I don't know." I sighed with the heaviness of it all. "I want to make it to the funeral home before they close and see if they have archive files."

"You think they would still have a file from that far back?"

"I don't know; maybe. Anyway, it's worth a shot."

We got back into the car and drove to the downtown area where the old buildings that had been built at the turn of the century still stood. I turned down a side street and pulled into the side entrance that ran between the funeral home and a tombstone company.

"Hmm," I said as I pulled the car to a stop behind the building. "How convenient, one stop shopping." We both got out and went up the back steps of the funeral home and went inside. "I've never understood why these places are so dark and quiet," I whispered to Gina.

"It's out of respect," she said as she shot me another one of her *'big sister'* looks.

"It's not like we're going to disturb the dead," I said a little louder than I intended. Gina elbowed me in the side and I let out a gasp.

"May I help you?" I sensed the woman behind the desk was perturbed with me before I even approached her.

"I hope so," I said as I reached her desk and lowered my voice. "Does your office have archive files dating back to nineteen fifty-eight?"

"Yes, as a matter of fact we do. What is the person's name you're looking for?"

"Virginia Avery."

"Are you immediate family?" The woman asked as she jotted down the name.

"Yes, she was our great-grandmother."

"I see. If you will just have a seat," she motioned towards two chairs against the wall, "I'll see if we can locate the file."

Gina and I went over to the chairs and sat down. "Wow," I said as I sat my purse on the table between us. "Wouldn't it be something if they really have a file on her?"

"That would be something alright." Gina crossed her fingers.

It seemed to take forever, but finally a man came walking into the room carrying an old, yellowed file folder in his hand. He went to the woman and leaned down and whispered something in her ear. The woman nodded. "Yes, I told you, she was their great-grandmother." The man turned then and faced us and motioned for us to join them at the desk. Gina and I jumped up and rushed over.

"I've located the file you were inquiring about," he said as he looked strangely at us. He opened it and laid it on the desk in front of us and only took two steps back.

"Thank you," I said giving him a look. I almost had to push him out of the way to be able to get close enough to read it.

"Can we get a copy?" Gina directed the question to the woman but was eyeing the man that was now acting very suspicious.

"I'm afraid not," He answered before the woman could say anything. "Company policy. You can take notes though."

I began to scan down the paper as Gina dug in her purse for a pen and paper. "Virginia Abbigail Avery," I read out loud. "Hmm," I said looking up at the woman. "Where it asks for her maiden name, the line is left blank. I wonder why the person supplying the information didn't know her maiden name."

"Not strange at all," Gina said pointing to the bottom of the page. "Look who gave the information."

"Addison Lipton? Why would he have been the one to handle her funeral?" Gina nodded in agreement. I turned the page and we both read the top line at the same time. I knew the shock on her face mirrored my own.

"Excuse me." I said rather loudly as I turned my attention squarely on the woman first and then to the man still hovering over my shoulder.

"Is there a problem?" The woman was clearly irritated with me.

"Well yes, I would say there is definitely a problem." I stood up straight and put one hand on my hip. "You show you buried her in three different cemeteries. I would say that's a problem, wouldn't you?"

"Let's take a look," the woman said nonchalantly as she turned the file around where she could see it. "Oh, that's just an error." She smiled at Gina implying I wouldn't understand such things.

"Three different errors?" I was almost yelling now.

"Ma'am," she said as she scolded me with her eyes. "You're going to have to lower your voice. You must understand this record is very old, what forty years? Whoever filled this out made a mistake. Besides, I'm sure you know where your great-grandmother is buried, don't you?"

"Yes ma'am, we do, and thank you so much for your help." Gina tried to escort me from the building.

"It's a good thing we know where she is because you people sure don't!" I yelled over my shoulder as Gina drug me out the door. Once outside she spun me around.

"What the hell is wrong with you? Are you trying to get us arrested?"

I jerked away from her. "Well, it's just not right! Who lists three different places where they bury somebody? Why would there ever be a mistake like that? Everything about this is just wrong! Especially what Mother said about Virginia!"

"That may very well be true, but you sure can't tell Mother that. Not yet anyway." Gina turned and headed for the car. "But I know one thing for sure, you have got to calm down. Give me the keys. I'm driving."

I tossed her the car keys and climbed into the passenger seat. "Look Gina, I'm sorry. I don't know why all of this is pissing me off the way it is, but it is! Everything Mother said about her is eating me alive. I can't explain it. I just feel like I need to defend Virginia."

"Okay, listen to me." She turned in the seat to face me. "I'm about to tell you something, but you have to promise me you aren't going to freak out further on me, okay?"

"What?" I stared at her, feeling a knot form in my stomach.

"I don't think you saw what was written at the bottom of the second page. You only saw the three-cemetery mess."

"What did you see?" I felt the knot in my stomach move up to my throat.

Gina sighed and pulled the paper she had made the notes on from her purse. "At the bottom of the page it listed where they picked up her body when she died." She hesitated for a moment. "Suzanne, they picked up Virginia from Terrell State Mental Hospital."

"What?" I yelled and I snatched the paper from her hands. My eyes raced over the information until I saw it. "Oh God no!" My hands were shaking. "Gina. Oh my God, she wasn't crazy!" I grabbed her by the arm. "I know she wasn't crazy!"

"How would you know that?" She asked in a semi-calm voice. "She ran off and left her kids for some reason."

"No, no!" I shook my head. "She wasn't crazy! You have to believe me!"

"Okay Suzanne, now you're really starting to scare me."

"I'm sorry," I said and began to cry.

"That's it, we're going back to my house. Now!" Gina cranked the car and pulled out onto the street. I couldn't say another word. The tears came from somewhere deep inside of me. All I could do was stare out the passenger side window as my mind kept hearing those words; *Terrell State Mental Hospital.* I felt like I was on the verge of having a nervous breakdown myself.

"Uh oh," Gina said as we pulled into her driveway. "What in the world is Doug doing home?"

We got out of the car and Gina's husband came out to meet us. "What are you doing home this time of day?" Gina asked as he got closer to us.

"Well, I'm glad to see both of you are alright." He sounded nervous. "Tony called asking how Gina was," he said looking suspiciously at me. "You look like you've been crying Suzanne. Somebody needs to tell me what's going on!"

"Oh man," I sighed as I remembered the lie I had told Tony about Gina being sick and might need surgery.

"I'm sorry Doug, I can explain," I managed.

"Where have y'all been?"

"We were at the funeral home," Gina began.

"Oh my God. Somebody died?"

"It's nothing like that," Gina said taking him by the arm. "Just come inside and I'll try to explain."

I followed them into the house and ran upstairs to my old bedroom and shut the door and fell across the bed and cried. I'd never felt such sadness in my life. When I finally calmed down, I went into the bathroom and washed my face. My eyes were red and puffy, and I started crying again at the sight of myself in the mirror. I came out of the bathroom and crawled into the bed and miraculously fell into a deep sleep.

I woke up an hour or so later and had to lay there for a minute and get my bearings. I'd temporarily forgotten where I was. After I regained my senses, I reached and picked up the receiver of the phone beside the bed and called Maggie. The house phone rang three times before she picked up.

"Hey Maggie, it's me. How are things going?"

"Everything is fine here. Tony called wanting to know if I had heard from you yet. He said he had tried to reach you at Gina's."

"I know, but we were at the funeral home and Doug just happened to be at home when he called."

"Funeral home? What on earth?"

"Oh Maggie, this has really turned into something bizarre and strange."

"It sounds like it and you sound exhausted."

"I am." I fell back across the bed. "Something about this whole thing just wears me out, and I don't understand it. I've had it out with Mother and then the woman at the funeral home too. I just don't know what's come over me." I sighed and she didn't say anything. "Is Max around?"

"You just missed him. He and some friends went down the street to another friend's house."

"Oh okay. So, Tony's not home yet?"

"No, but it's still early. Do you want me to have him call you when he comes in?"

"No, I'll try to reach him at the office. I'm sure he's worried since he called Doug and found out Doug didn't know anything about Gina being sick."

"So, Doug didn't know you were coming?"

"No, and Tony just repeated the lie I told him, so Doug thought Gina and I were keeping some health issue from him."

"Oh my," Maggie said followed by a deep sigh. "What will you do now?"

"I don't know. It's all such a mess."

"Maybe you should just come home."

"Oh Maggie, I couldn't hold up to a long drive right now. I'll leave sometime in the morning."

"Alright, well, try and get some rest. I'm dying to find out what you two have discovered that took you to a funeral home."

"It's terrible Maggie, but I'll wait and explain it all when I get home. Will you tell Max to give me a call when he comes in?"

"I sure will. Be careful honey."

I hung up the phone and called Tony's office and was grateful when it went straight to his voicemail. I left him a message telling him that Gina was going to be fine. It wasn't exactly a lie; she was fine. I got up from the bed and went downstairs. I found Gina in the den. She was sitting on the couch going through some mail.

"Hey, where's Doug?"

"Are you okay?" She asked as she looked up at me.

"Yeah," I said looking back towards the kitchen. "Did Doug leave?"

"Yes," she said with a nod as she looked back down at her mail. "After I explained, the best I could, as to what was going on, he went back to work."

"Look Gina, I'm sorry. I had to lie to Tony or I would have never been able to just take off and come here."

"Yeah, I get that, but did you have to lie and say I was sick?"

"Well, I couldn't think of a better reason, could you?" She just looked at me.

She patted the spot beside her on the couch and I went over and sat down. "Once I explained everything to him he was okay. Look, he knows if you're here, something must be wrong."

"I wish it wasn't like that."

"I know." She patted my back.

I got up and walked over to the mantle above the fireplace and pulled down a picture of me and Gina when we were young. "I miss them," I said looking back over at her.

She got up and came over to where I stood and took the picture from my hands and looked at it and smiled. "Me too. Whatever happened to those girls? All that innocence?"

"Who knows?" A ragged sigh escaped me. "I'm just tired of everything in my life being so complicated."

"So, do something about it." She put the picture back on the mantle.

"Oh yeah, just like that. You make it sound so easy." I headed to the kitchen to get something to drink and she followed me.

"Let's go out to eat dinner tonight," she said as she came in and sat down at the kitchen table. "Doug's got a meeting, so it would just be the two of us."

"You don't think we should wait on him so he could come with us?"

"Listen honey, it's not that Doug doesn't love you, he does, but he's not going to sit through two women talking non-stop through a meal if he doesn't have to."

"Smart man," I said with a smile.

Later that evening as the two of us sat in the restaurant waiting for our food, Gina asked the question I knew was coming sooner or later. "So, how bad is it with you and Tony?"

I shrugged my shoulders and poured sugar into my iced tea. "We just don't seem to get along at all anymore. We just tolerate each other."

"That's too bad. I know the last time we talked you mentioned y'all were having problems, I guess I hoped things had gotten better."

"Yeah, I was hoping for that too, but it didn't happen. He's so condescending when he talks to me, it just goes all over me."

"You shouldn't have to put up with that."

"If I say anything about it, he just says, *'you know I was kidding'.* I'm so sick of hearing those words. They are his answer to everything. I just don't care enough anymore to keep trying to keep the peace."

"Wow." She arched an eyebrow. "I know what happens when you get fed up."

"Yeah, me too. Let's change the subject for now. Shall we?"

We shared little more than small talk as we ate our dinner and then headed back to her house. Doug came in shortly after we got back and he and I visited for a little while and then I told them both good night and went upstairs and took a hot bath. I got out and slipped into my pjs and went back into the bedroom and called Tony's office. I got his voicemail again and hung up. I called the house and Max answered.

"Hey Mom." I immediately felt better just hearing my son's voice. I crawled into the bed and rubbed my bare feet against the soft comforter and felt all was right with the world, at least for the moment. "How's it going?"

"Everything's fine here, how was school?"

"It was okay. I made a ninety-eight on my algebra test."

"That's great. I'm proud of you." I scooted up in the bed and leaned against the headboard.

"So, you're coming home tomorrow?"

"Yes, I should be there when you get in from school. Let me talk to Tony for a minute."

"I don't think he's here, but Maggie's downstairs, do you want to talk to her?"

"Yeah," I said glancing at the clock on the bedside table; it read 8:45.

"Okay, hold on." I heard him yell for Maggie to pick up.
"Hello?"
"Bye Mom," Max said before hanging up the extension.
"Love you Max."
"Love you too Mom."
"Maggie?"
"Yes dear, I'm here."
"Max said Tony hasn't come in yet. Has he called?"
"No, but he did come home from work, he just didn't come in the house. Mark came by and picked him up and he hasn't come back yet."

I sighed. "Alright, well, I was just checking in, I'll see y'all tomorrow."

"I'm looking forward to it. Good night dear."

"Good night Maggie." I hung up the phone and scooted down into the bed and pulled the comforter up around me. I laid there and watched as the limbs of the oak tree outside the window swayed in the wind and the moonlight made shadows dance on the ceiling. I knew within minutes that sleep was not coming for me. I got up and pulled a chair over to the window and sat down. My mind immediately went into overdrive. I couldn't believe Tony was being bold enough to go out with Max and Maggie there. Not to mention he didn't know if Gina was going to be okay or not and clearly didn't care. Even if it was a lie, he didn't know that. I had to accept the fact that my marriage had deteriorated a lot more than I had realized. I'd foolishly thought that Tony had been truly concerned when he was calling trying to find me earlier, but now I think he just wanted to make sure I was really here; far enough away not to be able to check on him.

I suddenly tried to imagine what my life was going to be like once we divorced. Maggie would be the first casualty and just the thought of losing her hurt me to my core. But I knew I'd never be able to keep her on my salary alone. And then there's the house. I can't imagine someone else living in the English Tudor I have loved since the builder handed me the keys. I had wanted that house my entire life. I always felt so at home inside its walls and that's not something that has ever come easy for me. But, no house is worth selling your soul to keep and if I stay with Tony that's exactly what I would be doing.

I got up from the chair and pulled a cigarette from my purse and lit it. I watched as the smoke snaked through the moonlight coming in through the window. Why was it always me that lost in the deal? Why was I always the one that had to struggle to start over? I went back over to the window and stared out into the night. This was not how I envisioned my life to be at forty. A tap on the door rescued me from walking down the dark tunnel of my past mistakes.

"Suzanne?" I turned to see Gina open the door and stick her head in. "I thought I heard you talking."

"Sorry, I didn't realize I was actually saying what I was thinking out loud."

She came in and quietly closed the door behind her. She walked over to the window and stood beside me and we both looked out at the nothingness of the night. "Anything I can do to help?"

"No, not really."

She patted me on the shoulder.

"Oh Gina, why do I keep making such a mess of things?"

"It's not just your fault you know. It takes two."

I shook my head. "Yeah, but how do I keep finding the same one over and over. You know all my exes are typically the same, but I am the common denominator in all of this. I'm just not marriage material."

"I don't think that's true. You just haven't found the right one yet."

"Good Lord, Gina! Don't you get it? There's not a right one for me. I've wasted so many years finally coming to that conclusion. The only good thing that ever came out of any of my marriages are my kids. That much I know."

"Well see, there you have it. Maybe that's what it was always supposed to be, just for you to be able to have the kids." She hesitated for a moment. "I'm assuming you talked to Tony and that's what has you in this funk?"

"No," I said as I put my cigarette out in the ashtray. "He never came home. Maggie said Mark picked him up from out front of the house. He never came inside."

"Maybe they just went out to grab a bite to eat or something."

"Yeah, or *something.*"

"Oh, come on Suzanne, he wouldn't do something stupid with Max and Maggie there. He knows they would tell you."

"Did you miss the part where I said, *'He went out with Mark tonight?'*"

She pulled me by the arm. "Come on, we're going downstairs and I'm going to fix you some Chamomile tea."

"Okay," I sighed, "you talked me into it."

We got downstairs and Gina filled the tea kettle with water and put it on the stove and turned the burner on. "To be honest, I couldn't sleep either.

77

There's something I want to ask you."

"Shoot," I said as I sat down at the kitchen table.

"You know," she began as she came over and sat down across from me. "I've just been thinking. I know Mama really got into all that genealogy stuff. I mean she and I talked occasionally when she was working on it and she would tell me about the hours she had spent at some library somewhere in their archive department. I know she was thorough. Then all of these things you're finding that she never uncovered, and you're not even trying to find anything. It's like it's just falling in your lap. But even with all of that, there's still one thing that just flat out confuses me."

"Yeah, what's that?"

"The way it's affecting you. Suzanne, you're a very rational person and it takes a lot to upset you; always has. And I don't even remember the last time I saw you cry over anything, maybe Daddy's death, but nothing else."

"I know," I said as I got up to get us mugs for our tea. "But come on, you'd be freaked out too."

"That's not what I mean," she said as she got up and got the tea from the cabinet. "It's making you act like somebody I don't know."

I laughed. "Well who am I acting like?" I went back over and sat down in my chair.

She pulled the kettle off the flame before it began to whistle and poured the hot water into our mugs. "Okay, I'm just going to say it. "Do you believe in past lives?"

"A past life? Really Gina?"

"Don't look at me like I'm crazy, I know you've heard people on talk shows and other places talking about it. Come on, you work in a book store. You're telling me there's no books in Drexel's about past lives?"

"There are all kinds of books in the bookstore but it doesn't mean I've read them." I bobbed my tea bag up and down in my mug before pulling it out and laying it on the saucer in the center of the table. "But, okay, I have seen specials on television from time to time, but it's always been about kids that people say recall a past life, not a forty-year old woman."

"What does age have to do with it?"

"You realize how crazy it sounds for us to even be having this conversation, right?"

"Oh, come on, Suzanne. You're not one of those skeptical types."

"Alright, I will admit I do remember hearing a very compelling story about this little girl."

"What was it?" Gina asked as she crossed her arms and leaned on the table.

I lit a cigarette and got up and went over to the window. "Okay, so there was this little girl and every morning when her mother drove her to daycare they would go over this bridge. One day, as they crossed the bridge, the little girl said, *'I died on this bridge.'* The mother of course was freaked out and told her she had never died before, but the little girl was adamant and insisted it was true. Finally, one day the little girl added to the story and said it was *'all orange under the bridge'*. So, her mother dropped off the little girl at the daycare and then went back to the bridge. She parked the van on the side of the road and climbed down the embankment and sure enough, the underside of the bridge was painted orange."

"See! That's what I'm talking about." Gina turned in her chair to face me.

"Look, I'll be the first to admit how weird this is and how it's affecting me, but I can't let myself get too far out there or I'll be the one they pick up from Terrell State Mental Hospital."

Gina got up and came over and hugged me. "Nobody, and I mean *nobody* is ever going to do that to you as long as I'm alive! But seriously, it would explain so much about your life."

"Like what?"

"The way you have always been about your kids. Mama bear is an understatement, and maybe it's like we both said, maybe you only got married so you could have your kids. Plus, you had the dream on the day the woman died for Pete's sake! And then the question, *'who died the year you were born?'* All of this has to mean something."

I nodded my head. "I know. I must admit Mother saying Virginia abandoned her kids, got me the most. I can't imagine anyone just taking off and leaving their kids and never seeing them again. I know I couldn't."

The Chamomile tea began to kick in then and we both decided to try and get some rest and talk more about it tomorrow. I went back upstairs and crawled into bed but my mind just wouldn't shut down no matter how sleepy I was. I didn't want to admit to Gina that I had already thought about my bizarre behavior. I knew well enough that it wasn't like me to get so upset that it would push me to crying. I rolled over and looked at the clock; 12:30. I reached for the phone and called home. Tony picked up on the second ring. His words were so slurred I knew he was beyond drinking, but full-blown drunk. He asked a few questions that I could barely make out and I finally just told him I would see him tomorrow and hung up.

I closed my eyes and tried once again to go to sleep, but then my mind went in reverse, back to my childhood. I guess being back in this room brought it on, but I started to remember things that I had thought strange when I was a child. I suddenly remembered a little café called *Swiss Miss*. I didn't like it for the Kool-Aid type popsicles they sold, but for the building; inside and out. It reminded me of something I had seen before and I remember thinking, even as a child, how strange that was. The little Swiss boy dressed in the shorts with the suspenders and the little hat; it had all been so familiar to me. The way the eves of the building were carved into swirls. Every time we went there I would always get a funny feeling. The same thing would happen whenever I would see the red roofs of the Howard Johnson Hotel. But what was it? Was the feeling, Deja vu', but I was just too young to understand? But what did any of that have to do with Virginia? Those memories had come back to me many times as an adult, but I learned to just blow them off; just something strange that happened when I was a kid. Was that really all it was? Now I wondered. Then out of the blue I remembered something else; how lost I had felt as a child. I remembered a time I had gone into our living room and seen my reflection in the plate glass window and suddenly thought that these people I now lived with were not my real family and that somewhere, someone was trying to find me.

I opened my eyes to the darkness of the bedroom and wondered if those feelings had ever truly gone away or had I just pushed them down as I got older? I got up and tiptoed downstairs; back to that very same plate glass window. I turned on the lamp and once again saw the reflection of that little girl. I saw my tear-stained face and felt five years old all over again. I shook my head, and she disappeared and my forty-year old face replaced her. I turned the lamp off and tiptoed to the kitchen to fix some warm milk. Obviously, the Chamomile wasn't going to do the trick alone; not on this night. I took a mug down from the cabinet and poured the milk into it and put it in the microwave. I watched the timer closely and opened the door before the bell rang. I slipped quietly out onto the back porch and eased down into the porch swing. I wrapped my robe tightly around me and pulled my knees to my chest. My heart hurt. The depth of the sadness that plagued me when I was a child had returned. The swing gently swayed in the cold night as I sipped the warm milk. After a little while, I finally started feeling like I might be able to sleep and got up and headed back upstairs. I crawled into the bed and let the down comforter envelope me and I finally fell asleep.

Gina was surprised the next morning to see me coming down the stairs fully dressed, and carrying my overnight bag. "Where are you going so early?"

"I finally talked to Tony late last night and he was bombed."

"And I guess y'all got into it?" She let out a sigh of disgust.

"Not really, but I just think I need to get home and deal with everything."

"Oh Suzanne." She came over to the bottom of the staircase and hugged me. "Call me and let me know you made it home and that everything is okay."

"I will." I moved past her to the front door. "Do me a favor?" I paused and turned back to face her. "Don't do any more digging until I come back. Okay?"

"I won't." She patted me on the back. "This is your story, not mine."

As I got into my car and cranked it and pulled away, I knew I was going home to a royal battle with Tony. First, because I knew I would have to tell him the truth about why I had come to Marshall, and I knew that wasn't going to sit well. And secondly, I no longer cared what Tony's thoughts or views were, and that was only going to make matters worse.

I pulled onto the interstate that would take me back home, and despite the problems I knew were ahead of me, it was Virginia, who once again, took over my thoughts. I had to come back and find out the truth about her. I had to know what really happened to the woman who died in a mental hospital and then was buried in an unmarked grave. Forgotten for forty-years, by everyone, until now.

# Chapter 8

*Virginia*

*Dearest Diary,*

*I find my room at the Ginocchio Hotel to be quite satisfactory. Someone with taste, very much like Grandmother Abby has taken great pains in the placement of fine, ornate objects all about. The four-poster bed in the center of the room reminds me of my own back in New Orleans. I dare say I am already homesick. No one sent for me today, so I can only assume they will come for me tomorrow. I am weary now, dear diary, and I feel I must get rested for the journey that awaits me.*

*Dearest Diary,*

*I found myself quite famished when I awoke this morning, so I dressed and had a lovely breakfast in the dining hall of the hotel. I find the people of this town quite strange. Even though the hotel must have hosted many a traveler, the patrons gawked at me as though I was the first to do such a thing. Possibly it is because I travel alone, but that is perfectly acceptable at my age, so I do not understand their impertinence.*

   *I had returned to my room and began to unpack my trunk when I heard a loud knock upon my door. My heart fluttered in great despair, as I believed I was about to face a member of my own family for the first time since I was a child. A moment later, I stood staring at a man in my doorway that I contemplated must be my brother, Ralston. The roguish, ill-mannered man quickly informed me that I was mistaken. He said his name was Andrew Lipton, and that he had been sent by my father to retrieve me. The way in which he said the words made me sense I had not been summoned to come here, but I was a mere burden that had to be dealt with. I am aware that my parents are not able to afford help, but surely they can more carefully choose the type of people they associate with.*

*This man then turned, without saying another word, and left me standing in my doorway. He did not escort me in the proper fashion from the hotel, which gave the patrons more reason to glare at me when I descended the stairway back into the lobby. Upon searching the lobby, I could not locate Mr. Lipton. I went out the double doors to the carriage area and was about to return to the lobby when I heard him summon me from a loading dock near the train station. I tried desperately to hide my emotions when I saw that he was not standing beside a carriage, but a buckboard used for carrying supplies. As I approached him, he laughed in a sickening way and hoisted me up on the back of the wagon. He did not give care for the dress that I had chosen for the occasion of meeting my family. I will speak to my parents concerning the way this man has dealt with me.*

*The roads were very muddy from the rains that must have come during the night. He gave little care to the ruts in the road, and I was tossed precariously about the back of the buckboard, which seemed to give him much pleasure. I tried to steady myself, but I had nothing but a shoddy rail to hold on to, and it afforded me little or no stability. I judged by the houses in the area that we were traveling through, that my mother had in fact been forthright in her letters concerning their hardships. I was grateful, once again, for my room at the hotel.*

*I must say when Andrew Lipton pulled the buckboard to a halt I was greatly distressed by what I observed. The house my parents live in is nothing more than the shanties I have seen around the plantations in New Orleans. A woman, my poor mother, stood on the small porch in a dress yellowed with age. Her hair had course white strands running through the auburn of her younger years. Chickens ran freely around the grounds, and an old dog barked viciously at me from the side of the house.*

*As I approached my mother, I took notice of her eyes. They appeared to reveal a vast emptiness in her soul, clearly distressed over the loss of her youngest child. She did not speak, but rather stood in a stoic manner as I neared her. I did not know how to respond, so I simply hugged her haggard body while she gingerly returned the gesture. "Mother," I whispered as I held her, and I felt a shudder run through her body. She turned then, and without a word spoken, opened the screen door and turned the knob on the wooden door and went inside the house. I glanced back over my shoulder to see Andrew Lipton still sitting in his buckboard. His face displayed a wicked smile as if he was taking some pleasure in my plight. I followed my mother into the house and had to wait a moment for my eyes to adjust to the darkness of the room. Then, in the next room I could see a dim light flickering from an oil lamp. She quickly disappeared into the room, and I followed. There, I found the man I was sure to be my father, but he looked nothing like the photographs I had seen. He was extremely frail looking, and the oil lamp on the table beside him cast an eerie aura about his face. His eyes seemed to be sunken deep within their sockets, and his cheekbones protruded causing deep recesses in his jaws. A cane leaning haphazardly across the arm of the chair he sat in gave further attestation to his fragility. The sight of this man caused the hairs on my arms to rise.*

*He stared at me with a look of contempt. "So, you have decided to grace us with your presence." His voice was deep and his breathing seemed labored somewhat. I was aghast at the manner in which he spoke to me; it was as if I was an intruder. Had there been a mistake? Was I not summoned to come here by a letter from my mother? Did he not know the request had been made of me? I felt the sting of tears rising in my eyes. I had never dealt with a situation such as this, and I was not accustomed to such brazenness. I quickly recovered and inquired to the whereabouts of my brother, Ralston. My father just laughed in a wicked tone and stared at me. I turned to see my mother as she continued to stand in a stooped fashion in the shadows of a far corner of the room. "Like you," my father hissed, "he does not care for our way of life and has deserted us as well."*

*With that being said, I inquired of my father the reason they had sent for me if he clearly found my presence distressing. Then, with the help of his cane, he rose from the chair and approached me. I became so frightened that I feared I would faint. I staggered slightly, and then I felt his bony fingers on my arm. "You are my daughter!" he said in a low, cold voice. "You carry my name, and it is my blood, not your grandfather's that runs through your veins, and you will remain here with me, do you understand?" At that moment, I did, in fact, faint.*

*When I awoke later, I was still in the darkness of the shanty, and my mother sat in a chair next to the bed where they had put me. I immediately righted myself and found I was still experiencing light-headedness. I begged my mother to arrange for me to be taken back to the hotel, and she began to cry. "Your father is keeping you here," she said amidst her sobs. "I did not know his plans when I sent for you, Virginia, you must believe me."*

# Virginia's Diary

I heard my father and Andrew Lipton talking in the adjacent room. I gasped out loud when I overheard them discussing the dowry my grandparents have provided for my marriage. I do not know how they would be privy to such things, as I know my grandparents had never told them. "He believes it is his right, as your father, to arrange your marriage. I am so sorry, Virginia, please forgive me." My mother sat beside my bed and sobbed openly. I could not make myself believe what she was saying. Surely, my own parents had not betrayed me in this way.

Dearest Diary,

I have been so distraught since I have learned of my fate that I could not bring myself to write these words. Tomorrow I will become the wife of the treacherous Andrew Lipton. In the beginning, I attempted to run away, but it was to no avail. My father then informed me that he would have my beloved grandparents murdered if I did not comply with his wishes. Andrew was standing nearby when he made this threat and seemed to be more than willing to oblige my father of such a request. My father blames both of my grandparents for his station in life and the hardships he has had to endure, whereas I believe the choice he made was his own. He does not view me as his child, but rather a tool of vengeance against them. Grandmother Abby arrived today, but Grandfather was not with her. She said that he was ill. He may very well be, but I believe it must have been brought on by the news I telegraphed to them of my impending marriage. I realize this had to be their greatest fear, as well as my own. Texas would put an end to my happiness as it had with the ones that had come before me.

My parents or Andrew are my constant companions so that I am prevented from speaking the truth to Grandmother Abby. I know from the look in her eyes she suspects foul play in my decision to agree to this marriage, but she will not voice this in front of the others. I want so desperately to tell her the truth. I now recall the picture in my mind of Grandmother and Cissy standing in front of my beloved home in New Orleans the day I left. I wrote in this very diary that I felt as if I were viewing a funeral procession and I only hoped that it was not my own. I think now that my soul knew the truth, but it was my heart that refused to believe.

# Chapter 9

*Suzanne*

I got back to Brookfield and ran by the bookstore to check in with Tracy before heading home. I was in no hurry to have the argument I knew would take place with Tony as soon as he got in from work.

"Hey," Tracy said as I approached the sales counter.

"Hey, how's everything been around here?"

"Just fine, how is your sister?"

That one lie kept resurfacing everywhere, long after I had told it, demanding to be dealt with. "She's going to be fine. Thanks."

"That's great." She picked up a stack of books and headed toward one of the bookcases up front. "Mrs. Drexel called and asked that you call her when you get a chance."

"I will," I answered as I escaped the conversation and retreated to my office, closing the door behind me. I sat down in my chair and began going through the stack of mail on my desk. I couldn't concentrate so I got up and went back up front to the counter. I knew what I wanted to do and caught myself looking around at the people in the store to see who might be watching. I finally made my way over to the new age section. I glanced back once more to make sure Tracy was still in the other part of the store putting away books.

I couldn't believe I was trying to hide my interest in finding books about past lives, reincarnation, channeling or whatever would describe what I was experiencing. But, I knew I wasn't just bothered by what people might think, but more of what God would think of me. I had always considered myself a Christian, but what was I supposed to make of what I was going through? I needed answers and I desperately wanted to read someone else's experiences and see if they lined up in any way with my own. I said a silent prayer and asked God to please forgive me if I was wrong and ran my hand along the spines of some of the books. I came to one titled, *Many Lives, Many Masters,* and pulled it from the shelf. I stuck it under my arm and slipped back to my office without being noticed. I rushed inside and closed the door behind me. I eased down into my office chair and said another silent prayer that something, anything, would be among the pages of this book that would give me peace and understanding.

I flipped the book over and stared into the eyes of the white-haired man on the back of the book. I began reading the information under his picture. His name was Brian Weiss, MD. I was so relieved when I saw the *MD* behind his name. I don't know what I expected, maybe a two-headed circus freak? The man's bio went on to say he was a well-known and well-respected psychotherapist. He, too, had been skeptical until he stumbled onto a situation when he was attempting to help a client get over her phobias, and nothing seemed to be helping her. He decided to try hypnosis, thinking it might be something in her past that she had suppressed. When he put her under, she started telling, in detail, things that had happened to her in a *past life.* I felt my heart race with that little piece of news. Then, Tracy knocked on my office door. I quickly pulled some papers over the book and yelled for her to come in.

"Hey, is everything alright?"

"Yes." I heard the tone in my voice and I didn't like it. I felt like she was judging me even though I knew she didn't see the book. It was crazy but I couldn't help it. "I'm going to be leaving in a few minutes. Did you need something?"

"Oh, no. Everything's fine. I was just.." She stood there, mid-sentence, like she was waiting for something. "I'm sorry. I'll just go now." She turned and went out the door, closing it behind her.

I laid my head on my desk. *'What is wrong with me?'* I got up and stuck the book in my bag. I left my office and walked over to the section of the store where we displayed journals and diaries. I had kept a diary off and on as a teenager, but not since. But in my mind, since I thought I couldn't really talk to anyone about any of this, maybe I would just write it all down, surely that would help.

I stood in front of the display and a red leather journal on the bottom shelf caught my eye. I picked it up and thumbed through the pages. I liked the way it felt, and headed back to the counter to pay for it and my other *'secret'* book. I then headed for the front door and stopped when I saw Tracy straightening a shelf.

"Hey, I'm going to head home now." I hung my head. "Listen, I'm really sorry for snapping at you earlier."

"Oh," she dismissed my apolgy with a wave of her hand. "Don't worry about it. I'm sure you're just tired from your trip."

"I am," I said with a nod. "Anyway, I'll see you tomorrow."

As I headed to the parking lot I made a mental note to do something special for her to make up for my being an ass to her. I still wasn't feeling like myself as I climbed behind the wheel of my car. I couldn't put my finger on it, but I just wanted to run away, but I knew that wasn't possible. So, I pulled out onto the street and headed toward the ramp for the interstate. Then as I pulled to a stop sign on the corner, I decided to take the long way home and take the less traveled highway.

As I drove I began to relax some. I turned the radio up loud so it would keep my brain focused on anything except what I knew was ahead of me. When I finally reached my driveway, I was relieved to see Tony's car was nowhere in sight. At least I would have a little time before all hell would break loose. I pulled into the garage and turned the car off. I sat for a minute before I pulled my purse and book bag from the passenger seat and got out. I opened the back door of the car and pulled my overnight bag out and went inside.

I came in just as Maggie was pulling a casserole from the oven. "You're home," she said as she sat the dish on a hot pad on the counter. She wiped her hands on her apron and came over and hugged me. "You look tired honey."

"I am," I said as I turned and laid my purse and bag on the bar, and sat my overnight bag on the floor.

"You look like you haven't slept in days. Can I fix you something to drink?"

"No, I'm fine." I pulled out a barstool and sat down. "Have you heard anything from Tony?"

"As a matter of fact, I have," she said as she came over and sat down across from me. "He called and said he had to put his car in the shop so he will be late getting home. But, you don't need to pick him up, he said he would get a ride with someone from his office."

"Good." I pulled a cigarette from my purse and lit it. Without putting up an argument, Maggie got up and got an ashtray from the kitchen counter and put it on the bar in front of me, and sat back down.

"I'm guessing you coming home early has something to do with him?"

I looked at her and offered a weak smile and nodded my head.

"Okay, well let's change the subject. Tell me what you found concerning Virginia."

"We actually found out quite a bit. We went to the Catholic Church and they were extremely helpful. They confirmed that she is buried in their cemetery. Nobody paid for a marker, so the church placed a standard metal stake marking her grave, but that was forty years ago and there is no sign of it now. The woman at the church drew a map so we would know which one was hers. I put flowers on her grave."

"That was very kind of you."

"I just felt like we should do something."

"How was it that she came to be buried there if she really abandoned her husband and children?"

"I don't know, but, that's not all we found. The church also had records of her sister and brother going to school at their Catholic School, but no record of Virginia attending. And what really makes that strange is the brother was older and the sister was younger, so no one knows why Virginia wasn't in school."

"That is strange," she nodded in agreement.

"They also had a record of her younger sister dying when she was twelve."

"Oh my, what a shame."

"But, they had Virginia's marriage license when she married Andrew Lipton. He was my grandmother's father, so at least we know that part is right."

Maggie shook her head. "I'm surprised they had so much information on someone that lived so long ago."

"I know. The information Mother had on her said she was born in New Orleans, so the priest suggested we look there for her school records."

"Makes sense." Maggie nodded again.

"Yeah, but he also said we would probably have to go down there in person. He said they're not big on giving information over the phone. But, that's not the biggest thing we discovered."

"Oh?" Her eyes grew wide.

"We went to the funeral home that handled her funeral and they actually still had a file on her burial."

"You're kidding! You girls must have been elated!"

"Well," I sighed. "At first."

"What do you mean?"

I ran my hand through my hair. "First of all, they had listed three different cemeteries for where she was buried. But then…"

"What?" Maggie leaned closer. "What else did it say?"

Another deep sigh escaped me. "It said she died at Terrell State Mental Hospital."

"A mental hospital?"

"Yeah. I really lost it when Gina showed me. I hadn't seen it while we were still in the funeral home or otherwise I would probably be in jail right now."

"That's not like you at all, but I can certainly understand how upsetting it would be to hear that." She reached and laid her hand on top of mine.

I got up from the barstool and walked over to the kitchen counter and then turned to face her. "Maggie, I didn't lose it because they said that's where she died. I lost it because I *know* she wasn't crazy, and before you ask how I know, I'm going to tell you the same thing I told Gina. I don't know *how* I know, but I am certain she wasn't."

Maggie shook her head. "What does Gina say about all of this?"

"I think all of it has sufficiently blown her mind, but she has agreed to continue helping me get to the bottom of all of it." I laughed. "Of course, she said that while I was still in her house. That may not be the case now."

"Oh, I doubt Gina would have said it if she didn't mean it. I just wish there was something I could do to help."

"You're doing exactly what I need you to be doing; listening without judging me."

"I've got dinner ready. Do you want me to fix you a plate?"

"No, why don't you just go ahead and go home. I'm not really hungry right now."

"You're worried about what Tony is going to say when you tell him the truth."

"I know it's going to be bad and I would just as soon you nor Max be here to hear it."

Maggie began to gather her things and I followed her to the front door. "If you need to talk later, just call me."

"I will. Goodnight Maggie." I walked into the den and watched as she got in her car and pulled away and then picked up the cordless phone and dialed Tony's office number. I got his voice mail and left a message. I hung up and called Max at his friend's house and told him to stay put until he heard from me.

I trudged upstairs with plans of taking a hot bath before the battle.

The steam from the hot water bathed the bathroom mirror in an eerie mist. I pulled my hair up in a clip and got undressed and slid into the water and let it take me far away. I stayed in the tub for a long time and then got out and wrapped a towel around my body and went into the bedroom to find something comfortable to put on.

Just as I pulled a pair of jogging pants from the hook inside my closet, I heard a car door slam out front of the house. I walked over to the window and peered through a small opening in the curtain just in time to see Tony walking away from a sleek, black, sports car. At that very moment, the motion detector turned on the flood light by the driveway and I could see the blonde headed woman sitting in the driver's seat. Tony turned and waved and she slowly backed out of our driveway and took off down the street.

I stood there shaking from head to toe. When I heard the front door shut downstairs, I ran back into the bathroom and locked the door and turned on the shower. I knew what I had just witnessed, but who the hell was the woman? I could hear him in the bedroom, so I turned the shower off and waited a few minutes before I went into the bedroom.

"Hey, you're home," he said as I came out of the bathroom. He sat down on the bench at the end of the bed and pulled off his shoes.

"Yes," I managed.

"Gina's doing better, huh?"

"Yeah," I answered without a hint of guilt now. "Maggie said you had to put your car in the shop?"

"Hell yeah. It wouldn't start at lunch and I had to call a tow truck to take it into the shop."

I walked over to the dresser and started brushing my hair. "How did you get home?" I watched him closely in the mirror, waiting for the signs I knew all too well. The ones that are indicative of a cheating husband. The ones I had seen more times that I cared to remember from my past relationships; signs I swore I would never put up with again.

"A friend from work gave me a lift."

He never looked up and said it so nonchalantly it infuriated me. He opened the chest of drawers and pulled out a t-shirt and went to the closet and pulled a pair of jeans from a hanger and pulled them on. "What's for supper?"

"I don't know. Whatever Maggie cooked is on the stove. If you don't like it, you can get take out from somewhere."

"No, I'm sure whatever she fixed is fine." He came over to where I was sitting on the stool in front of the dresser and kissed me on top of the head. "I'll see you downstairs."

I felt my heart pounding in my head and chest. I watched in the mirror as he left the room. Did he really think I was so stupid not to notice the great mood he was in? He didn't even try to hide it. At that moment, I truly hated his guts. I could no longer deny my instincts. I knew he was having an affair. I got up and got dressed and sat down on the side of the bed. I was still shaking and furious. I had to calm down; but how?

My mind went back to last night when I had called from Gina's. He was obviously drunk. He probably didn't remember talking to me. I also knew from experience, that to kill the hangover I knew he would have had from getting that drunk, he would have had drinks at lunch; if not before. It made me wonder. Was he drinking more now to have the courage to cheat, or was this girl the bar type, and he had reverted back to his old ways when I had met him; the life of the party? I shook my head trying to get the thoughts from my mind. I was not going to let him get away with it. I went downstairs and found him in the den. A basketball game blared from the television.

"Can you turn that down?" I asked as I walked into the room. Without saying a word, he grabbed the remote and barely adjusted the volume, never taking his eyes away from the television screen. I sat down in the chair across from him so I could see his face. "So, where did you and Mark go last night?"

"Okay," he said as he finally muted the game. "I'm sorry, I know I shouldn't have gotten so bombed last night." He had never apologized so quickly since I had known him. Clearly, he just wanted to get this over with.

"You didn't answer my question." I stared at him, not intending to let him off the hook that easily. "My question was, where did you go?"

"Damn Suzanne! We went to a poker game; okay?"

"No, it's really not okay." My words came out flat.
He got up and went to the bar and poured vodka into a glass and drank it down. "You weren't here, so what difference did it make if I was here or not? It's not like I left you sitting at home alone."

"Is that why you went, because I was at Gina's?"
He looked at me and sighed. "No Suzanne, I went because I wanted to. There, now you can spin that any way you want."

I got up and walked out of the room and went to the kitchen. I heard the basketball game come back on the television. I pulled a glass from the cabinet and filled it with ice and opened a Coke and was pouring it into the glass when Max came in through the garage door.

"Hey Mom." He came over and hugged me and I felt the release of tension from my body. I held him in my arms a little longer than usual. "I hope it was okay for me to come home. Are you okay?" He asked as he pulled away from me.

"Yeah, I'm okay." I went over and sat down at the bar.

He went over to the refrigerator and opened it. "What's for supper?"

"Maggie fixed chicken casserole, it's on the counter."

He fixed his plate and came over and sat down across from me at the bar. "How's Aunt Gina?"

"Max," I started slowly, "Aunt Gina wasn't sick. I lied about the reason I went to Marshall." He looked at me in a way I had never seen before. I immediately wished I hadn't told him the truth. The hurt in his eyes was almost too much to bare. "I'm sorry. I just couldn't tell anyone the truth; not you or Tony."

"Tell me the truth about what?" Tony had slipped into the room unnoticed.

I jumped and turned to face him. My heart began to pound. I thought he was too absorbed in the basketball game to leave it.

Max stood from the bar and picked up his plate. "I'm going to my room." Tony moved aside in the doorway to let him pass.

He came over to the bar and stood facing me. "So, you lied about what?"

I lit a cigarette and took a long drag from it. "Gina wasn't sick." I got up from the barstool and got an ashtray from the counter, then turned and faced him.

"I knew it was a lie," he said shaking his head. "So, if Gina wasn't sick, what did you go to Marshall for?" His stare penetrated to my soul. "Spill it!"

"I had some business to tend to; that's all."

"What kind of business requires you to lie to your family?"

"Oh, Tony please," I said as I went back to the bar and sat down. "Don't refer to what we've got going on here as *'family.'* We haven't been a family for quite some time now."

"What the hell are you talking about?" He sat down across from me at the bar. "Just tell me why you went to Marshall?"

"I went to do some research on my family." I took a drag from my cigarette.

"What?" He asked and then I saw that familiar smirk and condescending look on his face. "Oh, wait a minute. That stupid dream you had! Right?"

"For your information, it turns out there may have really been something to that so called *'stupid dream'*.

"Oh damn," he said as he shook his head. "You can't be serious. You took off work, lied to me and Max and put Maggie out by asking her to stay the night, just so you could chase after some dream you had?"

I jumped up from the bar and went to the sink and poured the remainder of my drink down the drain. I spun around to face him again. "You don't worry about Maggie and Max, and as far as lying to you, well isn't that a little like the pot calling the kettle black?"

"Now what are you talking about?" He stood up from the barstool and stormed out of the room.

I followed him into the den and found him pouring another glass of vodka. I reached and picked up the remote and muted the game that was still playing on the television. He spun around to face me.

"Last Saturday you told me that you and Mark were playing racquetball; remember?"

"Of course, I remember," he said as he downed the drink and filled the glass again.

"Well then, you should remember that Kate and I were out that day too, and we went to the mall."

"As usual, spending more money," He said as he took a sip of the drink.

"I saw Mark at the mall Tony!"

He sat the glass down and looked at me. "I don't have a clue what you're talking about."

"Well then, let me explain it to you. At the very time, you and Mark were *supposed* to be playing racquetball, we saw him at the mall." I could tell by the look on his face that I had him. "Don't try to deny it Tony! After Kate said she saw him come into the mall, I found his truck in the parking lot. I know it was him!"

He stood stock still and I could see the gears in his brain spinning. He finally spoke. "For your information, I had a report to finish, and I had left the file at work, so we quit early so I could go by and get it." He looked pleased with himself, but I was in no way finished with him.

"Well then, explain how the two of you showed up here together and I don't recall you coming in with a file in your hands! I even asked you how the game went and you said *fine!* And you had been gone plenty long enough to have played all day!"

"Damn Suzanne, I didn't know I had to account for every moment of my day to you." He stormed out of the room and I followed him. He went into the kitchen and opened the refrigerator door and pulled out a bottle of water.

"And what about that *woman* that brought you home from work?" I saw the shock on his face. It felt good to catch him off-guard. "Yeah Tony," I said with a smirk. "I saw who let you out in the driveway."

"She's just a woman from the office that offered me a ride home! Big deal!"

"Oh, I bet!"

"What the hell is wrong with you?" He stormed over and got in my face. "You run off to chase some bullshit about a dream you have, lie to everybody because you know how damn crazy it sounds, and you want to interrogate me? I'm not the guilty one, you are!"

The doorbell rang then. "Who is that?"

"I ordered pizza," he said as he reached in his back pocket to get his wallet. "I didn't want that crap Maggie fixed. You and Max can eat it." He went to the front door and paid the delivery boy and took his pizza into the den. I heard the basketball game come back on.

I went upstairs to find Max. His door was closed so I tapped on it and went inside, closing it behind me. He had his back to me with his headphones on. I went over and tapped him on the shoulder and he pulled them down around his neck. "Yeah, what is it Mom?"

I could still hear the hurt in his voice. "I want to talk to you for a minute." He leaned back in his chair and just stared at me. I sat down on the side of his bed so I could face him. "Look, I'm sorry I lied to you. I just didn't want anybody, even you, to know exactly why I was going."

"But why? Why did you go if Aunt Gina really wasn't sick?"

"Do you remember that dream I had last week?"

"Not really," he said shaking his head.

"It was the morning Tony complained that I woke everybody up so early?"

He just shook his head. "Seriously Mom, I don't remember."

"Okay, just listen. I had a dream about my family and I felt like I needed to go to Marshall to check into something."

"You went because of a dream?"

I hated the way he looked at me. "Yes Max, but I think you know me well enough that it had to be more than just a *dream*. It was very real, but I'll tell you all about it later. Right now, I just want to tell you I'm sorry for lying to you and I won't do it again."

"Okay," he said as he stood up and took his headphones off and picked up his plate. "I'm going downstairs to get something to drink." He headed to the door as I stood up from the bed. "You coming?"

"I'll be down in a minute. I've got a phone call to make."

I followed him out of the room and went to my own room and closed the door. I sat down on the side of the bed and picked up the phone and called Mrs. Drexel.

"Mrs. Drexel, this is Suzanne."

"Hello dear. How is Gina?"

I let out a loud sigh. How could one little lie cause so much trouble. "She's fine, nothing serious."

"Oh good. Well listen dear, Paul and I have been going over the books and we're a little concerned."

"Oh?" I felt my chest tighten.

"I'm sure it's nothing, but you know my son, he's concerned because our sales are down by ten percent from this time last year."

"Yes, he said something to me about it a week or so ago. I told him the only thing I can think of is the teacher cutbacks this year. We haven't sold nearly as many classroom packets as usual, but I think it gives us an opportunity to do some special events this summer to make up for it."

"Ah, see, I told Paul not to worry that you would have a plan in place. Alright dear, thank you for calling me back and I'm so glad your sister is doing well."

I hung up the phone and fell back on the bed. *Why does everything have to get off kilter at the same time?* I laid there for a minute and then got up and went back downstairs. Tony had put the pizza box on the bar and it had one piece left in it. I sat down on the barstool and ate it. The phone rang and I got up and answered it. It was Gina. I told her to hold on while I fixed myself something to drink. I threw the last few bites of the pizza in the trash and headed back upstairs. I passed the den and saw that Tony was still watching the game. I went to my bedroom and closed the door.

"Okay, I'm back," I said as I sat down on the side of the bed.

"You forgot to call me and let me know you made it home and that everything was alright."

"Well, I guess I didn't call because everything is not *alright.*"

"I figured as much, that's why I called. What happened? I'm guessing things got ugly between you and Tony?"

"Very ugly. Everything is such a mess Gina. I admitted to Max that I had lied about you being sick. You should have seen his face. I know I really hurt him. But, while I was having my little confessional with Max, Tony overheard and all hell broke loose."

"So, he blew a gasket because you lied to him?"

"Actually, he was more upset because I went because of the dream. Can you believe that? I mean he did get mad about the lying part, but it really seemed to be more about why I came."

"Why would that bother him so much?"

"He just kept saying *how crazy* I was for going."

"I can't stand him!"

"Yeah, well me either, but that's not all. He had to put his car in the shop today and I was upstairs when *his ride* brought him home. It was a blonde-headed woman driving a sleek, black, sports car. He tried to say she was a woman from the office, but I know it wasn't. Anyway, once we started fighting, I brought up the fact that Kate and I saw Mark at the mall when they were supposed to be playing racquetball.

"Oh Lord. So, it was a knock-down-drag-out fight."

"Pretty much. Anyway, then Mrs. Drexel called and she informed me that Paul, her son, was concerned about sales at the bookstore. I swear Gina, it's always this way for me. One thing happens and then it's the domino effect."

"You should have stayed another night here," she said with a sigh.

"I can't hide from all of this; I have to face it."

"I just wished you lived closer."

"Me too. Listen, I'm exhausted. I'm going to bed."

"Alright, but if you need me, just call."

"I will. Thanks, Gina."

I hit the end button and put on a sleep shirt and got into bed. I laid there for a minute and knew right away sleep would not be coming for a while, so I got back up and got the book that I had bought and laid back down to read. At some point, I must have fell asleep.

When I woke up, I could see through the curtains that it was still dark outside. I rolled over and looked at the clock beside the bed and it read *4:44* in blazing blue neon. I sat up on the side of the bed and the book I had been reading fell to the floor. I glanced over my shoulder knowing fully well Tony wouldn't be there.

I got up and put on my robe and made my way downstairs. I could see the glow from the television before I reached the archway into the den. I crept into the room to find him passed out on the couch. An empty Vodka bottle sat on the coffee table. I wasn't sleepy anymore, so I went into the kitchen and pulled a bottle of water from the refrigerator and sat down at the bar.

As I sat there, in the stillness of the early morning, I tried to think of when, exactly, had my marriage slinked into the pit. I knew some of our problems stemmed from the pressure of Tony's sales job, but it was no longer a viable excuse, and I knew it. We were past that now. The condescending way he talked to me and the total lack of intimacy had slipped slowly into our relationship without me noticing. Now it was all I could see. I knew I wasn't doing myself any favors by going back like this, but it seemed impossible to stop my mind once it started its descent.

I suddenly remembered a time, not long after we got married. I had gone out of town for my job and was gone for a couple of days. When I arrived back home, Tony had surprised me with a night out and followed up the next day with flowers to my office. I wondered now if there was a guilty conscious involved, even then. Everyone that knew him had warned me that he would never truly settle down and be with just one woman. I had thought he just hadn't been with the right woman yet and that I could love him enough and he would change. How much was enough? And why in the world, with my track record, did I think I was even capable of loving someone enough to change them? Hadn't I tried that before and failed miserably? I glanced at the kitchen clock and decided to try and go back upstairs and lie down for just an hour or so before it would be time to wake Max up and get ready for work myself.

I awoke later to sunlight coming through the curtains of my bedroom. I stretched and actually felt good, that is until I rolled over and looked at the clock. It was way past time for Max and me both to be up. I jerked the covers back and jumped up and ran down the hallway yelling his name. I reached his room and his bed was empty, so I ran towards the hall bathroom.

"Suzanne!" I heard Maggie yell from downstairs. I ran to the top of the staircase and looked down at her. "Max has already left for school."

"How? Who took him?"

"He rode with a friend. I was about to come up and wake you. Come downstairs when you're ready, I have breakfast waiting." She turned and went back towards the kitchen while I just stood there in a stupor.

I went back to my bedroom and glanced at the clock again and called Tracy at the bookstore to tell her I would be late. I hung up and grabbed my robe from the end of the bed and went into the bathroom and took a quick shower. I got dressed in record time and came downstairs. I plopped down on the barstool. "Where's Tony?"

Maggie turned from the sink to face me. "He was leaving in a taxi when I got here."

"Oh, the *woman from the office* didn't come back to get him?"

"What woman?" Maggie asked as she dried her hands on a dishtowel.

"Doesn't matter."

"Max told me you and Tony got into it last night and that you were really upset. When he said a friend was taking him to school I thought you knew and that's why you were sleeping in."

"No, I woke up before daylight and I guess I must have turned the alarm off." I ran my hands through my hair. "Oh Maggie, my life is falling apart."

"Now it can't be as bad as all that," she said as she sat a plate of bacon and toast in front of me. "Tell me what's going on." She sat down across from me.

"Everything. All this stuff with Virginia, then Tony blew up when he found out I lied to him about why I went to Marshall."

"How did he find out you lied?"

"He overheard me admitting it to Max." I choked back tears at the memory of the look on my son's face.

"You need to eat," Maggie said pointing to the plate.

"Oh Maggie, I'm not hungry." I reached and pulled a cigarette from the package lying on the bar and lit it. "Everything is just spinning out of control."

"You aren't going to the bookstore today, are you?"

"I have to. When I called Mrs. Drexel last night she said Paul's upset about the drop-in sales."

"Oh dear. Paul needs to let his mother handle the affairs of the bookstore."

I looked up at her and rolled my eyes. "That's not going to happen. He knows he's going to inherit the store when she passes away."

"Yes, well, she's not dead yet!"

"I've got to get going, I called Tracy but I still don't want to be too late getting there." I went back upstairs to get my purse, and the minute I walked into the bedroom, I saw it. The book I had been reading, the one I had intended to hide from everyone, was now lying on the dresser. Tony wanted to make sure I knew he had seen it. *'I don't give a damn what you think Tony,'* I said out loud as I snatched it from the dresser and put it back in my bag. The phone rang then and I rushed to answer it. It was Kate. I told her I didn't have time to talk as I had to rush to work and we agreed to meet after I got off. Just knowing I would get to sit and visit with her later made facing the day easier.

When I got to the bookstore, relief washed over me. Whatever had caused Tracy to act strangely towards me yesterday was long gone as she greeted me with her normal cheery smile. Ever the optimist, I honestly believed things might be turning around. I temporarily forgot about the woman in the grave that was beckoning me to help her.

# Chapter 10

*Virginia*

*Dearest Diary,*

*On this eve of the new century, I find I can hardly write these words, but I know I must. Surely someday, and God only knows when that day might be, someone will have need to know the fate that has befallen me.*

*I am now of the opinion that greed is the strongest emotion of all. Not love, nor hate, but the love of money. I believe it has the ability to drive a person to act on the most hideous, dark recesses of one's mind.*

*I became Andrew Lipton's wife in a grave, solemn ceremony in the Catholic Church. It is my belief that I stood and took vows before my God to a man that is of no religion or belief whatsoever. Surely, he is one of the devil's own. I stood in somber silence as I watched my dear grandmother hand Andrew the leather pouch that held my dowry. There was no way for her to know that by doing so she spared her life as well as grandfather's and doomed mine forever.*

*I never realized that I possessed such strength. I did not faint not cry as I watched the scene before me. At the end of the service, I walked away from her. In the dark of the evening, I boarded the borrowed buggy with the monstrous man that I would now make my life with, whatever life there could possibly be with such a person. I couldn't bear to turn to see her face as we pulled away. I knew that she was scheduled to leave this God-forsaken place in the morning by train, and it may very well have been the last time I will see my beloved grandmother's face. My heart ached in such a way that I was sure it would cause my demise, at least I hoped for such, but alas, it did not.*

*I am to live with Andrew and his two sisters. The night of our wedding, I had not met them, and the two of them sat alone amidst the shadows in the pews of the church. I held out hope they might be a compassionate lot, but my hopes were in vain.*

*When Andrew and I arrived across town at his home, I stared at the structure aghast. The barren outer walls of the house were a dark, sinister brown. The trees that stood outside of the old, decrepit two-story house appeared to be dead instead of barren for winter. The gallery circled around the front and fell into darkness on both sides of the house. As I stepped upon the porch, the weathered wood creaked beneath my feet, causing me to shudder. I walked through the door into a foyer that was as barren as the outside, no paint nor wallpaper upon the walls and no furniture. I stood for a moment and tried to allow my eyes to adjust to the darkness of the room before going any further. There was a flicker of light coming from some other room and I was making my way in that direction when a mouse suddenly crossed my path, and I screamed. Andrew then appeared in a doorway off the foyer with what I was sure was a glass of liquor. He sat the glass down on a small table near the door and slowly walked towards me. My heart was pounding in my chest as he neared me, and my hands began to tremble. In one fluid movement, he slapped my face with one hand and ripped my dress open in the front with his other. I heard a whimper escape me before the second blow landed somewhere about my head. When I awoke, I was in a bed in a strange room, and he had taken me as his wife. I lay extremely still and looked slowly next to me to find the bed empty. I tried to raise myself up, but the pain was excruciating. My head and arms ached as well. I sobbed quietly, and for the second time in a day I wished for death to find me.*

*I finally managed to get up from the bed and went in search of the women of the house. Surely, they would help me as I found that my clothing was soiled with my virginity. Instead, I found Andrew sitting in front of the fire in the front room of the house. His shirt was unbuttoned and hung loosely about his back. His hair was disheveled as well, and I became ill at the sight of him. "Where are your sister's?" I implored.*

*He turned to me and offered the same wicked smile I had seen on numerous occasions now. "They are enjoying the finest suite that Ginocchio Hotel has to offer, compliments of your grandmother. Of course, it was supposed to be a gift to you, but that lifestyle is in your past now."*

*I turned to go to the kitchen to see if I could find food as my strength was waning even though it was in the early hours of the day.*

*"Where the hell do you think you are going?" Andrew bellowed. I explained I was in need of nourishment. He stood, and I was afraid he would strike me again, but instead he handed me a broom and said housework came first. It was at that very moment that I realized I would never be anything more to this man than a slave, sold to him by my father. I know now that they split my dowry between them.*

*When I finally met Andrew's sisters, I was not surprised to discover they too were evil in nature. Esther is a few years older than I am, while Mattie is a year younger. Both seem to hate me as much as Andrew. Surely, they must know I did not choose this marriage for myself. I know I will only be a servant for these people and nothing more. I fully understand the plan is to continue to acquire money from my grandparent's estate. I have overheard various conversations between my father and Andrew as to how they plan to achieve their goal. I am gravely sorry as I know my participation will be mandatory. Grandmother has sent a most beautiful gown for what she could only assume would be my attire at some New Year's Eve ball. I watched tonight as Esther put it on and left the house with a beau.*

*Please God, allow me to come to you now, before they do any more harm.*

*Dearest Diary,*

*I have been Andrew's wife for three months now, and yet it feels like an eternity. I have been ill for several days, and he finally summoned a doctor. He has not been kind, as he has continued to expect me to carry out my duties in this house. I have collapsed many times and fallen in a slump upon the floor only to be left there by him and his sisters until I regain my senses. My mother has called for me only twice since the wedding. Her interest in my hardship seems to be genuine. At times, I believe I witness traces of my grandmother's gentleness in her.*

*The doctor that came to examine me was quite old, and I found his ways to be unsettling. When all was done, he instructed me to get dressed, and he went into the adjoining room to speak with Andrew. I reached the door just as he was saying the words to Andrew that I had feared he would say. I am with child.*

# Virginia's Diary

*Dearest Diary,*

*My body continues to swell and the heat of this house stifles me. I feel the baby move inside of me quite often now. To my surprise, Andrew has instructed his sisters to help with the daily chores while he is away at work at the train yard. I am certain there is a reason, which I have not been made privy of, for this sudden compassion. I try not to think of this often and simply enjoy whatever reprieve there is for me. The baby is due in September, and I have written Grandmother Abby with the news. She has sent several parcels for both the baby and me. I am only allowed to wear the beautiful nightgowns that she sends. Andrew's sisters are the recipients of the dresses. At first, I shed many tears over the loss, but now, I find that I do not need them as I am not allowed to go away from the house. Andrew says it is not proper for a woman to be seen in my condition, and yet I find it amusing he displays a lack of etiquette in every other area of his life. Grandmother sent a telegram this week saying Grandfather was in ill health again, and I cried the entire day. It appears his health began to decline almost immediately after my marriage to Andrew. I miss all of them so very much and Cissy as well. I dream often of being back in New Orleans and being in the safety of their care, but I fear I will never again see that day. I spend my days reading the only two books I brought with me, as Andrew refers to them as an extravagance. I manage for myself quite well during the day, but I am still to be a wife at night even in his drunken state. It sickens me. I have convinced him I become ill due to my condition, but I do not know how I will justify my feelings after the baby arrives.*

*I find myself longing for the day that I shall give birth. Not just to put an end to the uncomfortable days that I must endure, but to have someone here with me that I can truly love. I have been so terribly lonely. If I should have a daughter, I wish to name her Elisabeth after my dear friend back home in New Orleans. Just to be able to utter her name again will bring me such pleasure. I pray now for God to sustain my days.*

*Dearest Diary,*

*My body still has life in it despite the doctor's predictions last night that I would die giving birth to my dear daughter. I write these words as I watch my precious Elisabeth sleeping soundly in her crib. I never dreamt I would be grateful to be alive in Andrew Lipton's house, nor have gratitude towards the man himself, but I find that to be my feelings at this moment. All the hardships I have endured to have Elisabeth seem naught now. I have never loved anyone so utterly in my life. The God I have prayed to daily has surely sent one of his own angels to be here with me. She has only been here one day, and I can find no words to measure the comfort and enrichment she has brought into my life.*

# Chapter 11

*Suzanne*

I should have known when one thing goes wrong in my life, it's inevitable, something else is coming right behind it. But, I was still shocked when I saw my daughter's name pop up on my caller ID at home. I snatched the phone from its cradle knowing she might change her mind and hang up. It was only the second time this year that Sam, short for Samantha, had called me. Unfortunately, my relationship with my only daughter mirrors my own with my mother.

Sam couldn't remember a time when I was married to her father because I had divorced him when she was two-years old. He had been very loving and caring when we dated, but after we married, he turned jealous and controlling. He took his insecurities out on me in very violent ways. I was scared to death my father would kill him before I could escape his tyranny. I never shared that part of my life with Sam because he had always been a good father to her. In the beginning, I had fought hard to keep him from seeing her without supervision, but without telling the courts of my hidden shame from the beatings, I couldn't present a reason that justified my request.

I never told her what he had done to me, and I refused to talk badly about him in front of her. I knew from experience what it felt like to have a mother hold how she felt about the father against the child. My mother had done it to me my entire life.

I always took over too much of the conversation in the beginning when Sam would call because I had so many questions since we didn't talk often. She usually tires of my tirade quickly and gives me just enough information before asking to speak to Max, then I've lost her.

This time was different. She didn't stop my interrogation concerning how school was going and if she was still seeing the guy she had been dating the last time we spoke. She was so cooperative I finally realized something must be terribly wrong. I was right. The next sentence she said felt like somebody hit me hard in the stomach. I lost the ability to breathe for a moment.

She called to tell me she had just left the doctor's office, and she was pregnant. My first thought was of fear of how her father, my ex-husband, would react. I was fearful this might be the time she would see the underlying monster that I knew existed. Sam then informed me she hadn't lived at her father's house for the last six months. She had moved in with the baby's father, off campus, and hadn't told him yet that she was expecting their baby. When I asked how she thought he would receive the information, she told me that she didn't intend to tell him because they had already split up. She had moved in with a girlfriend across town from the college campus. Sam said she wasn't planning on telling her father either because she didn't see him nearly as much as she used to because he was traveling a lot with his job.

My mind reeled, some with disbelief that I was the person she chose to share her secret with, and that I might be her confidant through her pregnancy. I asked what she intended to do about school. She quickly assured me she intended to finish. I shook my head. Surely, I had raised her to be smarter than to think she could continue school and be a single mother. Of course, her next comment made me realize it was me that was uninformed.

"Oh Mother, really. You don't expect me to keep the baby, do you?"

I heard her words, but I couldn't believe the nonchalant way she said them. This was her baby, my first grandchild we were talking about. "Samantha, please let me adopt the baby." I knew my lips moved, but I swear it sounded like somebody else talking. I didn't know who was more shocked by my statement; me or her.

"Mother! You have got to be kidding!" There it was, that *'tone'* that always found its way into our conversation no matter how hard I tried to keep it out. "You're forty-years old!"

"I'm aware of my age Sam, but honey, please, this is my first grandbaby, and I can't stand the thought of someone else raising it."

"Why do you have to complicate things?" The exasperation in her voice was clear. "I just thought you would want to know. That's the only reason I called to tell you, not so you could make this harder."

"It won't be difficult. I promise. You don't intend to ever move back down here; you've said it a thousand times. You wouldn't have to be reminded of anything. I would never bring it up; I swear. Let me do this, Sam, please." There was a long silence on the line, and I knew better than to say anything else, so I waited.

"I'll think about it. I don't want you telling Max or Matt about it, or Aunt Gina, okay?"

"I won't say a word to any of them. I promise."

"Okay." She said and then there was another long pause on the line. "I'll get back with you after I give this some thought."

"Okay," I said exhaling a breath I hadn't realized I had been holding. "Just let me know." I hung up the phone and plopped down in the chair in the den. What in the world had possessed me to offer to take the baby and raise it? I got up and paced the floor. But then, moments later, a calm came over me and I just knew in my soul it was something I was supposed to do.

I had promised Sam I wouldn't tell her brothers, Max or Matt, or Gina, but I hadn't said anything about Maggie or Kate. Since it was Saturday and Maggie was off, I dialed Kate's number. When she answered the phone, I asked if she was going to be at home for a while. When she said she was, I told her not to leave. I grabbed my purse and raced through traffic to her house. I pulled into her driveway and jumped out and ran up the front steps. She flung the door open just as I reached to ring the doorbell.

"What's going on?"

"I'm going to be a grandmother!" I said as I hugged her.

"That's fantastic," she said as she hugged me tightly. "I bet Matt and Leah are ecstatic."

"Oh, it's not Matt and Leah," I said as I pulled away from her. "It's Sam, she's pregnant."

"If it's Sam," she said with a frown, "why are you so happy? This will ruin her chances of finishing college."

"Well," I said as I stepped past her into her living room. "It would if she kept it, but I'm going to adopt the baby." I've known Kate since I was in my twenties and I have never seen her speechless; until now. She backed away from me and turned and closed the front door. She turned back to face me but still wasn't saying anything. She walked over to the couch and sat down; never taking her eyes off me. I went over and sat down in the chair across from her. "Well, say something."

"I would, if I knew what to say. Suzanne, surely you know the last thing you need to do right now is to be thinking about adopting a baby. Especially Sam's child. You two have never gotten along; this is only going to make y'alls relationship worse. And then there's this business about Virginia and your marriage is in the toilet."

I got up and paced the living room floor. "Look, I know this all sounds crazy…."

"That's because it is crazy! You can't do this. You just made a comment the other day that you were worried about losing Maggie when you and Tony get a divorce because you know you won't be able to afford to keep her. Now you're talking about raising a baby? You'll be adding another mouth to feed, not to mention diapers, daycare…"

"I realize it's a lot of expense, but…"

"No," she said as she came over and put her hand on my arm and stopped me from pacing. "You don't realize. That's just it, you're not thinking rationally. Listen, I haven't said anything, but I've been worried about you."

I stared at her. "Worried about me, how?"

She let out a loud sigh like what she was thinking should be obvious to me and maybe it should have, but I wasn't expecting this from her. Not my best friend.

"I love you to death Suzanne, but this whole Virginia thing has me really worried about you. It's changed you somehow."

"Well, wouldn't it change you too if you thought there was a possibility of being your great grandmother in a past life?" There I had said it, out loud, to somebody besides Maggie or Gina.

"Is that what you think this is? *Reincarnation?*"

I don't know if it was the look on her face or the way she said it that upset me the most, but it felt like a knife had been plunged through my heart. I grabbed my purse. "You know, I don't need this from someone that is supposed to be my best friend." I stormed out the door. She followed me yelling for me to come back inside. I got in the car and never looked her way as I backed out and gunned the car out of her driveway and down the street.

I drove around Brookfield in a stupor. I had started the morning with almost a full tank of gas, so the ding indicating I needed to stop to refill, surprised me. I pulled into a gas station and filled the tank and called Maggie from the payphone.

"I think I'm in trouble," I said into the receiver as I choked back tears.

"Where are you dear?"

"About five minutes from your house."

"Well, come on over, let's talk about it."

It was the loving concern in her voice that I desperately needed to hear. She was waiting on the porch when I drove into her driveway. I got out of the car and walked up the steps to the porch.

"Oh Maggie." I broke down and sobbed as she took me into her arms.

"Come on," she said, taking me by the hand. "Let's go inside and I'll fix us some tea and we'll talk."

I followed her into her cottage style house, into a kitchen that felt the way a loving grandmother's kitchen should feel. It smelled of the soup cooking on the stove and a fresh batch of cookies sat under a glass dome on the counter. I don't know how long I cried, but it felt like forever. Maggie just sat holding my hand while I rambled on and on, lamenting over all my troubles. When I ran out of tears, I crossed my arms on the table and put my head down.

"What is it that you really want to do?" she asked as she rubbed my shoulder.

I raised up and reached and got a napkin from the holder in the center of the small kitchen table and dried my eyes. I leaned back in the chair. "I think too much is happening all at once," I sighed. "It's just too much to handle."

"I agree. You're bound to be overwhelmed, but we have to start somewhere on getting you back on track and headed in the right direction."

I looked down and a deep sigh escaped me. "I think I need to see somebody; a professional, you know?" I slowly looked back up at her.

She smiled. "There's no shame in that. I think it might be a good idea to run all of this by a stranger, someone with no dog in the fight; so to speak. But, I would definitely find a woman to talk to, not a man."

"Hmph," I said shaking my head. "There is no way I would want to talk to a man about all of this!"

We sat and talked some more before I told her what had happened with Kate. She quickly took up for my friend saying that when people don't understand something someone they love is going through, they get scared and sometimes react in ways that seem harsh, but they really are trying to help. I knew she was right. I had totally freaked Kate out about everything. I had always been the one that had it together, no matter what came down the pike, but I didn't now, and she knew it even before I had come to the realization. Still, I knew deep inside of me, if Sam called me back and agreed to allow me to adopt the baby, I would do it. That's the one thing that felt entirely right at the moment.

It was almost dark when I finally left Maggie's house and headed home. As I drove, I tried not to let my mind wander onto anything. I finally got home and pulled into the garage and got out and went into the kitchen. Max was sitting at the bar looking at a car magazine that had come in the mail.

"Hey, where have you been?" He asked.

"I've been over at Maggie's house, hope I didn't worry you." I laid my purse on the bar and went over to the refrigerator and pulled out a can of Coke.

"Aunt Kate has called a couple of times. She said you were over at her house earlier and you got real upset and left."

I popped the top on the can. "She say *why* I was upset?"

"No, but she wants you to call her. Why did you go to Maggie's?"

"Oh, I was just out and about so I decided to go by her house. She's been inviting me to come by and see a new sofa she bought." I walked over and picked up the phone. "I'll be right back; I'm going to call Kate."

I went into den and called my best friend and apologized profusely for running out the way I did. I asked her not to say anything to Max about the baby and she assured me she wouldn't. I intended to keep my promise to Sam and not say anything to her brothers or Gina. I certainly wasn't going to say anything to Tony; I knew he wouldn't still be around in nine months. Before we hung up, Kate and I agreed to try and get together again in the next day or so.

"Why don't we go out to eat," I said as I came back into the kitchen.

"Sure," Max said as he hopped off the barstool. "You don't want to wait on Tony?"

"No, I don't," I said bluntly.

"Cool. Can we get Mexican food?"

"That's fine," I said as I picked up my purse and we went out the back door.

We beat the dinner crowd to the restaurant so we were seated as soon as we came in. Once we were settled and the waiter had brought our drinks and chips and hot sauce, I leaned a little closer across the table. "So, how is everything going with you?"

"Uh-oh," he said as he dipped a chip in the hot sauce and popped it into his mouth. "Am I in trouble?"

"Should you be?" I said with a laugh.

"Not that I know of." He popped another chip in his mouth.

"Max," I said shaking my head.

"What?" He asked looking at me as hot sauce dripped from his chin.

"Uh manners?" All I could see was the six-year old boy he used to be and not the sixteen-year old young man he was now.

"Oh, sorry," he grinned and unrolled his napkin and wiped his mouth.

"I know I've been preoccupied lately, and I just want to make sure you're okay."

"Everything's fine with me."

"Well, that's good to hear."

The waiter brought the food over and even though Max had finished off a whole basket of chips and a bowl of hot sauce, his plate of food disappeared just as quickly. When he finally looked up, he spotted a friend across the room at another table. He asked to be excused and went over to visit while I continued to eat. When I finally finished my meal, and got the ticket, I got up and went over to the table where he now sat with his friend and his family. Max introduced me to everyone and then asked if he could stay and go to the movies with them when they left the restaurant. The other boy's father assured me he would bring Max home later so I gave my permission and left him there.

I made my way out to the parking lot and got into my car and a thought crossed my mind. *'I hope I'm not just wanting to adopt Sam's baby because my own 'baby' isn't a baby anymore. Am I scared to be without a child? I had spent my entire adult life as a Mom to three children. Was I afraid not to be that person?* I shook my head and quickly dismissed the idea and drove home. When I went into the house there was still no sign of Tony and I was glad.

I went upstairs and got the book I had bought and brought it back to bed to read. I was really enjoying reading the stories of others that had experienced something like I was. It was a couple of hours later when I heard Tony come in downstairs. I didn't try to hide the book. I no longer cared what he thought about all of it.

"What are you doing in bed so early?" He asked as he came into the room.

I lowered the book and looked at him. "Just relaxing and reading."

"Yeah," he said as he unbuttoned his shirt and took it off, "I see you're still reading *that garbage*." I just kept reading; never acknowledging that he had said anything. I heard him shut the bathroom door. Then, moments later he came back out and stood over me. "You're not even going to try and hide it from me?"

"No, I'm not." I lowered the book again and looked him dead in the eyes. "This happens to be written by a well-known and well-respected psychiatrist."

"Well, you need one." He walked out of the bedroom and then minutes later I heard the television come on in the den.

*"Ass,"* I mumbled and kept right on reading.

For the balance of the weekend I managed to stay away from him. I worked in the yard, even though I wasn't sure how much longer I would be able to call it *my yard*. But, for right now, I intended to enjoy it while I was still here.

The one thing reading Dr. Weiss's book had done for me was it had made me feel more comfortable in my own skin. I came to understand that other people, lots of them apparently, believed they had been here before too. And, just from what little I did know about Virginia's life, I was certain if given a chance, I would have chosen to come back to set things straight.

When Monday rolled around I got Max off to school and thanked Maggie for letting me come to her house and vent.

"Honey," she said as she hugged me. "Anytime you need me, I'm here."

The next morning as I got into my car and headed to the bookstore, even though I still had a lot on my plate, it felt like it was now somewhat manageable. I still wanted to talk to someone, so as soon as I finished my morning routine, I slipped into my office and closed the door. I went through the yellow pages and found an advertisement for a woman, Counselor, Diedre Long. Her advertisement simply stated; *'Here to help when life's ups and downs happen a little too often.'* I didn't know how she would feel about reincarnation, but I figured the rest of my ups and downs might be something she was accustomed to hearing and could help. I called to make an appointment and to my surprise, her receptionist said she had a cancellation and could see me after lunch if I could make it. I assured her I could and left for her office as soon as I hung up the phone.

On the drive over I began to feel a little apprehensive. I had never seen a counselor before, but probably should have, if nothing else to learn to deal with the issues I still had with my mother. My multiple failed marriages were another area that I knew needed to be addressed. Even if she couldn't shed any light on this *'past life'* business, maybe the time had come to try to straighten out other areas in my life.

By the time I pulled into the parking lot of Deidre Long's office, the apprehension had gone away and I was actually looking forward to the meeting. I was pleasantly surprised when I got off the elevator and walked into her office. The décor was beautiful. There were upholstered chairs with matching ottomans in the waiting room. I gave the receptionist my name and she handed me a clipboard with papers to fill out. I went over to one of the chairs and sat down and had just begun to fill out the papers when the receptionist called my name.

"You can go on back now. Just finish filling out the papers before you leave and drop them back off to me," she said smiling as she held the door for me. As I entered the room, a very attractive, middle aged woman stood from behind a desk and walked over and extended her hand.

"Hello, I'm Deidre Long."

I shook her hand. "It's nice to meet you."

"Well, come on over and have a seat," she said motioning to two chairs that sat across from each other. "Can I get you something to drink? Bottled water?"

"Yes, that would be great," I said as I took my seat and sat my purse on the floor next to the chair.

When she brought the bottle of water over, she also had a box of tissues she sat on the table between us.

"Am I going to need those?" I asked as she held out the bottle of water to me.

"I hope not," she said as she sat down in the chair and slipped her heals off. "I hope you don't mind if I get comfortable. It will teach me not to wear a pair of new shoes to work before they are broken in."

I immediately liked her. "No, that's fine."

I felt somewhat uneasy at first, answering all the personal questions she was throwing at me, but before long I relaxed and it felt good to let it all out. I found being honest with a stranger that you knew would never repeat what you were saying was very freeing. Plus, she was so busy writing she hardly ever looked directly at me until we were close to the end of the session.

"You know," she said as she raised up and slid one of her legs underneath her. "It's odd that you chose me."

"Why do you say that?" I was scared she was about to tell me I was just too big of a mess for her to tackle.

"I've only recently started studying people that claim to have past life memories. A colleague of mine had a client that experienced something very similar to Dr. Weiss's client, and she's written a paper on it. I read his book after she made reference to him in her paper."

"Wow," I said as I felt the tension in my shoulders release. "Well, I admit I prayed hard for God to let me find the right person to talk to."

"Well, He must have heard you," she said with a smile. "I find it all very fascinating."

'*Fascinating*', but not crazy?" I winced.

"Not crazy at all," she reassured me.

I felt I could trust her with the whole story, so I let it all out, even the part I hadn't told anyone. "Something really bizarre has begun to happen. I bought a journal at work thinking I just wanted to keep a record of all that was going on," I began.

"Okay, that sounds like a good idea.

"Well, I thought so too, but something strange started happening when I began to write in it."

"What do you mean?" she asked as she leaned in closer.

"Something came over me and I began to write really fast and I can tell you now they are not my words. Words like '*attestation*'. I had to look the word up. Anyway, it's not my life that's pouring onto the pages. I think it's Virginia's."

"Oh," she said as her eyes grew wide. "I would love to see them sometime."

I reached into my purse and pulled out the journal and handed it to her. She almost snatched it from my hand and began reading. "This is amazing Suzanne! I've only talked to you," she glanced at her watch, "a little over an hour, and I know you don't talk like this."

"So, you won't use it to have me committed?" I laughed nervously.

"Oh, don't worry; things are a lot different now than they used to be. To get one committed to a mental hospital takes quite a bit, and trust me, I don't think you're crazy at all. I think you're experiencing something very rare, but that doesn't make you crazy." She reached over and patted my hand. "It makes you interesting," she said with a smile.

"Try telling that to my husband," I said with a laugh.

"We'll get to him next session. You know what we '*in this business*' say?"

"No, what's that?"

"You spot it; you got it."

"I don't understand," I said making a face.

"In other words, if you're husband thinks you're crazy, maybe he's really the crazy one."

I laughed. "Okay, now I really like you."

"Good," she said as she stood up. She handed the journal back to me and I put it in my purse. She walked over to her desk and came back with her business card and handed it to me. "This has my office and home phone number on it. If you need to talk before our next appointment, just call me.

"Her offer surprised me. "Thank you," I said taking the card from her. "I really appreciate it."

As I left her office, I knew I had made the right decision in seeing someone and I thanked God out loud in the car for letting it be her. As I drove back to the bookstore, I felt a weight had been lifted from me.

# Chapter 12

*Virginia*

*Dearest Diary,*

*My heart is breaking as I write these words. Grandfather has passed away. Andrew delivered the telegram from Grandmother Abby to me yesterday. I sobbed with the knowledge that I will never see him again. Andrew has shown no sympathy, quite the opposite. He has sent a telegram back to Grandmother Abby stating that Elisabeth is ill, which she is not, and that we will be unable to attend his funeral. I fear by telling such things, we somehow bring them to pass. I can only pray that my Lord knows this was not of my doing and will protect my darling Elisabeth.*

*My father came to our house after I received the news. I foolishly thought he was coming to check on me, as he and Mother must have known how distraught I would be. On the contrary, he came to see Andrew. The two went into another room away from me and were talking in very low voices. I was unable to hear their discussion, but I fear I know the reason for their secrecy. I know it has something to do with the money they believe Grandfather has left for me. I shudder at the thought of such crassness but, I must say I am no longer shocked by their insolence. I shall miss Grandfather so very much. I only wish I could be there to comfort Grandmother Abby.*

*From my earliest memories, I remember Grandmother telling me that Grandfather was her true love. They had first met in their homeland of Germany. They both came to America by steamer ship after wars had continuously broken out, and Grandfather wanted to protect his bride. He had drawn up the plans for the house they would eventually build in the Garden District of New Orleans while they were still on the ship. I cannot imagine losing a person that has shared so much of your life. I pray for you, dear Grandmother, and may you feel my arms wrapped around you, even though I am so very far away.*

*Dearest Diary,*

*Andrew gave so little reprieve after the baby's birth before he began assaulting me again. I've attempted to learn the things that seem to bring about his fits and to avoid them at all costs, and yet, still there are times when he assaults me for no good reason at all.*

*I have now learned that I was correct in my assumption that father's visit after Grandfather's death was to plot, once again, with Andrew. They hope to gain quite a substantial amount of money left on my behalf. The two are such loathsome men.*

*Dearest Diary,*

*I write now when Andrew is away and hide these words in the keepsake box Grandmother Abby gave me. I keep it stowed away under the bed. I believe Andrew has forgotten that it exists.*

*I lost another child due to one of Andrew's violent attacks. He did not send for a doctor as I was badly bruised and bleeding. I believed I would surely die from the loss of blood, but I kept Elisabeth at the forefront of my thoughts. I believe she is the sole reason I am writing these words and did not succumb to death.*

*The beating occurred after we received word Grandmother Abby has decided not to sell Grandfather's business as yet. She has made the decision to allow his assistant to continue to handle his affairs for now. She forwarded a small amount of money and a book Grandfather had known was my favorite from childhood and had read it to me often. I will now read those same words to my darling Elisabeth and tell of her of the man that gave them to us. When Andrew realized he and father would not gain the sum they had discussed, he took his wrath out on me. He threw the book*

*Grandmother sent and it struck me in the face. I am better now, but I believe my nose is fractured. Amidst great pain, I have attempted, from time to time, to straighten it myself. While it does appear more in line now, there is still a small lump on the right side.*

*I continue to will myself to live if only for the bright smile that Elisabeth welcomes me with each morning.*

*Dearest Diary,*

*Father has died! God forgive me as I cannot say I am grieved in any way. Andrew did not attempt to hide his relief. He now believes Father's death will allow him sole control of whatever money I might inherit from my grandparent's estate in the future.*

*I live for the day Andrew will die as well. I know I should not say such things, but it is true. I believe my God forgives me for saying such things as He knows the trauma I suffer daily as his wife. Someday I plan to take Elisabeth and escape from this place that I hate. I cannot let Grandmother Abby pass away without seeing her again, and I will not allow Andrew to gain from their demise.*

# Chapter 13

*Suzanne*

It has been almost a month since I cut my fact-finding expedition to Marshall short to return to my troubled marriage. It did little good as it has continued to deteriorate no matter how hard I have tried to stop it.

"What are you going to do?" Kate asked as she watched as I put another box of winter clothes into the closet of the guest room.

"I don't know." I shut the closet door and turned to face her. "I keep thinking something will happen that will make things better between us, but I think I'm just kidding myself. I think our marriage is toast."

"Do you really believe Tony's having an affair?"

"Yes," I nodded. "And so does everyone else, including you."

"Oh Suzanne," she said as she plopped down on the side of the bed. "I had so hoped y'all would make it."

I sat down beside her. "Yeah, I know; so, did I. Just once I wish things would go right for me and I could just live in peace. The very thought of starting over, again, makes me physically sick. I hate to admit this, but a part of me still loves him and I don't know why. I can't deal with the thoughts that go through my mind when I think of him with someone else especially while we're still married. But to be honest," I said as I stood up from the bed, "being divorced won't change that either."

"I just wish there was something I could do," she said as she followed me from the room.

I stopped and turned around. "Actually, there might be," I said slowly. "Just hear me out before you say no, okay?"

"I already don't like the sound of this," she said as she arched an eyebrow.

I headed down the stairs and she followed. "I need to go back to Marshall while Max is on Spring break from school. He's going to stay the week with a friend and Maggie will be taking off that week as well. So, Tony will be home alone." I went into the kitchen and she came in behind me and sat down at the bar.

"Okay, so where do I come in?"
I turned back to face her. "I want you to go out with Mark and…"

She jumped from the barstool. "You must be out of your mind! You're my best friend, and you know I would do anything for you, but I won't go out with that obnoxious jerk!"

"Wait," I said holding my hands up to stop her rant. "I probably said that wrong."

"Any way you say it, it is still going to be wrong and the answer is still going to be no! You know I despise that man!"

"Listen! I don't really want you to *go on a date with him*. I just want you to casually run into him at that bar he goes to all the time. I've seen him when he goes out, and he drinks a lot. I just need you to flirt a little and see if you can get him to spill the beans about Tony, because I know he knows what's going on."

Kate leaned against the kitchen counter. "Oh Suzanne, I don't know."

"Please?" I walked over and took her hands in mine. "You know if there was another way to find out what Tony is up to without involving Mark and you, I would do it."

"What happens if he takes this flirting thing to heart? I'll never get rid of him."

"Don't worry. Once Tony and I split up, Mark will never give you the time of day out of loyalty to him. You'll be nothing more than a casualty of the divorce."

"You're pretty sure you're going to catch him, aren't you?"

"You forget," I said with a sigh, "I've dealt with an unfaithful husband before. I know I'll catch him. Right now, it's simply a matter of when and where." The tears I had been fighting to hold back betrayed me and rolled down my cheeks.

Kate hugged me. "I just hate him for what he's done to you." She released me then and smiled. "You can count on me; I'll do it. Hell, I'll get him in the sack, as repulsive a thought as that is, if that's what it takes to catch Tony."

"That won't be necessary, I assure you."

The next two weeks flew by as I made all the necessary arrangements to return to Marshall to search for Virginia. I finally told Mrs. Drexel the truth and I must say I was surprised by how interested she was in all of it. She made me promise to let her know what I found.

I knew this wasn't just about finding Virginia anymore. I was giving Tony enough rope to hang himself and put the final nails in the coffin of our marriage. I had no choice. I couldn't live like this any longer. Waiting for the other shoe to drop was driving me crazy.

I went over everything one more time with Tracy to make sure she was comfortable with running the bookstore while I was gone. She convinced me she could handle it, putting my worries to rest. I had finally finished telling her about the dream and everything Gina and I had found. She too made me promise to fill her in when I got back. I was truly relieved not to feel like I had to lie to anyone about what I was doing; well to anyone besides Tony. I knew the less I told him, the better. I got home in record time since it was in the middle of the afternoon. I came into the house and found Maggie dusting the furniture in the den.

"You're home early," she said as I came into the room.

"Yeah, I wanted to make sure everything was set for me to leave tomorrow."

She stopped dusting and came over to where I stood going through the mail. "Are you sure you don't want me to hang around here while you're away?"

"No, Maggie," I said looking up at her. "I want Tony to be here alone. I need him to drop his guard. If he's going to mess up, I want it to be now. The stress is killing me living like this."

"I have to agree with you there," she said with a sigh.

"I'm so sorry you've been caught in the middle of all of this." I choked back a sob. "And, the saddest part of all, is I know I'll lose you too."

"Oh, my dear." She hugged me. "You aren't going to lose me. I will always be your friend and I will stay with you and Max as long as you want."

"I could never afford to keep you on my salary alone."

"Is that what you're so upset about?" She cupped my face in her hands. "Now listen to me. I don't do this solely for the money. I come here every day and do these things mainly because I love you all, including Tony, for the time being. However, if you find your suspicions to be duly founded, my loyalty will lie with you."

I pulled away from her and patted her shoulder. "I just don't know how many times this can happen to one person in a lifetime. What is it that I do that makes the men in my life betray me?"

"Now you stop that this instant. I know you know this, but I'm going to say it anyway. If a man decides to become a philanderer, it's usually because he has always been one. I've seen nothing to indicate to me that you're the cause. Now, get upstairs and lie down until I get dinner ready.

I sighed. "I am tired."

"I know you are. Now go on up and I'll wake you in a bit."

My legs suddenly felt like they weighed a ton as I pulled myself up the stairs. I went into my room and thought I would just lay across the bed and rest, never intending to fall asleep. It was dark outside by the time Maggie came into my room to bring me a tray of food.

"What time is it?" I asked, rubbing my eyes.

"Seven-thirty. Sit up and eat this before it gets cold."

I shoved the pillows up behind me and scooted up against the headboard of the bed. She set the tray across my lap. "Any sign of Tony?" I asked as she sat down in the chair in the corner of the room.

"I'm afraid not, dear."

"He knows I'm leaving for Marshall in the morning. I told him the truth this time. I guess he figures since I stood up to him about going, he doesn't have to come home tonight. That's the part I just don't get."

"What don't you get?"

"If he really is seeing somebody, why would he raise so much hell about me going out of town? Wouldn't me being gone make it easier for him?"

She shook her head. "I wouldn't dare attempt to know what the man is thinking and you shouldn't trouble yourself with it either. I just really hate the idea of you making this trip alone in the state of mind you're in."

"I have to Maggie." I spoke in a low voice, just in case Tony might come in undetected and hear us. "Kate and I have a plan, and I have to be gone for it to work."

"Ah, I see." She got up from the chair. "Well, if you insist on going alone, then I insist on tagging along with you."

"What? Oh, Maggie, I couldn't ask you…"

"You didn't ask me," she interrupted. "And besides, it's been a long time since you and I did anything together. It'll be fun."

I smiled. "Well, if you're sure."

There was a tap on the door and I jumped. Maggie held a finger to her lips and went over and opened the door. We were both relieved to see Max standing on the other side.

"Is Mom okay?" He asked as he leaned around Maggie and peered into my room.

"Yes Max, I'm okay. Come in and close the door." Maggie moved aside and Max came over and sat down on the edge of the bed. "If you're okay, what are you doing in bed so early?"

"I was just tired and Maggie insisted I come up and rest. But really, I'm fine." I reached up and pushed the hair out of his face.

"Are you still going to Marshall in the morning?"

"I am, and I've just learned that Maggie is going with me. Isn't that great?"

"Yeah, it is," he smiled at Maggie. "I won't worry if Maggie's with you."

"I'm going to be with Gina too."

"I know, but at least you'll have somebody riding with you there and back. Terry just called and he and his Dad are on their way to pick me up."

I reached and hugged him. "I'll miss you."

"I'll miss you too Mom." He glanced over at Maggie. "Remind her to call and check in with me while y'all are gone."

Maggie smiled. "She won't need me to remind her, she thinks of you always."

He leaned over and hugged me. "Okay, well, I'll see you when you get back." He left the room and closed the door behind him.

"He's a good lad," Maggie said with a smile. "Now, I'm going to run home and pack. I'll come back and spend the night in the guest room so we can leave early in the morning."

"Sounds good," I said with a smile. After she left the room, I got up and sat the tray on the table beside the bed and walked over to the window. I watched as she got in her car and drove away and then my mind began to play its familiar tricks.

I had really believed the past five years had been good ones between me and Tony. I thought we had been happy for the most part. I began to rack my brain and tried to figure out when all our trouble had started, but I just couldn't pin it down. But one thing was for sure; it had been long before the mystery of Virginia, even though that seemed to be where he liked to lay the blame.

It was also before the woman brought him home from work. His notorious bad moods over the past several months and the late nights at the office had all seemed to start about the same time. Yet, no matter how hard I tried, nothing I did seemed to make things better for us. He was always condescending and blamed me for all our arguments. The streetlights began to flicker on and I felt a tear run down my face. *'Tony, where are you?'*

I went into the bathroom and washed my face. I was hanging the hand towel back up when I heard the front door close. I walked to the landing at the top of the staircase just in time to catch sight of Tony as he went into the den. I decided to take the opportunity of us being alone and try to talk to him. I walked slowly down the stairs. He was pouring himself a drink when I walked into the room.

"Hey, what are you doing?"

"What does it look like I'm doing?" He kept his back to me.

"I didn't mean at this very moment." I sighed and sat down on the arm of the sofa. "We need to talk."

He turned to face me then. "No, Suzanne, we don't." He had such a cold look in his eyes. "We've talked this to death. Don't you agree?"

"No, I don't agree."

"Why doesn't that surprise me? We haven't agreed on anything in months."

"And that's my fault? I've tried to talk to you for weeks, and I'm always met with arrogance and attitude. What's really going on with you?"

"Look, you seem determined to make an idiot of yourself in this quest to *'find Virginia'.*" He threw his head back, taking all the liquor in the glass at once. "But, I don't have to like it or condone it." He picked up the liquor bottle and filled the glass again.

"And you think drinking is going to help us? Do you even realize how often you are drinking these days?"

He laughed. "Living with you would make any man drink."

"Why are you always such an ass?"

"Seriously, Suzanne, you really don't realize how all of this makes you look? You just don't get it, do you?"

"This whole thing with Virginia has only given you an excuse to escalate everything between us. Our problems didn't start with me looking for Virginia."

"You believe whatever the hell you want to believe. But, I promise you, I'm through talking about all of this." He walked past me and headed for the kitchen and I followed him.

"Don't walk away from me when I'm trying to talk to you."

He spun around and I almost ran into him. "I just told you I was done with this. You refuse to see anything, and I'm sick to death of talking about it because you clearly don't care what I think.

"I do care what you think." I reached and touched his arm.

"The hell you do," he said as he pushed my hand away. "Anyway, I don't give a damn where you go. I've made plans of my own."

"What plans?" I felt my stomach start to churn.

"I'm going with Mark up to his Dad's lake house to go fishing. Maybe then I can unwind because I sure as hell can't around here anymore. And one more thing. Don't ask for the telephone number because you're not getting it. I don't want to be bothered by you or anyone else."

"So, we aren't going to talk at all for the whole week?"

"That's the plan." He walked back into the den and fixed another drink.

"I can't believe you are being this way," I said as I followed him.

"Well, you better believe it. I've had it, Suzanne."

I felt like we were playing a game now, and somebody had changed the rules and I no longer knew how to play. "Are you saying you want a divorce?" The knot in my stomach moved up to my throat. I dreaded to hear his answer, but I needed to know.

He let out a loud sigh. "I don't know the answer to that yet," he said flatly. Car lights flashed across the front windows of the den. "Who the hell is that pulling in?"

"It must be Maggie," I said as I brushed away tears I hadn't realized had streamed down my face.

"What is she doing coming over here so late?" The coldness in his voice chilled me to the bone.

"She wants to go with me tomorrow. She's worried about me."

He laughed a sickly laugh and got in my face. "Well, she needs to be worried, because you're crazy," he said through clenched teeth. "Don't come home early from your little trip, and I mean it!" He stomped off towards the staircase. He stopped and turned to face me. "I'm going to bed. You can sleep down here or in Max's room!" He stormed up the staircase and I heard him slam the bedroom door. I sat down on the arm of the sofa and put my face in my hands and sobbed.

For a large portion of the remainder of the night, Maggie tried to console me. I couldn't believe the way he was acting; it was if suddenly I was his worst enemy instead of his wife. I knew for certain I had to go through with my plan and go to Marshall; I had no choice, even if it meant leaving our heated words hanging between us.

The next morning, the sun was just coming up as we pulled onto the interstate. Maggie somehow convinced me that letting Tony have this week apart might help in the long run. "You need to give him time to think about what he's doing."

"What he's doing is blaming me for everything, and I know this is a two-way street."

"Of course it is, but it's just easier to blame you than to take responsibility for his part in all of this."

"He's not much of a man if you ask me." I stared straight ahead at the endless interstate in front of us. "I know from past experience when I lose respect for a man, well, it's pretty much over for me. I won't fight to save the relationship."

"It would be that way for anybody; not just you."

"I know the woman that brought him home from work that day is more than just somebody from the office. But, of course, he's never going to admit it."

"I know you really didn't believe he would," Maggie said with a laugh. "Look, let's just try not to think about him or your troubles. Let's just try and enjoy this little trip. What do you say?"

"I'll try."

"That's half the battle," she said with a smile.

After what seemed forever, we finally pulled into my sister's driveway and once again, I felt an instant release of tension. Gina came out onto the porch and I could tell she was surprised when she saw Maggie get out of the passenger side of the car. She immediately came down the front steps and rushed out to greet her. They hugged and then Gina helped her with her bag.

I cleared my throat. "I'm here too, you know."

They both laughed. "I know silly, but it's not every day that I get to see Maggie."

"Before I had the dream it had been over a year since you had seen me," I objected.

"Whose fault is that?" Gina asked as she looked back at me as she and Maggie made their way up the sidewalk to the front steps of the house.

"Now girls," Maggie intervened.

We all laughed and I followed them inside. "Well, come on in," Gina said as she sat Maggie's bag down at the bottom of the stairs. "I've made some chicken salad for lunch. Just come on back and we'll visit." I sat my bag down next to Maggie's at the foot of the stairs and followed them into the kitchen. I sat down across from Maggie at the table while Gina fixed us all a glass of iced tea. She brought the glasses over to the table and sat them in front of us before sitting down next to me.

"How was the trip?" Gina asked.

"It was good," Maggie answered for both of us. "But, I am glad to be out of the car."

"I can imagine." Gina smiled. "Okay, I know you're anxious to get started; where do you want to begin?"

I took a drink of tea. "Well, something occurred to me the other day. Mother said Andrew Lipton remarried; right?"

"Yes, that's right," Gina nodded.

"Well, if that's the case, there should be a divorce decree on file at the courthouse."

"Oh Suzanne, I don't think so. Mother said she abandoned them, remember? I don't think there was ever a divorce."

"I realize that, but I still think we should check it out anyway. So, the place I want to begin is the courthouse."

"I guess you mean right now," she said with a laugh.

"The trip was a little long for me," Maggie said as she slowly got up from the chair. "If you'll just tell me which room you want me in, I'll get unpacked and settled in while you girls go and check things out. Then when you return I'll fix us some lunch. If it's okay with Gina if I take over her kitchen while we're here."

"You're kidding, right?" Gina smiled and looked over at me. "You won't hear any protest from me."

"Now Maggie," I said smiling at her. "You were the one that said we were to act as if this was a mini vacation, so no cooking for you."

She walked over and patted me on the back. "Now don't you worry. I won't do anything I don't want to. You and your sister go snooping and let me do what I do best."

"Okay then. Gina, are you ready?"

She jumped up from her chair and grabbed her purse. "I'm ready if you are."

When we got in the car, Gina didn't waste any time and started questioning me about what had happened between me and Tony. I didn't really want to talk any more about it, but she was a good listener, so I vented.

"So," she said after I told her everything, "you're really thinking he will do something while you're gone?"

"I think he's been *doing* something with me there, so yeah, I do."

"Do you have any idea who he might be seeing?"

"Well, I would say I think it's the woman that brought him home from work that time, but really, that's almost too easy. He would have to be an idiot to let her bring him home if he was secretly seeing her. I mean he had no way of knowing who all was there that evening. I had pulled my car into the garage and the door was closed." I looked over at her. "I mean, come on, nobody would have their mistress bring them straight to the house where he was still living with his wife; would they?"

"I have no idea. I would kill Doug in his sleep if he ever pulled something like that."

"Don't think I haven't wanted to kill him," I said as I pulled to a stop at a red light. "But, then there are nights, where my mind plays back all the good memories we've had and it really hurts. That's the part I hate. It makes me sick because I know all it would take to turn all of this around is for him to say he's sorry and mean it. It makes me feel like such an idiot."

"Don't beat yourself up; we're all like that. I'm always the first to apologize when Doug and I fight."

"Oh, please." I said as I pulled through the intersection when the light turned green. "Your *petty misunderstandings* with Doug don't qualify as a fight by anybody's standards."

"Yeah, I know," she said with a grin. "But, I still wouldn't put up with it, I can tell you that."

I pulled into the parking lot and got out. I looked over at the old courthouse that had been closed since they built the new one across the street. "I wonder what they plan on doing with the old one."

"There was an article in the newspaper last week that said the city is about to start renovations on it. It said when they finished it would house a museum," Gina said as she glanced back over her shoulder at the old building.

"Good, at least they aren't going to tear it down."

We went through the double doors of the new courthouse and once inside, we went through security. I asked the deputy on duty what office we should go to find archive files and she suggested we start with the District Clerk's office and told us where it was located. As we walked down the hall, I suddenly remembered the last time I had been in the building. I shook my head.

"What is it?" Gina asked as we walked down the hallway.

"The last time I was in this building was when I divorced Eric."

"Oh wow," she said raising her eyebrows. "That's a bad memory."

"You're not kidding," I agreed as we reached the office we were looking for. I opened the door and went in with Gina right behind me. A young man got up from his desk and came to the counter.

"May I help you?"

"I hope so," I said smiling at him. "I'm not sure this is the office we need to be in, but I'm trying to locate an old divorce file from the early nineteen hundreds."

"Well, you're in the right place." He reached and pulled a scratch pad from his desk and pulled a pen from his pocket. "What's the name of the party?"

"It would be a divorce between Virginia Barrister Lipton and Andrew Lipton."

He scribbled down the name. "Give me just a minute and I'll check the system and see if we have anything." He turned and went back to his desk and Gina held up crossed fingers and winked at me.

Within minutes the man returned to the counter. "Okay, I've located the file. If you'll just come on back this way," he motioned us through a swinging door at the end of the counter. Stunned and speechless, we followed him back to an area that was lined with bookshelves. "Just have a seat and I'll pull the file."

"So," Gina whispered. "Mama didn't know Andrew filed for divorce before he got remarried."

My mind was reeling. I hadn't told Gina what made me want to come and check to see if there was a divorce on file. The man came back over to the table where we were waiting and laid the file in front of me. "Just let me know if you need copies," he said before returning to his post at the front counter.

I opened the file and felt like something sucked the breath out of me as I read the top line: *Petitioner: Virginia Abbigail Barrister Lipton.* I quickly closed the file and slid it to Gina. "Take this to him and get a copy. I can't do this here."

Gina slowly rose and picked up the file and took it back to the counter. I didn't need to stand to know that my legs felt like Jell-O. She came back a few minutes later and stood beside me. "Okay, I've got the file. Are you ready to go?"

I slowly rose and walked out of the office as if I were in a trance with Gina right by my side. "Why don't you let me drive?" She asked as we reached the parking lot. I reached into my purse and pulled out the keys and handed them to her. We got into the car and closed the doors and then it was Gina that spoke first. "I cannot believe you just found a divorce decree and Virginia had filed it!" I just sat staring out the windshield of the car. "What made you think to come here and look?"

"I just knew," I said as I fought my emotions.

Gina sighed and I turned to see the look of total disbelief on her face. I looked down at the papers in my hand and tried to read the words written in calligraphy. I could make out about every third word. "We're going to need help with this," I said as I folded the papers and put them in my purse.

"I agree." She said as she looked away from me and nodded her head.

I didn't know if we were still talking about deciphering the words in the divorce decree, or if she thought she was going to need help with me. She put the key in the ignition and cranked the car and pulled away. Neither one of us said anything on the drive back to her house. When she pulled up in the driveway, we both got out and went inside. I followed her into the kitchen where Maggie was standing at the counter.

"You're back already?" She asked as she turned to face us. "No luck, I guess?" Gina and I sat down at the table. Maggie cocked her head to the side and looked at me. "Suzanne, what's wrong?"

I pulled the folded papers from my purse and held them out to her. She came over and took them from my hand. I watched as she unfolded them and began to read. "She filed for divorce?" She put one hand to her bosom as she handed the papers back to me. "What on earth?"

"If you're wanting an explanation, I don't think there is one," Gina said as she got up and went over and pulled glasses down from the cabinet. "You want ice tea or Coke, Suzanne?"

"Coke please. I need something to settle my stomach."

"Good idea," Gina said as she filled the glasses with ice. "What about you Maggie?"

"Coke's fine for me too," she answered without taking her eyes off me. She slowly lowered herself into the chair across the table from me. "Suzanne, this changes everything," she said so low I almost didn't hear her. Gina brought the glasses over to the table and sat down.

"What do you make of this?" Maggie asked as she looked over at Gina.

She sighed. "I have no idea. I don't even understand what made her think to look for a divorce decree. We had no reason to believe there was one." They were talking like I wasn't sitting there, but it was just as well, I was still in shock myself. I sat looking at the document in front of me wondering how something like this happened and nobody knew. I looked up and Gina was staring at me. I couldn't understand the look on her face; she appeared mad.

"Are you alright?" I asked.

"No, not really. I just can't make heads or tails of all of this," she said, never taking her eyes from me. "I've been with you since this whole *dream* thing began, but this is really starting to freak me out. It's scaring me if you want the honest truth!"

"Now Gina," Maggie reached and patted her hand. "There's no reason to be scared. This is all very strange, no doubt, but I don't think it should scare us."

"I didn't ask for all of this to happen," I said as I got up from the table and started pacing the floor. "You must know that! Yes, I realize it was my decision to pursue it, but I'm telling you I didn't feel like I had a choice."

"What do you mean, *you didn't have a choice?*" Gina barked.

"Girls," Maggie pleaded. "Let's all just calm down."

Gina looked down and then raised her head and looked back up at me. "I didn't mean to snap at you like that. I'm just…I don't know how I feel. It just blows my mind."

"Don't you think I feel the same way? How would you like it if this happened to you?"

"Tell me, what made you go and look for this?" She asked as she picked up the papers from the table and held them up to me. "There was no reason for you to believe there had been a divorce. If anything, it would have been the opposite because of what Mama told us."

Without answering her I went to my bag sitting at the foot of the stairs and pulled the book by Dr. Brian Weiss and the journal out and went back into the kitchen. I sat down across from Gina and handed her the journal.

"What is this?" She asked as she took it from my hand.

"Just read it." My voice cracked.

She kept her eyes on me for a minute longer before she opened the journal and began to read. "What the hell is this, and where did you find it?"

"I didn't find it, I wrote it."

"No, you did not, Suzanne! These are not your words, where did you find it?" She stared at me like I was suddenly a stranger.

I glanced at Maggie and saw the look of total confusion on her face. "I bought the journal at the bookstore last month." I said as I choked back tears. "I thought if I wrote down my feelings about what was happening to me it might help me make sense of everything. But," I slowly continued. "When I opened it and began to write, it was like somebody else was doing the writing. The words just spilled out of me." Maggie got up and came and sat beside me and put her arm around me.

"Oh, Suzanne," Gina said as she reached across the table and put her hand over mine.

"I don't know what's happening to me." I leaned into Maggie and cried on her shoulder.

I hated the way Gina continued to look at me. I got up and walked over to the kitchen counter and she followed. She reached into the cabinet above the sink and pulled down a bottle of liquor and walked back over to the table and opened it. "I need a drink," she said as she poured rum into her glass of Coke.

Maggie slid her glass over to Gina. "You might as well fix me one too."

My eyes got big and Gina turned to look at me and we both busted out laughing. Maggie began to laugh hysterically too. None of us could stop. Gina came over and hugged me as we continued to laugh. I went over to the table and picked up my glass. "Well, don't leave me out." Gina and I finally sat back down at the table and it was Maggie that brought us back to the moment.

"Let me see that journal," she said. I handed it to her and she opened it and began to read.

*'Dearest Diary,*

*Today is my birthday and I know I should be happy, but to the contrary, I find myself quite sad. Grandmother and Grandfather arranged a grand party for me, and I had a lovely time, but it was later that I became grief stricken.'*

"This has numerous entries in it," Maggie said as she flipped through the pages. "How long have you been writing these and why haven't you mentioned any of this to me?"

"I didn't want to say anything to anybody until I could come back here and see if what I had written was true."

"How long has this been going on?" Maggie asked.

"The writings started almost as soon as I bought the journal. I bought it and this book at the same time." I laid the book *Many Lives, Many Masters,* on the table.

Gina picked up the book and flipped it over and read the back cover, just as I had when I bought it. "I mentioned to you awhile back that I thought it might be past life memories you were dealing with and you wouldn't even consider it."

"I know, but I just couldn't give into any thoughts of something I thought of as being so outlandish and plus, I consider myself a Christian and I don't think they believe in reincarnation."

"Well, it's in the Bible," Maggie spoke up.

"What do you mean?" I asked. "Where?"

"In the book of Matthew."

"Will you show me?"

Maggie looked over at Gina. "Can you bring me a Bible?"

"Sure," she said as she rose slowly from her chair and left the room.

Maggie looked over at me. "You didn't ask for any of this. You remember I told you when you first told me about the dream that I thought you had it for a reason."

"I know you did."

"Well, I think we are all seeing the reason now. Someone had to clear this woman's name."

Gina came back into the room carrying her Bible and handed it to Maggie. She took it and opened it up to the book of Matthew and ran her finger down the page until she found what she was looking for and slid the Bible over to me. I began to silently read what she was showing me.

"Wow," was all I could manage.

"Read it out loud," Gina said as she sat back down at the table and leaned forward.

*Jesus replied, "They are right. Elijah must come and set everything in order. And, in fact, he has already come, but he wasn't recognized, and was badly mistreated by many. And I, the Messiah, shall suffer at their hands. Then the disciples realized he was speaking of John the Baptist."*

"So," Gina looked over at Maggie. "John the Baptist was Elijah reincarnated?"

"I think that's exactly what it says," Maggie said softly. "I don't know how else you can take it, and I for one believe the entire Bible. But, I especially take note of the words written in red, spoken by Jesus Himself, and I know you do too, Suzanne."

"I do," I said nodding my head. "But, to be honest, I already knew this had to be of God because I begged Him to take it from me if it wasn't of Him. Instead of taking it from me, all of this began to happen," I said pointing to the journal.

"I couldn't agree more," Maggie spoke up. "He could have certainly put a stop to it any time He wanted to if it wasn't of Him. And besides, this divorce decree alone speaks volumes about the lie they told saying Virginia just ran off. We know now that is not what happened."

"I agree," I said running my hand through my hair. "But why did they lie? What were they trying to hide?"

"Okay," Gina held up the book by Dr. Brian Weiss. "How much of this book have you read?"

"Some, but it's basically about people he regressed."

"What is that?" Maggie asked.

"That's where he hypnotizes them and under hypnosis they remember a past life and he records it."

"But you're getting this information by writing journal entries, you're not being hypnotized, and this all began with the dream?" Gina asked, before tipping up her glass to finish off her drink.

"Right," I nodded.

"But the people in the book, when they are hypnotized, they just start talking about being alive in another era; another time?" Maggie asked.

"Yeah, that's pretty much it."

Gina reached and picked up the journal again and opened it. "All these entries start with *Dearest Diary?"*

I nodded again. "It's almost like dictation. I began keeping the journal in my purse to keep Tony from seeing it. But then, I would be driving down the road, or sitting at home or at work and something would happen and the words would just come to me. I would pull the journal out and start writing." I sighed. "There's an entry about the divorce, that's why I went to look for the decree at the courthouse today."

"Ah," Gina said nodding her head. "Now I get it." She laid the journal down and picked up the divorce decree and looked over it. She reached the last page. "Oh, that's strange."

"What now?"

"Look at the date," she said as she pointed to the last line.

"April fourth, nineteen o'four. So?"

"Well think about it," Gina said looking up at me. "Didn't you tell me you woke up from the dream at 4:44?"

"Yes," I answered slowly.

"Oh dear," Maggie spoke up. "Fourth month, fourth day, and fourth year of the new century. Four, four, four."

I sat down and laid my head down on the table. I raised back up and sighed. "I just don't understand. Four boxes in the dream, I woke up at 4:44, and now this. What does it mean?"

"Four generations of women that had issues with each other. Virginia, your grandmother, your mother and you," Maggie said as she shook her head.

"Okay," Gina said as she got up from the table. "We need to find somebody that can read this divorce decree."

"I agree, but who are we going to find in Marshall that knows how to read this stuff?"

"I know you don't want to hear this," Gina began. "We're going to need Mama's help. She's bound to have ran into this type of writing when she was doing her genealogy research. She must have found somebody to help her."

I let out a deep sigh. "Okay, she needs to know about the divorce decree anyway."

"Yes she does," Maggie said in agreement.

"So, can I call her now?" Gina asked.

"Yeah, go ahead." I picked up the journal and the book from the table. "But not a word to her about the journal entries; not yet." Then I looked at both of them. "And not a word about the *'past life'* theory."

"Oh no," Gina raised her eyebrows. "I totally agree with you on that!" She got up from the table and went into the living room to make the call.

"It's going to be alright," Maggie said as she reached and squeezed my hand.

Gina came back into the kitchen. "She's on her way." She came over and hugged me. "We'll be right here with you."

"Alright," I said as I pulled back from her. I'm just going to put these back in my bag and take it upstairs. I'll be right back down. I'm ready to face her now."

# Chapter 14

*Virginia*

*Dearest Diary,*

*I did not want to record these words until I was certain of my condition. I am once again with child. A part of me is grateful for the opportunity to have yet another child to love. I pray this one will love me the same as my dear Elisabeth. I hope they will be very close, as she has just begun to toddle about. I have never told anyone this, but when I was growing up, I dreamt of a sister that would play with me. At times, I imagined her into real life, during my waking hours as well. It was only when I began school and met friends my own age that I allowed my imaginary sister to go back into her world, and I remained in mine.*

*I secretly hope this child will be a boy. I hope he will grow big and strong and protect all of us from his father. Then, I give this thought more attention, and I fear a boy might succumb to Andrew's ways and be a horrible tyrant like his father. It is difficult to know what to wish for when your days are filled with such uncertainty.*

*Andrew has not beaten me since I told him of my condition. I long to say it is because he has softened because of Elisabeth, but my words would be untrue. I know that Elisabeth and I both carry a bounty on our heads, and this child will as well. Andrew believes each birth secures more money for him from Grandmother.*

 *Mother comes to visit every other week now. She has moved to Jefferson, a nearby town with her sister. I have finally come to trust her. She has spent many hours explaining how things came to be, and in the end, resulted with my being left in New Orleans. She still tries to convince me that my father was not always the evil person I came to know in his last days. I must admit the photographs she has shown me are from a time when he was young and strong, and his eyes sparkled with joy. That bright light had burnt out by the time I came to know him. Mother gave me one photograph of my father holding Ralston, my brother, and she was holding me on the day of my christening. I had never seen a photograph of the four of us before.*

 *I know a hard life can change a person. I remember I would read Mother's letters, and even though I was young, I did not want to live the life she described. It is my belief that hard times can cause a person to hate everything and everyone. Eventually, that hate can creep into a person's soul and slip unnoticed into the crevices until the day it grows so large it takes over the person completely. I pray that doesn't happen with me and the children.*

 *I want desperately to confide in Mother and tell her my plans to run away. I long to be able to say the words aloud to someone; anyone. I dare not say anything in front of Elisabeth as she has begun to talk and mimics my words. Andrew still doesn't have anything to do with her, and she appears to be frightened of him as well. I have always attempted to shelter her from witnessing the violence, but I know in my heart it has still affected her.*

 *I only pray that once I escape, God will restore my heart. But, even if I live to be a very old woman, I shall never forget the horrors I have known in this house.*

*Dearest Diary,*

*The weather and my condition have both been dire. I have almost lost this child on two separate occasions. Both times Andrew has sent for the doctor, which greatly surprised me until I remember what he stands to gain. Mother is not able to come for a visit as the roads are in such bad condition. Because of my illness, I am not able to care for Elisabeth nor attend to my household chores. Andrew's younger sister, Mattie, has been assigned the task of caring for Elisabeth. I greatly dislike this arrangement, but I have no other options. I hope the difficulties I am experiencing are not a sign as to the character of the child I am carrying. I can only believe it is because of all the beatings I have had to endure and the lack of medical attention I had during the loss of the last child. I pray God will not let me conceive again.*

*Dearest Diary,*

*My son has made his way into this world screaming and thrashing about. His name is Jonathan, named after Andrew's deceased father. I did not want to name my child after a man I have never known, but I had no say in the matter. It's quite clear to me now, that I am of no value whatsoever to Andrew. I am only here to produce heirs to my Grandmother's estate. His violent rages began again shortly after Jonathan's birth. Mattie continues to care for Elisabeth and has extended a form of kindness to me. I have grown to care for her, but I could never trust her; not completely. I constantly remind myself she is still Andrew's sister. I contemplate now of a way to escape from him.*

*I must constantly rock Jonathan, as he is a very colicky baby. I miss my time alone with Elisabeth. Both of Andrew's sisters care for her, and I find it very unsettling. She has appeared at the end of the day with scratches and bruises, evidence they are not attending to her as they should. I also fear they will pass along their feelings concerning me to her. Grandmother continues to send dresses for me that I must see Andrew's sisters attired in when they go out. I am left with only the nightgowns.*

*Dearest Diary,*

*I fear Andrew's patience is waning waiting on Grandmother to die. He reads all correspondence from her before I am allowed to see them. He was so exuberant when she wrote that she was ill, but then beat me when the letter came reporting her recovery. Jonathan's constant crying also brings on his attacks. I have tried to tell him I have no control over his ailments, but he doesn't care to hear my words.*

*Mother has finally begun to visit again now that our world has begun to thaw from the long and dark winter. I wish my gay mood would return as well, but I fear it is lost forever. I fear I will never again be the girl I once was in New Orleans.*

*Grandmother sent a photograph of herself standing in front of the wall of books in Grandfather's study. I yearned so desperately to go home when I saw her and the room again. I sobbed for hours. She sent money for a photograph to be taken of the children and myself. It was the first time I have had the luxury of wearing one of the many dresses she has sent. The one Andrew chose for me to wear would no longer fit after being altered to fit his sister. Grandmother will never know that the back gaped open as I was instructed to smile for the photographer. I can only hope she doesn't notice the small knot on the side of my nose, where I believe the book Andrew threw at me, fractured it.*

*Dearest Diary,*

*I have, at last, trusted Mother with the truth concerning my plan to leave Andrew. I have sworn her to secrecy, and she has agreed to help in any way she can. She broke down and sobbed when she took notice of the bruises upon my wrist.*

*I have asked her to write to Grandmother and tell her the truth, including the part my deceased father played in all of this. I have instructed her further, to tell her of my plans to leave as soon as I feel it will be safe for me and the children. I have also asked her to tell Grandmother to continue to correspond with me here as she has, but also through secret letters my mother will write and receive for me as well. I do not know how I will find the courage to escape when just the notion of secrecy frightens me so, but I know I must. Without such courage, I fear the children and I will perish after Andrew receives whatever money he hopes to gain when Grandmother passes.*

# Chapter 15

*Suzanne*

I sat by Gina's kitchen window and watched as my mother pulled her car into the driveway. She rushed up the sidewalk and disappeared onto the front porch. I heard the front door open and close, and before I was ready, she was standing in the doorway to the kitchen.

She looked first at me, and then, to Gina and Maggie. "What's going on? Why the urgency for me to get here? Gina?"

"Mama, we found a divorce decree," Gina said as she held out the papers to her.

"What divorce decree? Are you and Tony getting a divorce?" She took the papers from Gina. "Well, I never thought it would last as long as it did."

I just shook my head as she came over and sat down across from me at the table. Gina walked over and stood behind her and Maggie came and sat down next to me.

"Not Suzanne," Gina said slowly. "It's Virginia's divorce decree. The one she filed against Andrew Lipton."

She looked down at the papers and then threw them on the table and jumped up from her chair. "What? Virginia didn't file for divorce; she ran off with another man. She abandoned her family!"

"No, she didn't." My voice was so calm I barely recognized it as my own. "She divorced him."

Mother reached and picked up the papers from the table. As I watched her, it was as if everything began to move in slow motion. I saw her mouth open with astonishment as she read the papers, but nothing came out. I had never known her to be speechless in my life. I suddenly felt bad for proving her wrong.

She plopped back down in the chair as if her legs would no longer support her. "Where did you find this?" She asked without looking up at me.

"It was on file at the courthouse," I answered.

"I don't understand. I researched for years. How could I have missed this?" The shock of it all made her voice sound strange. I suddenly realized it was the way she must have always sounded to everyone else, except me. The malice was suddenly missing from her speech.

"You couldn't have known to look for it," Maggie said, with a look of compassion on her face.

"How did you know to look for it? What made you think there was a divorce decree?" My mother asked as she glared at me.

I sighed. "Just a hunch."

"Why are you suddenly so interested in this woman?"

I leaned back in my chair. "Do you remember when I came to town a few months back and I told you I had a dream about Mamaw?"

"Yes," she answered hesitantly. "You're telling me that's what made you look for this?" She held up the papers.

"Well," I began slowly, "I didn't tell you all of the dream. Mamaw and Aunt Margie were both there in my dream." I saw the tears form in her crystal blue eyes at the mention of her sister. I had always known she loved her. "Mamaw came to me and told me she was having an *estate sale*, and she had something she thought I was going to want. She had a keepsake box with a mirrored lid and there were three more identical boxes inside; four in all." I took a deep breath and continued. "Mamaw was opening each box as I watched. When she got to the last box, I had to lean over to see inside. I thought I would see my own reflection in the mirror as I looked down into it, but what I saw in the mirror was the face of another woman; someone I had never seen before. Then a voice from behind me asked, *'Who died the year you were born?'* and I woke up. I had never seen the woman that I saw in the mirror in my dream, until you dropped those papers and pictures on Gina's table that day. Mother, the woman in the mirror was Virginia."

The silence at the table was deafening, then Mother started to shake her head. "This is impossible." She looked at each of us, one by one, looking for any sign that any of us would agree with her. Finding none, she turned back to me. "So, you're saying this dream is what pushed you to come here.

It's just a foolish dream! What exactly have you come here to do?" The cold blew back into the room with her words.

I didn't have the energy to fight her. "I just need answers."

"Answers to what?" She got up from the table and walked over to the cabinet and pulled a glass down and filled it with tap water from the kitchen faucet. She took a drink and then faced me again.

"I need to know what really happened to her."

Gina and Maggie didn't say a word. I so desperately wanted one of them to intervene, but I also understood why they were silent; this was between me and my mother.

"You know," she said as she came back over and sat down across from me. "This divorce decree doesn't prove anything."

"How can you say that?" Gina suddenly spoke up. "It proves she didn't abandon them."

"I don't mean she didn't divorce him; clearly she did. But, she still sent her youngest child back on a train, alone, with that horrible note penned to him."

"Mother," I heard the sternness in my voice and tried to control it, "If Mamaw's father and aunts lied about her abandoning them, how do you know they didn't lie about that part too?" I got up from the table and went over to the counter and pulled a glass down and put ice in it. I needed to put some space between us. I looked back over at her as I opened a can of Coke and saw the confused look on her face.

"Olivia," Maggie finally broke the heaviness of the silence. "Right now, we need your help with all of this." Her voice had always had a calming effect. "We can't read the divorce decree. As you saw, it's written in calligraphy. Gina thought you might have run across this writing before, in other documents you found doing your genealogy."

"I have," she nodded. "I wasn't able to read it either, but there is a judge in town; he's a historian as well, and he helped me." She thought for a minute. "Judge Price; that's his name." She seemed to drop her guard at the thought she might be needed. "I could call him."

I came back over to the table. "Oh, would you? Please?"

She nodded her head. She dug into her purse and pulled out a small book and flipped through its pages. "Yes, I still have his number." She got up and went into the living room to make the call.

I looked over at Gina. "I think she's temporarily forgotten that it's me she's helping."

She came back and stopped in the doorway of the kitchen. "He said he can see us in twenty minutes. Can we make it by then?"

"Absolutely," I said as I looked at both Gina and Maggie.

"Yes, that's great," Gina agreed as she grabbed her purse from the kitchen counter.

We all rushed out to the car. Gina got up front with me, as Mother and Maggie got in the backseat. I drove as Mother gave directions to Judge Price's office. Moments later, I pulled into the driveway of an old Victorian house that now served as his office. We all got out and went up the steep front steps into the receptionist area. My mother went in first and approached the receptionist that sat at a desk in what was once a parlor or sitting area. The woman escorted us down a long hallway and into his office at the back of the house. The windows behind his desk looked out over a lush, green garden.

The old, white-haired man, dressed in a starched white shirt with red suspenders, rose from his chair when we entered the room. "Good afternoon," he said in a deep, baritone voice. "You ladies come on in and have a seat."

"Judge Price," Olivia said as she shook his hand. "It's good to see you again, and I really appreciate you seeing us at such short notice."

"Always glad to help," he said with a smile. "Now, who are these lovely ladies you have with you?"

"These are my daughters, Gina and Suzanne. And this," she patted Maggie on the arm, "is Maggie, my daughter's…"

"Friend," I spoke up.

"Well, it's nice to meet you all. Now, I understand you have some papers you need help reading?"

"Yes," I said as I pulled the divorce decree from my purse and handed it to him.

He picked up a pair of round, wire rimmed glasses and put them on. "Well, you ladies have a seat."

Gina and Maggie sat down on a sofa against the wall. My mother and I sat down in the two chairs in front of the judge's desk.

"Ah, yes," he said with a smile after looking over the papers. "I've seen quite a bit of this gentleman's handy work. Quite impressive, isn't it?" He looked over his glasses at all of us.

"Yes, it is," I agreed.

"Hmm. Who is Virginia Lipton?"

"She was my grandmother," my mother said with a sigh. "I never knew her. She…"

"Was severely abused," the Judge said before she could finish her sentence. "Did you know that?"

143

The gasp that escaped us all answered his question. "Abused?" My mother barely whispered the word.

"Terribly," he sighed. "The abuse was both verbal and physical."

"Dear God," I barely heard my mother say.

I glanced over at Maggie. She had one hand over her mouth and the other clutching the neckline of her dress. The shock on Gina's face was evident as I'm sure my face revealed as well.

"Somehow, I feel like they lured this poor girl to Marshall under false pretense. Maybe an arranged marriage. It used to happen frequently, I'm afraid. Although, I feel there is something about the way this attorney handled this case."

"What do you mean," I asked.

"I don't know exactly. It seems he was very careful at the words he chose. It's as if there is still some fear his client feels and he's trying to weigh his words to keep from provoking this *Andrew Lipton*. Very peculiar. Of course, divorces were so rare back in that day, maybe the attorney just didn't have a lot of experience. Hard to say, but no doubt, she definitely had a rough go of it. It says he beat her on a regular basis."

I heard a gasp escape from my mother. I looked over at her, but she never took her eyes off the judge as he continued to look over the papers. "She is asking for custody of her two children. She states she is Catholic and understands she will lose her place with the Church, but fears if she doesn't get away from this man, her children will never know the God she serves with all her heart. She also says he is capable of killing all of them, and that his sisters were brutal at times to her as well." The judge laid the papers back on the desk in front of him. "Quite the story, I'd say. I take it you just discovered these papers?"

"I found them at the courthouse just this morning," I answered as my mother sat speechless for the second time since earlier at Gina's.

He shook his head. "Well, judging by the looks on all of your faces, I'm assuming you all weren't aware of any of this." I sat quietly, knowing the words describing this life had already been written in my journal.

"No," My mother finally regained her voice. "We weren't, but we needed to know." She stood and he handed her the papers and she handed them to me. "I can't thank you enough for your time."

"You're very welcome, Olivia. Glad I was able to assist you again in your family tree search."

I stood and shook his hand. "Thank you so much."

We all filed out of his office and went back to the car and got in and sat for a moment; the silence weighing heavy on all of us. "I just can't believe it," Olivia said as I cranked the car.

I took a deep breath. "Since we're this close, I would like to drive by the house."

"What house?" My mother asked from the backseat.

"The house that was in my dream, the one Mamaw took me to, is just up the road. I'd like to go by if no one objects."

"That's fine," Olivia managed. "I'm not in a hurry." The shock of all of it was still prevalent in her voice.

I backed the car out of the driveway and began to drive down the street. "On second thought, why don't I take y'all on the exact route of my dream?"

"Yes," Maggie spoke up from the back seat. "I would love to see how it all happened."

"Yeah," Gina added. "Why don't you just start at the beginning of your dream and tell us what happened as you go."

I nodded. I drove until I reached Lafayette Street as I remembered that had actually been the street where it started. "Okay, it was right about here," I said as I pulled onto the street. "I…"

My mother spoke up. "You do realize you just passed Aunt Mattie's house."

"Yes," I said as I looked at her in my rearview mirror. I remembered all too well the old woman that had given me the creeps on the few occasions I had been around her. We had stayed at her house for a month during the summer before I turned thirteen after my mother and father had divorced. Mother had left me there with her one day and I had started my period. She had made me sit in the hot bathroom until my mother returned, so she could *handle* the situation, as she had put it. "How could I forget?"

"I don't think you realize what I'm telling you," My mother spoke again.

"What? I know she was your aunt."

"My *great aunt*. She was Andrew Lipton's sister."

I slammed on the brakes of the car and pulled over to the curb. The revelation sent me reeling as another memory of that house slammed into my brain and chest at the same time. "Wait!" I yelled. "We went to that house when I was little! There was a casket in the front room, there was an old woman in it!"

"That would have been Aunt Esther," Olivia said as she nodded her head.

"Oh! I remember now, when we lived there I snuck into that room. I wanted to see it again, and it was exactly the way it had been that day, except the furniture was draped with white sheets." Suddenly it all hit me. I had, in this lifetime, lived with one of the same women that had tortured Virginia. And why hadn't it upset me when I was so little to see a dead woman in a casket? Was it some type of relief to know she was gone? I looked over at Gina and could tell by the way she looked back at me, the same thoughts were going through her mind. She reached across the seat and took my hand and squeezed it.

"Why don't you go ahead and take us the rest of the way." She forced a small smile.

I put the car in drive and drove away from the house that held such terrible memories for me and Virginia and continued on to the next intersection. "When I got here, I turned right. I was going to that bank," I said pointing to the motor bank two blocks down the street. "But, when I reached just about here," I said slowing the car, "I could see the lights were off in the bank and it was closed. So, I pulled onto this street," I said as I turned the car beside the bank building. "And I pulled in this driveway and turned around, to go back the way I came." I put the car in reverse and backed up and then pulled back onto the street. "I came to this stop sign," I said as I stopped the car. "That's when I saw Mamaw," I said pointing across the street. "She was standing right over there and she was motioning for me to pull over to where she was. So, I pulled over to the curb, and rolled my passenger window down. She leaned down and said, *'Park your car and follow me. I'm having an Estate Sale and I think I have something you are going to want.'*

I slowly inched down the street in the car. "We walked down this sidewalk and crossed the street here, and then when we reached this house," I said as I pulled the car to the curb again. "She went inside and I followed." I turned the key and killed the engine and got out. The others followed. "What are you doing?" Gina asked as she came up behind me.

"I'm going to see if anybody is home," I said as I made my way up the sidewalk to the front door. The feeling of retracing my steps of the dream was surreal. I reached the front door and knocked.

A man opened the door and had a surprised look on his face when he saw all four of us on his porch. "Can I help you?"

"My name is Suzanne Peyton. I know this is going to sound incredibly strange, but this house was in a very strange dream that I had that has led me on a journey to discover my great-grandmother. I was just wondering if you might allow us to come in. I just want to see if it looked the way it did in my dream."

"Oh, Suzanne," Gina whispered. "Let's just go back to my house."

"No," the man looked strangely at me. "I don't mind if you come in and look around. Really."

"Thank you," I said as he stepped aside and let us in. The minute I was inside, and able to look around, it took my breath. "Oh, wow! I just can't get over it. It's exactly the way it was in my dream." Then I looked down the hallway where I had seen my mother's sister standing. "Well, all but that," I said pointing to a wall at the end of the hallway. "In my dream, my aunt was standing back there, but I remember she was standing in front of two windows."

The man suddenly looked shocked and it looked as if all the blood had drained from his face. "Come with me," he said as he headed down the hallway. We all followed him. He reached the end of the hallway and went around the wall. I was right on his heels when he suddenly stepped aside and asked, "Are those the windows you saw?"

Seeing them again took my breath. "Yes," I whispered.

"I just remodeled this area of the house a few months ago. Before that you could see these windows when you came in the front door, just like you're describing."

"Oh, my," Maggie uttered and Gina reached and gently patted my back. I suddenly felt weak in the knees and felt the need to get out of the house. I took off in the wrong direction and found myself going through the kitchen. The man and the others were right behind me. As I rounded the corner from the dining area back into the living room, I stopped, dead in my tracks. There by the front door were four nesting boxes stacked on top of each other. They were in the exact spot where my grandmother had stood when she opened the four keepsake boxes.

"Oh Jesus," I managed to get out.

Gina saw what I was looking at. "Oh, no. How in the world?"

"What is it?" The man asked as he looked over and tried to see what we were staring at.

My knees gave out and I dropped into a dining room chair.

"Are you alright?' The man asked. "Can I get you some water?"

"How long have you lived here?" I managed.

"My wife and I bought the house four years ago because it reminded us of one we had seen in New Orleans."

"New Orleans," my mother repeated, just loud enough for me to hear her.

The man laughed a nervous laugh. "To be honest, when I opened the door and saw all of you standing there, I thought y'all were with that committee."

"What *committee*?" Gina asked.

The man ran his hand through his hair. "Well, apparently, some committee in town has uncovered some information about this house being used during the underground railroad days. They say there are tunnels running under it where people were hidden until they could escape."

I jumped up from the chair. "Thank you so much for letting us come inside," I said as I quickly shook his hand. "But, we have to go now." I rushed to the front door and opened it and ran back to the car. I threw the car keys to Gina as she caught up with me and climbed into the passenger side. I knew I was in no shape to drive. Gina got in and shut the door before the others reached the car.

"I've already written about the tunnels under this house in the journal. This is the house she escaped from," I said as I ran my hands through my hair.

"Oh my God!" Gina threw her hand to her mouth.

I held my finger up to my lips as Mother and Maggie reached the car and climbed into the back seat. She drove us back to her house and as soon as the car stopped, I got out and ran inside. I rushed up the stairs to my room and closed the door and leaned against it. My heart was pounding. Moments later Gina was knocking on the door and pleading with me to let her in. I finally opened the door just a crack and she pushed inside and closed it again behind her.

"What is happening to me?" I asked as I began to sob.

She put her arms around me. "Please don't cry, Suzanne. It's going to be alright. Please."

I couldn't stop. The shock was one thing, but suddenly I felt as if I was reliving Virginia's days and they were getting all mixed in with my own. Had my life and hers always been so parallel? How could I make it stop? What could I do to stop history from repeating itself?

I don't know how long we stayed in my room and I truly don't remember what all I said to her through my sobs, but eventually she calmed me down enough to go back downstairs. When we reached the kitchen my mother and Maggie were sitting at the kitchen table. Mother rose to her feet when she saw me. She held out her hand to me as I made my way over to the table and I took her hand in mine. I could not remember the last time we had physically touched and I felt a shudder run through my body.

"Are you alright?" she asked with such concern in her voice that I had to fight back more tears.

"I think so," I managed.

"Maggie filled me in. She told me about the journal."

"I'm sorry dear," Maggie said as she patted my back. "I think she needed to know."

I nodded my head and sighed. "It's okay; I don't mind"

"Come on over here and sit down." My mother led me to the chair next to her own and sat back down next to me. "Why were you scared to tell me? I do have a television you know? I've seen stories like this before."

"Maybe," I sighed, "but that doesn't mean you believe in things like reincarnation."

"Well," she said as she glanced at the others, "it doesn't mean I'm so closed minded that I can't see when there is little or no other explanation that would explain this either."

"Then you believe I could have been her? In a past life?" I was shocked.

"Look," she said as she turned in her chair to face me. "I know how thorough I was in my research. I didn't ignore her. I looked as hard for anything on her as I did on anyone else in the family. It just wasn't there." She sighed. "I don't think I was the one that was supposed to find it; I think you were."

"You don't know how relieved I am to hear you say that." Something in me softened towards her then. "I mean it, Mama." I had not called her by that name since I was a child.

She patted me on the back. "I'll say this too. The minute I heard Judge Price say Virginia had been Catholic, all I could think about was how obsessed you had been as a child with the nuns."

"We've already thought about that," Gina spoke up.

"Well," she continued, "It would certainly make sense if this is what *we* think it is. But, there is something else that Judge Price said that is very confusing to me."

"What's that?" I asked.

"He said that Virginia was asking for custody of her *two* children. Why was she not asking for Addison?

Just then the phone in Gina's living room rang and she got up and rushed to answer it. She came back into the kitchen a few minutes later. "Suzanne, you better take this call."

"What is it?"

"It's the courthouse."

I rushed into the living room and they all followed.

"Hello?" I said hesitantly.

"Mrs. Peyton?"

"Yes, this is she."

"This is Mark, I'm the one that helped you this morning at the courthouse."

"Yes?"

"After you left today, I was about to put the file you asked for away and I discovered there was some more paperwork in it that I hadn't noticed when I made your copies."

"What type of paperwork?" I felt my hand begin to shake as I held the phone receiver to my ear.

"Well, it appears to be *another* divorce decree for Virginia Lipton."

"Another one? I don't understand."

"I'm not sure I do either, but I thought you might want a copy of it too."

"Yes, of course. We'll come back up there now."

"I'll have it ready for you."

"Thank you," I said and slowly hung the phone up.

"What is it?" Gina asked.

"They found another divorce decree," I said as I looked at all them.

"What?" My mother almost yelled. "Another one? How can there be two? And how did they know how to reach you?"

"I can answer that," Gina piped in. "When Suzanne told me to take the file and get a copy, the man realized he had let us go back into the file area without signing in. So, I signed the ledger while I was up there. It also required a phone number so, I just put mine down."

We all went back to the kitchen and grabbed our purses and filed out to the car. I got in and cranked the car. "Mother, I said as I backed out of the driveway. "Do you think we can go back to Judge Price's office and show him this one as well? Just in case it's written in the same handwriting, I want to be able to know what it says."

"If we hurry we might be able catch him. I don't know what time he usually leaves his office."

With that being said I gunned the car down the road. I told everyone else to stay in the car when we reached the courthouse and I ran inside and got the copy. I came back and jumped in the car and drove straight to Judge Price's office. We all ran up the front steps and were relieved when his receptionist told us he hadn't left yet. He heard all the commotion and came out of his office and saw all of us and motioned for us to come back to his office. We rushed down the hallway and he had just sat down behind his desk when we came in.

"We found another divorce decree," I said breathless.

"Another one?" He reached and took the paper from me.

All of us remained standing, I don't think any of us could have managed sitting down as we waited for him to tell us what it said. "This is a forgery," he said after he read some of it.

"What?" I gasped. "How do you know?"

"Yes ma'am. See right here?" He turned the paper so we could all see what he was referring to. "It says they had to make notice of it in the newspaper."

"I'm not understanding what you mean," I said shaking my head.

"It says they did try to locate her, but that's the part we know is not true, because you see, she filed. You don't have to put notice in a newspaper trying to find someone when it was that person that filed the petition. I tell you, it's a forgery."

"Why would anyone do that?" Gina looked as confused as I felt.

"If I had to guess," he began as he looked over his glasses at us. "It would have something to do with this third child." He looked back down at the paper. "This *Addison* wasn't mentioned at all before."

"But what does that mean?" I asked.

"Are you saying Virginia was not Addison's mother?" My mother asked.

"If I were a gambling man, that's where I would place my bet. That's the only reason I can find for them to forge a divorce decree. The only difference between the two are the dates and the addition of this third child."

We all stood there with our mouths hanging open. Mother was the first one to finally speak. "Well, this changes our entire family history."

"Yes, I would think it would," the Judge spoke softly.

He handed the papers back to me. "Thank you so much for all of your help," I managed.

"You are more than welcome," he said with a somber tone.

We filed silently out of the office and got back to the car and got inside. The silence continued all the way to Gina's house. I pulled the car to a stop in the driveway and everybody got out.

"I'm going to run home and see if I can find any more information for us." My mother said as she got out of the car.

"Okay, thanks," I said as she rushed away. She got in her car and waved at all of us as she pulled away. As soon as we got into the house I told Maggie and Gina I was going upstairs to lie down.

As soon as I got in the room I fell across the bed. Sleep took me quickly. I awoke later to Gina rushing into my room. "You need to come downstairs! Mama's back and she's got something for you."

I jumped from the bed and followed Gina. Mother was standing at the foot of the staircase. "I found it!"

"What is it?" I asked as I reached her.

"Addison's birth certificate! He registered his own birth in 1957!"

"Why 1957?" I asked as she handed me the paper.

"I don't know, but that was the year before Virginia died! It lists Andrew Lipton as the doctor and the only witness! Addison registered his own birth!"

"But why? Why would he do that?"

"I think she found him and told him something; something he didn't want to hear! I think he's the one that threw her in that mental hospital!"

# Chapter 16

*Virginia*

*Dearest Diary,*

*It has been months since I have dared to take my journal out of my keepsake box and write my thoughts, but now I must.*

*So many things have happened, beginning with the loss of yet another child. Jonathan was only eight months old when I discovered I was with child again. I cannot say I was pleased, as with each child my health has surely deteriorated. The loss of this child came by the same means as the other, Andrew's wrath. He discovered the secret correspondence Grandmother and I have had through the letters mailed by my mother. This beating was very vivacious.*

*I believe he began to suspect, as my moods had grown light with the release of the dark secrets I have been forced to keep from her. The doctor had to be summoned because the bleeding would not cease. It wasn't Andrew that summoned him, but my mother. Andrew then threatened her life if she attempts to interfere again. He lied to the doctor and told him I had fallen down the stairs. The doctor examined me and told him the damage was great, and he does not believe I will be able to conceive another child. When I first heard the doctor's words, a sense of relief flooded over me. But then, I realized what this would actually mean for me. If I can no longer* bear heirs to my Grandparent's estate, I will no longer be of any value to him at all. In my absence, Elisabeth and Jonathan will inherit Grandmother Abby's estate. I truly believe he is now contemplating killing me.

This past week, Mother and I both sustained a beating from Andrew. She had once again gone against his wishes and delivered what I know will be the last letter I receive from Grandmother Abby. In our secrecy, I had successfully hidden the letter under a loose floor-board in my room and denied I had received another. He struck Mother twice as she was trying to leave the house. I attempted to get between them, but he knocked me to the floor, and ran down the front steps after her. A man was passing in front of the house and stopped him, or I believe he would have surely taken her life. Andrew began screaming to the man that he had caught my mother stealing from our house. She broke free from both of them and fled down the street. I know she will never come here again.

Since that day, Andrew has kept me locked in the attic. He only allows me to have short visits with the children and only when he is present to oversee such times. He has forced me to write to Grandmother Abby and say it was my mother who wrote the letters of the past to her and forged my signature. I know in my heart Grandmother will not be fooled by this. She told me in her last letter that Mother delivered to me that she wants me to escape without the children and come back to New Orleans alone. She said she will assist me in getting them away from Andrew at a later time, when it can be done safely. She said he might hurt them if I try to take them with me now. She also gave me the name of a colored family that lives in town that are related to Cissy. Grandmother said they have already written to them, and they have agreed to help me if I can make it to their home. As the days passed, I became hesitant to go through with my plans until Andrew showed me how far he was willing to go to have his way.

He came home with a telegram that he said was from Grandmother Abby informing me of her impending visit. It said I was to meet her at Marshall Hotel where she would be staying. I had no knowledge if it was truly from her as it was a telegram instead of her own handwritten letter.

When the day of her visit arrived, Andrew supplied me with a dress Grandmother had sent in the past that had not yet been altered to fit one of his sisters. He had his sister, Mattie, help me with my dress and hair. She seemed genuinely happy that I was being allowed to go on an outing. I believed it might be because she knew I have never been allowed to go anywhere since I married her brother. I have been confined to this house and the sparse yard since the day I arrived, three years ago.

I was so foolish to believe Andrew, but I left the house alone and *briskly walked the four blocks to the hotel. It was dusk when I entered the building through the beautiful double doors. I climbed the staircase that led to the dining hall, where I was told I was to meet Grandmother for dinner. I told the maître d' that I was meeting someone so he would seat me immediately.*

*I was in heaven, anxiously awaiting the time when Grandmother would arrive. I glanced around the room at the women in beautiful dresses and the men looking quite dapper as well in their vested suits. I was so lost in my thoughts that I did not immediately notice the ruckus at the maître d' post. Before I could turn in my seat to see what the commotion was, I heard his voice. Andrew stood shouting my name across the room. I turned slowly in my seat and was horrified by what I saw. Andrew was wearing a torn and dirty pair of overalls; the likes of which I had never seen him wear before. Beside him, Elisabeth stood with a dirty tear-stained face wearing a torn and tattered dress that was much too large for her small body. And poor Jonathan, was wearing a sleeping gown that was filthy as well. I had never seen Andrew or my children in the clothing they now wore.*

*I slowly got to my feet as Andrew continued to shout my name and beg me to return home to take care of the children so that he wouldn't lose his job. The full knowledge of what he was doing slowly crept up my spine. As I began to make my way to them, I felt the hot tears stream down my face. As I passed the tables between us, I heard the women whisper 'tramp' and the men boldly called me a 'harlot'.*

*I walked in stoic silence back to the house and Andrew jeered that no one would help me now. Elisabeth began to cry for me as we reached the steps leading up to the gallery of the house. I reached for her, and Andrew swung his fist at me, but struck her instead. Her head struck the gallery post, and blood trickled down her precious face. I begged him to let me take her and her brother inside. He then beat me, in the most violent fit of rage and drug my lifeless body back up to the attic. He threw me into the room and slammed the door and locked it as he left.*

*I lost consciousness several times during the days that followed, and he wouldn't allow me food or drink. As soon as I could make my mind think straight, I knew that I must get away as soon as possible. The whole incident was a lie. Grandmother Abby had never sent the wire. He sent me there so he could make the people of this town believe I am of no worth.*

*It's been a week now since I have seen the children. If I lie on the floor of the attic and press my ear against it, I can hear my sweet children's voices and conversations between Andrew and his sister's as well. I now know it was Andrew that summoned the doctor for Elisabeth's injury. He lied to him and said it was I that had harmed her in my anger for being forced to come home from the dining hall of the hotel.*

*I have a plan now for my escape. I will never let him hurt my children again. I know I will have to do as Grandmother says and leave them here for now, but I will not rest until I have them with me again.*

# Chapter 17

*Suzanne*

We spent the last few days in Marshall going over everything we had learned about Virginia. I was somewhat relieved when there had been no new revelations since the divorce decree. That was enough to digest for now. We were all able to just visit and enjoy the balance of the visit; well almost. I couldn't shut my mind down concerning Tony. I had to fight myself to keep from calling Kate to see if our plan had worked. She had made me promise I wouldn't call until I returned from Marshall. She begged me to take a break, and I was trying; truly I was.

When Friday finally rolled around, and we prepared to leave, I shared with Gina that I could honestly say I was going to miss my mother. Over the last few days her entire attitude towards me appeared to have changed. I saw it as a miracle and decided if nothing else came out of this quest to find Virginia, that one thing would be enough.

Gina helped Maggie and I load the car and we hugged with me promising I would stay in touch with her and come back to visit as soon as I could. Once we were in the car and on the interstate headed home, Maggie began to question me concerning my decision to adopt Sam's baby. It seemed a lifetime since I had that conversation with my daughter. I knew I had just conveniently tucked it away in the back of my mind. I told Maggie, once again, that I still intended to follow through with my offer to Sam, and I wouldn't be changing my mind. She kindly suggested I run the idea past my counselor and I promised that I would.

We were back home by the afternoon. I pulled up beside Maggie's car in the driveway and we got out and moved her bags from my car to hers. Knowing that Max wouldn't be home until Sunday, she offered to spend the night, but I insisted she go home. I knew she was as anxious to sleep in her own bed as I was. I waved as I watched her pull away. I got back in my car and hit the remote to the garage door and it raised and I pulled my car inside, next to Tony's. I knew it meant nothing for his car to be there, as I knew he and Mark would have taken Mark's truck to his father's lake house. I got out and pulled my bags from the trunk and pulled them through the door into the kitchen. I sat them on the floor. I went room to room, making sure Tony wasn't there.

I came back downstairs and went into the kitchen and got my cigarette case from my purse and lit one. I slowly walked into the den to check to see if there were any messages on the answering machine. I stopped short when I saw the blinking red light, indicating *there were* messages, and said a silent prayer that Tony had at least called since I told him I would be coming home today.

I took a drag off my cigarette and slowly made my way over to the machine and pressed the button. *'You have two messages.'* The automated voice broke the silence of the room. I sat down on the arm of the chair to listen. The first message had come in on Tuesday evening from Carol, Mrs. Drexel's daughter-in-law. *'Suzanne, this is Carol. I'm afraid I have some bad news and I hate to break it to you like this, but I didn't have another number to reach you. Mom's had a stroke. It's pretty bad, she's still in ICU. I know you're out of town until Friday, but just call me when you get in.'*

I gasped out loud and jumped from the arm of the chair and put my cigarette out and immediately dialed Carol's number. She answered on the second ring and I listened as she brought me up to speed on the extent of the damage the stroke had caused my dear friend.

"Suzanne," Carol spoke so low that I had to really strain to hear her. "She can't talk."

I gasped and then began to cry. "Oh Carol, I'm so sorry."

"I'm sorry too," she said through muffled sobs of her own. "I know how much she means to you. You can come to the hospital tonight during visiting hours if you like," she said before hanging up.

I felt it then, the tremors starting deep inside of me. They began to build into what felt like an earthquake inside my body. Everything that had happened in the last few months caved in on me. A deep sob left my body then, and the tears came and wouldn't stop. My body was racked with grief; it felt like somebody had died. I cried so hard I had to run to the bathroom and throw up. I fell to my knees and held onto the rim of the toilet. I heaved, still crying and gagging at the same time. I was scaring myself now. I managed to finally get up and go back into the den and call Kate. She answered immediately. "I need you," was all I could manage and then I just hung up the receiver.

I held the banister tightly as I made my way upstairs to change clothes. I was passing Tony's closet when I stopped. I slowly opened the closet door, knowing fully well what I would see. His fishing poles were still leaning in the corner; right where they always were. They hadn't been touched. He had not even attempted to cover his lies. I heard the front door open just as a loud hiccup from crying escaped me.

"Suzanne?" I heard Kate call out from downstairs.

"I'm up here," I managed to yell.

She came barreling up the staircase and almost ran over me when she rushed into my room. "Oh my God, what's happened?" She asked when she saw the shape I was in.

"Oh Kate," I cried as I grabbed her.

"What is it? What's wrong?"

I went over and sat down on the side of the bed and pulled a Kleenex from the box on the nightstand. "Everything," I said as I blew my nose and then wiped my eyes.

"Where's Tony?"

"I don't know, but he's not fishing." I motioned towards the closet. "Look for yourself."

She got up and went to the closet and opened it and then glanced back at me. "What am I looking for?"

"Look in the corner. His fishing poles are right where they always are."

Kate leaned in and looked and then shut the closet door and came back and sat down next to me on the bed and put her arms around me. "Okay, look," she said as she took my chin and turned my face to meet hers. "You've got to stop this! You can't let him control you this way. Suzanne, you're better than this," she said gently.

"It's not just Tony," I said as I tried to fight back the urge to cry again.

She let out a deep sigh. "Well, what else is going on?"

"Mrs. Drexel's had a stroke, Sam's pregnant and I've offered to take the baby, and Virginia filed for divorce, she didn't just run off." I fell back on the bed.

Kate stood up and grabbed me by the hand and pulled me up from the bed. "We're going downstairs, and I'm going to fix you something to drink."

"Wait," I said. "I've got to change clothes. I got sick earlier."

Kate let go of my hand and went over and pulled a t-shirt and jogging pants from my chest of drawers. She came back over and began to undress me and helped me get into clean clothes. "Now come on," she said taking my hand.

She led me down the stairs and into the kitchen. I sat down on one of the barstools and laid my head down. The coolness of the bar felt good on my face. My mind refused to stay focused on any one thing. It was like a movie reel that had jumbled all the recent events in my life together and now ran, unorganized and rampant, through my mind. I raised my head up and watched as Kate fixed me a glass of Coke and was opening a box of crackers and I suddenly felt guilty for laying all of this at her feet. I didn't feel like I had that right since I had stormed out on her that day at her house.

"I shouldn't have called you," I said as I began to cry again.

"Suzanne, we've been best friends for twenty years, who else should you have called? I'm not much of a friend if I'm only available for the good times." She sat the glass of Coke and a small saucer with crackers between us on the bar and sat down across from me. "Now, take a deep breath and start with telling me what happened in Marshall."

I took a drink of Coke. "Okay, but first, would you please get me an aspirin out of my purse?"

She got off the barstool and rummaged through my purse that sat on the kitchen counter. She found the aspirin and opened the bottle. She came back over to the bar and handed me two and sat back down across from me. "Now spill it. Tell me what you were talking about upstairs. You said Virginia filed for divorce? How did you find that out? I thought your mother said she abandoned her husband and kids."

"I found a divorce decree on file at the courthouse and Virginia had filed it. We also found a forgery of the same decree. We think it was to cover the birth of the third child."

"Oh my gosh!"

"Yeah, but it just complicates things even more."

"How so?"

I shook my head. I don't think I can go into all of it right now. But, I do have one question. Did you have any luck with Mark?"

"No," she said shaking her head. "I'm sorry. I actually went a couple of different nights to the club you told me about, but he never showed up. Maybe they were telling the truth this time; maybe they really went to the lake house."

I sighed. "I don't believe it or he would have taken his fishing poles. But, I guess I'll never know."

"Listen, it's getting late. Tony's probably not coming home tonight, so I'm going to spend the night. I'm sure you've got a sleep shirt I can borrow." She came over and patted me on the back. "I'm not leaving you here alone like this."

"You'll get no argument from me. I'm glad you're staying."

Kate helped me take my bags upstairs and I unpacked and then took a hot bath. The headache that had my head in a vise finally let up. I called and checked in with Max and then went downstairs and found Kate in the den.

"Hey," she said as I came in. "I hope it's okay, I ordered a movie." She was wrapped up in the throw I kept at the end of the couch and she had a big bowl of popcorn on her lap. As I walked over to the couch, she lifted one side of the throw and I sat down and pulled it over me. "Here," she said as she handed me what I thought was another glass of Coke. I took a sip.

"Whoa!" I made a face. "What's in this?"

"Something to help you sleep," she said with a laugh. "Did I mix it too strong?"

"Not if your goal is to knock me out." I said with a laugh.

"Good," she said and held up her glass and we tapped them together in a toast.

We watched the movie and had a few more of her concocted drinks. I was more than ready for bed by the time it was over. We staggered up the stairs laughing at nothing and everything. I barely made it to the bed before I passed out.

I awoke the next morning feeling better than I expected. The smell of bacon cooking wafted into the room. *'Good ole' Kate,'* I muttered to myself. I got up and pulled my robe on and went into the bathroom to wash my face and brush my teeth. My reflection in the mirror shocked me. My eyes were puffy and swollen and it looked like I hadn't slept in a week. I brushed my hair and pulled it up into a loose pony tail and headed downstairs.

"Something smells good," I said as I stepped off the last step and walked towards the kitchen. "You didn't have to…" I stopped midsentence when I saw Tony standing in front of the stove. I gasped. "You're home." I struggled to push the words out.

"Yes, Suzanne," He said as he turned to face me. "But, I wouldn't say I'm *home*; let's just say I'm back; shall we?"

I went over to the counter and got the tea kettle and filled it with

161

water and put it on the stove and turned the burner on. "Well, I can see the week apart didn't do anything for your attitude." I reached and pulled a mug down from the cabinet.

"See any *ghosts* while you were gone?" He took a plate of food he had cooked over to the table and sat down.

"You don't give a damn what I found while I was gone, so why ask?"

"Well, the reason I'm asking," he said, and then hesitated for a moment and took a sip of his coffee. "I'm wondering how long you'll be needing to see your *'shrink'.*"

I froze. I could feel the piercing of his eyes on my back. I slowly turned around to face him. "What are you talking about?"

He laughed. "Thought you'd slide that one past me, huh? Not that I don't think you need one; I absolutely do. But, next time you might make sure you don't give them my insurance card." He then shot me a cold look. "I don't want people at work to know you're nuts, so use your own damn insurance!"

The teakettle began to whistle as I bit down on my lip to gain control of what I was about to say. Instead I turned and said, "She's not a *'shrink',* she's a counselor. Big difference."

"I don't give a damn if *she's* Peter Pan! Don't put it on my insurance! But, I am curious; when were you going to tell me?"

"It's none of your business."

"Oh, it's definitely my business. I don't want everybody at work to think I'm married to a flake!"

I put a tea bag in my cup and bobbed it up and down for a moment as I tried to calm down. "I'll have the charges reversed and put on my card."

"That's not the point, Suzanne." He got up and brought his empty plate and put it in the sink. "I think we need to talk about this." There was that condescending tone again.

"You listen to me," I spun around to face him. "If I need a counselor or even a shrink, you are ninety percent the reason why!"

"What the hell? You're going to try to blame your insanity on me?"

He was so close I could feel the heat of his words on my face. "You know, I held out hope that this week apart would help us, but I can see now it hasn't. Of course, for a fishing expedition to be effective, one would need to take their fishing poles; wouldn't you agree?" I turned to walk away, but he grabbed me by the arm and the tea in the cup sloshed onto the floor. I slammed the cup down on the counter.

"What the hell are you talking about now?" He squeezed my arm.

"Get your hands off me!" I jerked away from him.

"You've completely lost it! You're going to wind up in a loony bin just like that great-grandmother of yours; or should I say *like before*." He laughed an evil laugh that I had never heard before and it sent a chill down my spine.

"You've been snooping through my things! I knew it! I want you out of here! Just leave! Go stay with your girlfriend!"

He pushed me into the wall and held me there and got in my face. "You listen to me bitch," he gritted his teeth. "This house belongs to me too and you won't stand a chance in hell of putting me out when I tell a judge what you've been up to!"

"That's enough, Tony!"

I looked over his shoulder to see Kate standing in the doorway of the kitchen. I pushed against him and he pushed back. "I'll leave for now, but you better get a lawyer because I plan to have your ass locked away!" He gave me one last push and stormed past Kate and went upstairs.

"Are you okay?" Kate asked as she rushed over to me.

"Oh God Kate! I thought he was going to hit me!" I fell into her arms.

A few minutes later we heard Tony stomping down the stairs. He came back through the kitchen. He had an overnight bag and his shaving kit in his hand. "You better enjoy your stay while you can! You won't be living here much longer! I'll send for my things!" He went out the kitchen door into the garage, slamming it behind him. I heard the motor of his car rev and Kate and I rushed to the kitchen window just in time to see him back into the street and speed away.

I turned to Kate. "I'm so sorry you had to witness all of that."

"Don't worry about it. I'm just glad I was here."

I was shaking like a leaf and suddenly exhausted from the onslaught of adrenaline. I sat down on a barstool and ran my hands over my face. "You know he's serious; right?"

"About what?" She said cocking her head. "I hope you don't mean that business about having you *locked away,* because I'll tell you now, it will be over my dead body!"

I got up from the barstool. "I've got to call my counselor's office and have them reverse the charges from Tony's insurance to mine. I can't believe I gave them the wrong card." I headed to the den to get the phone.

"Suzanne, wait. It's Saturday, you're going to have to wait until Monday."

I stopped and turned around and a deep sigh escaped me. "I just can't think straight."

"Is it any wonder? Come on, just come back in here and sit down and let me fix you something to eat."

I came back over to the bar and sat down while Kate started cooking us breakfast. I suddenly realized it was really over between me and Tony now and a part of me was relieved. "Hey, do you have any plans today?"

"No, not really. What do you have in mind?"

"Will you go with me to the hospital to see Mrs. Drexel?"

"Oh," she said turning to face me. "I forgot all about that. Sure, I'll go. I need to run home first and get some clothes. You want me to stay another night?"

"Would you?"

"Absolutely," she said smiling at me. "We'll order another movie and I'll make more of my special drinks."

"I don't know if I can handle any more of your *special drinks*," I said as I held my head in my hands.

Kate and I ate breakfast and she left to go home to get her clothes and I eventually made it upstairs to take a shower. I got out and wrapped a towel around my head and pulled my robe on. I went into the bedroom and sat down in front of my dresser. I stared at the picture that was just to the left of the mirror. It was of me and Tony on our wedding day. I reached and got it and was looking at it when the phone rang. I reached and picked up the receiver from the bedside table.

"Hello?" I could hear noise in the background, but nobody said anything. "Hello?" I repeated. Still nothing. "You can have him!" I screamed into the receiver before slamming it down on the base. I walked back over and got the picture of the two of us and flung it across the room. "I hate you!" I screamed.

I wasn't remotely prepared, later that day, when Kate and I went to see Mrs. Drexel. She still couldn't talk and she looked at me with such panic in her eyes that it broke my heart. I took her hand in mine and assured her everything was going to be okay, even though at the moment I didn't believe a word of it. Carol walked me out to the waiting room where Kate was waiting for me. She rose when she saw us and walked over to join us.

"How is she?" Kate asked.

"The doctors are semi hopeful she will regain some of her speaking ability with therapy, but it's going to be a long road," Carol said as she choked back tears.

"I hate seeing her like this," I said as I tried hard to fight the tears, but lost, and they streamed down my face.

Kate drove as I sat on the passenger side looking out the window at the lights that were on in the houses we passed. I wondered what those people's lives were like. Were they enjoying being together on a Saturday evening or was their life as messed up as mine. Were they laughing or crying? A feeling of doom fell over me; I felt totally defeated. I had no idea where I would begin to start over. My life felt shattered into a million tiny pieces; scattered all over the place.

When we got back to my house, I begged off from the movie and drinks and went to bed early. I lay in bed for hours watching the shadows from the tree outside my window, dance across the ceiling every time the wind blew. My mind would not shut down and took me back over all my mistakes; back to my first marriage to Eric.

He had been a good guy, or so I thought. Shortly after we were married, he too had become violent. He beat me and locked me away and burnt all my clothes so I couldn't leave him. I gasped at the thought. Wasn't that marriage so very much like Virginia's marriage to Andrew Lipton? Had I been on a collision course my entire life as I relived hers? How could I stop it? I had almost died before I got away from Eric. I had been admitted to the hospital when I weighed only seventy-nine pounds. The doctors said my body was over producing adrenaline and it was killing me from the inside out. I remember being so afraid my Father would find out about everything and kill Eric and then spend the rest of his life in prison.

I got up and walked around my room in the dark. I had to stop my mind from going back; I had to move forward. Max needed me. Then as if I had not instructed my mind to stop, it went back to my marriage with my second husband, Ralph. Years after my marriage to Eric was over, I finally told my father everything. I will never forget the look on his face and how mad he was that I hadn't told him when it was happening. But, in time, he forgave me, but he could have never known what was going to happen later.

Ralph and Daddy had gotten along really well, but my Father made no bones about what he expected the night Ralph talked to him about marrying me. He had told him, in no uncertain terms, that if he ever touched me or the kids, he would kill him. Ralph had laughed about it at the time and assured my father he would never have to worry about that. And his words were true until we put Daddy in the ground. Our marriage had been on the rocks for a long time. Two days after we buried Daddy, Ralph grabbed me by the throat and shoved me into a wall when I told him I was leaving.

I got back in bed and tried desperately to go to sleep. It wasn't working. Then, with no prodding from me, Virginia hit my brain and hit it hard. Hadn't her life been exactly like this? Except as far as we knew she only had to go through it once as far as the beatings went, but the pain of losing her children had lasted an entire lifetime. I decided then and there that Tony would be my last husband. I would never do this again. I didn't care if I had to hold down three jobs, I would never let anybody else do this to me.

I knew I was getting nowhere tossing and turning and dragging myself down memory lane, so I got up and went downstairs. I walked through the dark shadows of the house I had lived in for five years. I remembered how excited I had been when we moved in at all the promise it held inside its walls.

I went into the kitchen and sat down on a barstool in the dark. Light from the glow of the street-light filtered through the kitchen window. *'Lord, I don't know what to do with myself.'* I began to cry. *'You know I didn't mean for any of this to happen. I need you to tell me what to do. Please. Just guide me out of this mess and help me get my bearings. You know I don't mind working, but just please leave me enough time to be with Max. I can't disappear on a teenage boy.'*

I dried my eyes, went back upstairs, and got into bed and miraculously fell sound asleep. When I woke up, a sense of clarity came over me. I sat up in bed and turned to look at the clock; it read 4:44 in neon blue. I smiled, got out of bed, and went downstairs. I went into the den and pulled a spiral notebook from my desk. I went into the kitchen and filled the teakettle with water and put it on the stove and turned the burner on. I went back over and sat down at the bar and pulled the spiral over to me and began to write.

By the time Kate came downstairs, hours later, I had written the first two chapters of the book I knew I was destined to write. I left it lying on the bar as I cooked breakfast. When Kate sat down at the bar I saw her glance over at the spiral and pull it to her and she read the title, *Virginia's Diary.* She looked at me and smiled and we both knew I was going to be fine. But, neither she nor I knew the rest of that story was yet to come; in New Orleans.

# Chapter 18

*Virginia*

*Dearest Diary,*

*My hand trembles as I write these words. If Andrew does not catch me, this will be my last night in this horrible house. I truly know he will take my life if he discovers my intentions. But, I also know he will take my life if I stay. I have no choice in leaving as I had no choice in being brought here to begin with. Either way, I will not awake to the trickle of light through the attic window tomorrow morning.*

*Today, as I sat contemplating my escape, I heard the children's voices coming from outside where they were playing. I went to the small window and marveled at how much they had grown since the last time I saw them. I gently tapped on the glass trying to get their attention without Mattie, who was sitting nearby, noticing me. Both of my darling children looked up at the window, squinting from the glare of the sun. I waved, but neither of them responded. I fear the things their father and his sisters have told them have tainted their feelings for me. I know I can win back their affections once I am able to take them away from here.*

*When Mother risked her life to bring me the last letter from Grandmother Abby, she brought something else as well. She delivered a bottle of ether that I am to use if I am to gain the time I need to escape. Mother said I am to pour the liquid onto a cloth, and being careful not to breathe it myself, hold it over the person's nose and mouth, and they will lose consciousness. It grieves my heart to think of hurting anyone, even those that have hurt me, but I must if I am to do this without being caught. My life, as well as my children's, is at stake. I must remember this.*

*I know I must wait until Andrew goes out drinking again, as he does every night, and Esther must be turned in for the night, because her compassion would never extend to me. Then, it is Mattie I must depend upon. When I listen through the floorboards of the attic and hear her checking on my children, one last time, as she does every night, then I must act. I will appear to be violently ill and call to her and beg her to assist me. When she comes to me, even though I have never attempted to overtake anyone before, now, I must succeed.*

*I won't allow myself to dwell on the possibility of being able to be with Grandmother Abby again. I fear if I ponder too long on the hope, something will go terribly wrong and I will fail. The sheer possibility the children and I could be free of this place and these people is so much to hope for. To be cared for by Cissy again is only a dream in my mind. To linger in the gardens of my home and to be able to watch my own children play there makes my heart leap with joy. I have dreamt so many times of being at home again in New Orleans. If I should succeed, I will never again take for granted the peace and tranquility I once knew.*

*I must stop writing now, as the time for my actions draw nigh. Please God, forgive me for what I must do and protect my children until I can come back for them, and we can be together again.*

# Chapter 19

*Suzanne*

When I got out of bed Monday morning, I felt more alive than I had felt in a long time. I got to the bookstore on time for the first time in a month. I had written several chapters of the book and with each chapter, I felt a sense of accomplishment. Something deep inside of me told me I had finally found a purpose for the balance of my life.

I had a plan now, and it seemed to fill me with energy. I rushed through my morning routine of getting the bookstore ready to open and then I went into my office and called my travel agent. She called back within the hour to tell me she had booked a room for me in *The Columns Hotel*, in the Garden District of New Orleans. I was giddy with excitement. I had already cleared the time with Carol and my bags were packed.

Just after lunch on Wednesday, I pulled onto the St. Charles Avenue exit in New Orleans, with Gina in the passenger seat. The branches of massive, ancient Live Oaks draped over the street, creating a shadowed tunnel. A dark green trolley car came down the median towards us. Victorian homes with lush green lawns stood side by side separated by black, lacy wrought iron fences. The large white blossoms on the Magnolia trees stood out against their deep green leaves, and azalea bushes bloomed in vibrant shades of pink against every expansive porch we passed. Time stood still as my soul was filled with a *'knowing'* I couldn't explain.

I kept driving down St. Charles Avenue until we reached the hotel. I pulled up to the curb in front. Gina and I got out and just stared at the

Victorian House that now served as a Hotel. "Remind me to send my travel agent flowers or something," I said as I took in the massive estate that rested on a knoll in front of us.

"Definitely," Gina agreed as we began to pull our bags from the trunk of the car.

We made our way up the sidewalk and climbed the steps to the wrap around porch. We entered through a beautiful, old wooden door that had *'The Columns Hotel'* etched in the glass that was in the center of the door. We followed the deep red-carpet runner that protected the ancient hardwood floors to the hotel desk located at the end a long hallway. There was a stunning staircase that rose next to the desk and I could see a landing just above, with a stained-glass window, depicting the Garden of Eden.

"Hello ladies," an older black woman sitting behind the desk greeted us. "How may I help you?"

"My name is Suzanne Peyton. I have a reservation."

She never looked at a book or anything. "Well, my name is Georgia, and yes ma'am, you do, most certainly, have a reservation." She turned in her chair and pulled two keys from a peg hook behind her and handed them to me. "You ladies are on the second floor; Room 17."

I took the keys from her and turned to hand one to Gina and saw she was no longer standing next to me. "Gina?" I said as I turned in a circle.

I saw her then as she came out of a doorway nearby and back to the desk. She took the key from my outstretched hand. "You are going to love that room," she said pointing to where she had just been. "It's a library."

"Yes, it is and you are welcome to use it any time you would like," Georgia said with a smile. "You can check out books and take them to your room if you like, but the upstairs porch is my favorite place."

"I noticed it when we were coming in," I said as I smiled at her.

"I think you'll find it very private and enjoyable. You can watch the trolley cars go by. We have a bar and restaurant just through those doors," she said pointing across the hall from the library. Breakfast is from 6 am until 9 in the breakfast dining area. It's back this way," she said pointing to another door that opened next to the staircase. We have live music at night in the big room just to the right of the front door. If you need anything; anything at all, don't hesitate to let someone know."

"Thank you so much," I said as I picked up my bag. Gina and I climbed the beautiful staircase to the second floor. We passed French doors that led to the second-floor porch, and made our way down the hall and found our room. I stuck the key in the lock and turned the knob and opened the door and we both gasped.

A massive four-poster bed was against one wall while an equally large armoire stood in the corner of the room. There was a bench seat at the end of the bed and Gina and I both sat our bags and purses on it and turned to take in the beauty of the room. It all felt so familiar; I felt goose bumps rise over my body. I immediately went over to the floor to ceiling windows and pulled back the gauzy curtains and looked out into the limbs of one of the massive oak trees that lined the property.

"Come in here and look at this," Gina called from an adjoining room.

I went into the bathroom and found her sitting in an empty claw-foot tub. "If you get to looking for me while we're here, this is where you'll find me! Can you believe this?"

"It is truly stunning! I am so impressed with the entire place."

"Can you imagine living like this?"

"Yes." The word came out of my mouth without hesitation. I shook my head to bring me back to the present. "Come on, let's check out the porch."

She got out of the tub and followed me out of the room and back down the hall to the French doors. I opened one of them and we stepped into an absolute oasis. The porch ran the entire length of one side of the house, and true to Georgia's word, a trolley car came lumbering by and the engineer rang the bell. It took my breath. Flashes of what I could only assume would be *'past life memories'* consumed me. It affected my vision momentarily. The trees seemed to blur, St. Charles Avenue suddenly looked slightly different. The cars in front of the hotel disappeared from my vision. I suddenly heard faint piano music. I shook my head and ran my hands through my hair.

"What is it?" Gina asked, bringing me back with a jolt.

"Whoa," I said as I sat down in one of the chairs on the porch. "That was weird."

"What?"

"I don't know how to describe it. Maybe I'm just a little dizzy from being in the car so long. I'm sure it's nothing." I slowly stood back up. "Let's get unpacked, I'm hungry and I can't wait to try the food here."

We got back out to the car, and I made the block to go back to a restaurant we had passed when we were headed to the hotel. I pulled to a stop sign and suddenly felt I knew the area. I pulled slowly through the intersection and then spotted a house on the next corner. I pulled to the curb and turned the car off and got out.

"What are you doing?" Gina called after me.

I walked slowly over to the sidewalk that ran in front of the huge estate that was surrounded by a wrought iron fence. A longing filled my soul. I could see the servant's quarters that still stood behind the house. Gina was now following me; taking pictures with her camera.

I reached out and touched the wrought iron fence and ran my hand along it towards the gate. Suddenly another flash hit me, like the one that had happened back at the hotel. I suddenly felt small; like a child. I could hear myself humming a tune, but I didn't know where it came from; I had never heard it before. I yanked my hand back from the fence and ran back across the street to my car. I got in and shut the door. Gina finally caught up and came over and got in the passenger side.

"What just happened back there? You've got that same strange look on your face as you did when we were on the porch at the hotel! You're feeling something, aren't you? Something about this place."

I took a deep breath. "Something is definitely happening. Just now I felt like a little girl. It was weird. That tune I was humming…"

"You weren't humming a tune. I was right behind you; you weren't making a sound."

I shook my head and cranked the car and pulled away from the house and pulled to the stop sign. One street sign read *Carondolet* and the other read *Napoleon.* I turned right and turned back onto St. Charles Avenue at the next red light. I only drove a few blocks before I found a little diner and pulled into the parking lot. "Maybe I'm just hungry," I said as we got out and went inside.

We got a table and placed our order with the waitress. Gina sat staring at me for a moment before she spoke. "I'm not sure coming here was a good idea," she said hesitantly.

"Well, we're here now," I said as I looked out the window and watched as people walked by. "Besides, coming here was inevitable. I had to come sooner or later; it's where she grew up."

"You mean *it's where you grew up,*" she said with a smile. "I'm convinced, Suzanne, you were her."

I shook my head. "How does this happen to a person that just had a dream?"

She laughed. "That wasn't a dream you had. It was some kind of a message, but this just doesn't happen. You're meant to find what you're finding. I just know it."

Our food came and we didn't discuss Virginia any further. I was grateful I had never been to the city and hoped it's beauty would distract my thoughts somewhat. I didn't want to go through all of this and miss something. I knew we were both tired, so after we ate I suggested we not begin our search for Virginia until the next morning. Gina agreed and we went back to the hotel.

I went out onto the porch and sat down. It was especially beautiful when the sun finally set and the lights of the Garden District came on. I had never been in such a magical place. I watched as a trolley car came down St. Charles Avenue with the light on inside. I saw the smiling faces of the people as they passed and stared at the beautiful hotel we were blessed to be staying in. I finally got up and went to our room. Gina took her bath and then I went in and filled the tub with warm water and bubble bath. I crawled in and soaked until my weary bones said it was time for bed. Gina was already asleep in the Queen size bed when I came back into the room. I turned off the lights and pulled the heavy curtains back from the window so the moonlight could come through the gauzy sheers. I crawled into bed and I don't think my head hit the pillow before I was sound asleep.

I woke up the next morning with a jolt. Gina rolled over and pushed her night mask up on her face. "You okay?"

I rubbed my eyes. "I had a weird dream," I said in a low voice as I tried to concentrate on the details.

"What was it?" She asked as she scooted up in the bed and leaned against the massive headboard.

"I dreamed I was back in my apartment. The one I had before I married Tony, you know the one that was a loft and had all glass in the front?"

"Oh yeah," Gina shook her head, "I remember that place."

"I was upstairs in my bed and I remember sitting up and seeing this huge monk, you know in a brown robe, and he was walking through the tree tops. He was carrying this big book in his arms and somebody said, *'All the answers to your questions are in this book.'* And I woke up."

Gina got up from the bed and headed for the bathroom. "You and your dreams," she said just before she shut the bathroom door.

I pulled the journal from my bag and sat down at the desk that was in front of one of the windows and recorded the dream. Something just told me it was important. I closed the journal and put it back up and grabbed my cigarette case and went out onto the porch to smoke. I sat down in one of the chairs and smelled the scent of the blooming flowers that I figured must surround the house. I noticed there was not an ounce of the tension in my shoulders that had weighed on me for the last several months. A part of me felt so at home; a feeling I had never completely had before, no matter where I lived.

173

I went back to the room and found Gina already dressed. "I'm going to go ahead and go downstairs to the breakfast room. Just come on down where you're ready. I'll save you a seat," she said with a smile.

I went to the armoire and pulled out a pair of jeans and a shirt and put them on and brushed my hair and rushed downstairs to meet her. The breakfast room was painted a light yellow and antique tables and chairs were scattered about the room. Gina waved me over to where she was sitting. "Check this out," she said as she handed me a menu. "You get to choose what you want from this list, and it's all compliments of the hotel! I swear you owe your travel agent; big time!"

"I agree," I said as I looked over the menu. "Everything sounds heavenly." The waitress came over then and asked what we would like to drink and I ordered hot tea and Gina did as well. We took our time and savored the quiet of the room and the delicious breakfast before we laid out our plans for the day. I had reached a research group that was in the French Quarter and had decided that would be the best place to start. Georgia, the night desk clerk, had told us the best way to go to the French Quarter would be to take a trolley because of the parking situation, so we walked to the corner to catch the next one.

As I stepped up the steps onto the trolley, my heart sang. I was flooded with an indescribable joy. I glanced back at Gina and she smiled. We found a seat towards the back and sat down. As the trolley rolled down St. Charles Avenue I could truly enjoy the sights since I wasn't driving. We eventually went through the streets where the buildings rose towards the sky all around us. The trolley finally came to a stop at Canal Street and we got off and continued to follow the directions the woman had given me to *Williams Research Center.*

We found the building and went inside. A clerk was seated at a desk just inside the door. We were instructed to sign in and put our purses in lockers that were located on a far wall. Then we climbed the staircase to the second floor of the building. I was amazed when we entered the room. It was wall to wall bookcases filled with all kinds of books. Old maps of Louisiana hung on the walls. Gina and I approached a woman sitting at a desk in the center of the room.

"Can I help you?" she asked with a smile.

"I'm looking for information on my *great-great-great* grandparents," I said with a smile. "Their last name was Fontenot."

She jotted down the name on a piece of paper and then keyed their name into the computer on her desk. "I have information on Abbigail and Henry Fontenot. Is that the right one?"

"Yes," I replied a little louder than I planned in my excitement. "Yes, that's them."

"Okay," the woman slid a piece of paper and pencil towards me. "I can't print out the information, but you can write it down."

I grabbed the paper and pencil. "Okay, I'm ready."

"I don't have very much," she said with a frown, "but maybe this will help. I show they lived on the corner of Carondolet and Napoleon in the Garden District."

Gina and I both gasped.

"There's not an address, it just gives the location; the Northwest corner of Carondolet. Then I have a record that both are buried in Lafayette Cemetery #1. It's also located in the Garden District." She looked up at us. "That's all I have."

"Thank you," I said as I turned and all but ran from the room with Gina right behind me. We rushed back downstairs, got our purses from the locker, and left the building before either of us said anything. Gina wheeled around to face me as soon as we were on the sidewalk out front.

"Napoleon and Carondolet! That's the corner where the house is that we went to! Oh, Suzanne! You knew it was theirs! You are Virginia!"

I couldn't say anything. I just grabbed her by the arm and headed towards the trolley stop. We got back to the hotel and both of us were giddy with excitement that we had found the very house Virginia had grown up in. With this now being a certainty, we got back in my car and drove back around to the house and Gina took a picture of me standing in front of it.

"What do you want to do now?" She asked as we got back into the car.

"Let's go to the Cemetery."

I cranked the car and drove as straight as an arrow to the cemetery. When I pulled the car to a stop outside of its concrete wall, Gina just looked at me and shook her head. We got out and went through a beautiful black, wrought iron gate. I stared at all the above ground tombs. They stood side by side with barely enough room to go between them. There was a main walkway down the center with smaller paths in between the rows.

As we walked down the main path, we passed tombs that time and elements had aged, but not destroyed. There were names on some of the tombs I couldn't pronounce and then I stopped when I saw one for children from an orphanage. "Oh, how sad," I said as I reached and ran my hand over the children's names. We continued until we reached the back wall and I instinctively turned and within minutes we were standing in front of the Fontenot tomb.

I stood and read the names of Abbigail and Henry and some of their children that were buried in the tomb with them. Some of the children had died young, but then there were others that I knew my mother knew nothing about. Gina took out a pad of paper from her purse and wrote down the information. When she was finished, we walked silently back to the car.

We decided to find a place for lunch. I turned down a side street, intending on getting back onto St. Charles Avenue, but instead drove straight across and in the middle of the block, underneath the shadows of the Oaks, I spotted a gate. I slammed on my brakes and was grateful no one was behind me. "Look!" I screamed to Gina. "I know that gate! I've walked through it!"

Gina turned around in her seat and looked behind us. "It's part of a building that faces St. Charles Avenue. Make the block and let's see what it is."

I drove the car back around the block and pulled to the curb in front of a Catholic Girl's School. The building was well maintained but we could tell it had been there for a very long time. I turned the car off and we got out and walked up the long sidewalk, passing a beautiful fountain midway. We reached the front door and rang the buzzer as was instructed by a sign that was bolted to the brick wall.

"Can I help you?" A charming voice echoed through the speaker.

"Yes ma'am," I answered as I inched closer. "I am trying to find some information on my great-grandmother and I believe she might have been a student at this school in the late 1800's. Do you have records that go back that far?"

"Wait just a moment and someone will come and let you in."

Gina grabbed my hand and squeezed. Within a few minutes a very sweet-faced nun came and opened the door and invited us inside. We stepped into the building and I immediately felt something again. Was the entire trip going to be this way? Dejavu' overload?

The nun instructed us to follow her to the office. As we walked behind her we passed classrooms filled with girls in plaid skirts and white blouses. I had never been this close to a nun before. The closest I had ever been was when I watched them, as a child, through my binoculars from my hideout in the tree in the side yard of our house; now Gina's house.

"You must be in heaven," Gina leaned close to my ear and whispered.

I smiled and nodded. "I think I would have enjoyed going to an all-girls school like this one."

Gina giggled. "Well, your grades would have probably been better."

We reached the end of the hallway and followed the nun into an office where another nun was sitting behind a desk. "Sister Madeline." The nun addressed the other one. "These ladies need to speak with you about our archive files."

Sister Madeline stood and smiled at us. "What can I do for you?"

"We are trying to find information on our great-grandmother, Virginia Barrister. We believe she might have attended your school, but it would have been in the late 1800's."

"Do you have any documentation to prove you're related?"

"Oh," I said, suddenly remembering the warning the priest in Marshall had given us about the Catholics in Louisiana requiring proof before they would give me any information. "Yes ma'am," I said as I pulled the paper we had just received from the research center out, along with the paperwork my mother had given me on Virginia. "I hope this will work."

Sister Madeline looked over the papers and then smiled. "Give me just a minute." She went over to her desk and sat down and keyed something into her computer. I watched as her lips moved as she silently read something on her screen. She picked up a pen and jotted something down; read more and made more notes. She eventually got up from her desk and came over to where we were standing. "She was a student of ours." I grabbed Gina's hand. The nun held out the paper she had made the notes on and I took it. "I don't have a lot of information, but I can tell you she intended to take her vows of lifelong service to our Lord. But, of course, you know she changed her mind."

A solemnness fell over me. "She wanted to become a nun?"

The Sister nodded her head. "I'm sorry we don't have any more information for you. She must have left the area after graduation."

"Thank you so much for your help," Gina said.

"You're welcome," she said with a slight smile. "Now," she motioned to the other Nun that stood nearby. "Sister Francis will escort you back."

Gina and I followed her back to the front and thanked her for her help and went back out and got in the car. I was suddenly exhausted. I cranked the car and looked over at Gina. "Virginia just lost on all fronts." I felt such a heaviness on me.

Gina reached over and patted me on the shoulder. "Sounds like someone else I know."

The next morning, I awoke just as the sun was coming up. Gina was still sleeping, so I pulled on my robe and picked up my bag and crept, quietly from the room. I went out onto the porch and sat down at one of the tables. I lit a cigarette and pulled the papers mother had given me out of the bag. There were three pictures of Virginia in with the papers. One was of her standing in front of a filling station. She was an old woman in this one.

I wondered why there was such a gap in the timeline of the pictures. The other two I had were obviously taken when she had been young, but this one had to have been towards the end of her life.

I was still staring at the pictures before me, when I heard one of the trolley's coming down the track with the bell ringing. The heaviness from the day before was still hanging on me like the moss on the live Oak trees. What was it? What was here, in this beautiful area of the city, that was producing the feeling?

Gina came through the French doors onto the porch and sat down next to me. It startled me, I had been away in my own little world. "Oh hey," I said with a jump. "I didn't see you there."

She pulled the pictures of Virginia over in front of her and looked at them. "I didn't notice these other two. Were they in the papers Mother gave you?"

"Yeah, they were stuck in the bottom of the envelope. I guess I never thought to look in there. When she poured it out on your table, I thought everything came out."

Gina picked up the same one I had been looking at. "She looks old here."

"Yeah I know. Mother wrote Carrollton on the back of the picture. I guess Mother thought she was still living there since that's where she mailed all those letters from."

"Yeah," she said nodding her head. "I guess so." She put the picture back on the table and stood up. "I'm going downstairs to eat; are you coming?"

"No, you go ahead."

"You want me to bring you something back?"

"A cold Coke would be nice," I said smiling up at her.

"Sure thing," she said as she walked away and disappeared through the French doors.

I leaned back in my chair and looked out over the front terrace of the hotel. I saw a couple walk hand in hand down the front steps and followed them with my eyes until they disappeared down the sidewalk in front of the hotel and my mind went back to Tony. Had he ever really loved me? Had I really ever loved him? I got up from the chair and grabbed my things and went back to the room to get a shower. I refused to spend one minute surrounded by all this beauty with any thoughts of my failing marriage.

I ran into Gina at the foot of the staircase. "Hey," I said as I stepped off the last step. "I thought you'd still be eating."

"No, I just had toast and coffee. Here," she handed me a Styrofoam cup. "Your Coke."

"Oh yeah," I took the cup. "Thanks."

I walked over to the hotel desk and smiled when I saw Georgia was back on duty. "Good morning, Georgia," I said smiling at her.

"Good morning," she smiled back. "Is everything going well with you ladies?"

"Oh yes, this place has been wonderful." I reached and patted her hand. "And that upstairs porch is divine; just like you said."

She smiled, "I told you."

"I need to get gasoline, where is the nearest filling station?"

"Just follow St. Charles all the way to the end," she said as she made a gesture with her hand. "When you reach the end, there will be a 'V' in the road, just make a right and there is one up there on the left."

"Great; I have one more question."

"That's what I'm here for," she said with her now familiar smile.

"We're here doing some family research. We've already been to the Williams Research Center; is there another place we should try?"

She thought for a minute. "I believe the downtown library has an archive department; I'd try them. You should be able to take your car down there. There are parking lots across the street where you can pay to park. But be careful down there. A lot of homeless people hang around the library, so go early."

"We will. Thank you, Georgia."

Gina and I got in the car and headed down St. Charles Avenue. We hadn't gone this way yet, so the scenery was new and interesting. We passed both, Loyola and Tulane Colleges. Their campuses were gorgeous. They matched the beauty of Audubon Park across the street. I reached the end of St. Charles Avenue and veered right like Georgia told me too. I was so caught up in the beauty I missed turning to get to the gas station on the other side of the street. "Oh well, I'll just go a little further down and turn around." The *'familiarity'* of the area hit me, but this time it was more like a jolt of electricity. My body actually jerked.

Gina looked over at me and I guess from the look on my face she knew it was happening again. "You want to pull over and let me drive?"

"Not yet," I said as I slowly made my way down the street. We reached a park and I slowed almost to a stop. *'Palmer Park'* was written in the stone archway above the entrance. A car behind me honked and I sped up, intending on finding a place to turn around so I could go back and get a better look at the place. I pulled to the red light, and just up ahead, a building caught my eye. "Oh my God, Gina! Look!" I screamed as I pointed ahead.

"It's the filling station in the picture! The one Virginia was standing in front of!"

# Chapter 20

*Virginia*

*Dearest Diary,*

*I have escaped! My last hours in Andrew's house were most frightening. I waited for him to leave, and then for the next few hours, I kept my ear pressed to the floor of the attic and waited. I knew Esther had gone out earlier, as had Andrew, so I knew I had to hurry. I listened intently as Mattie put my children down for the night. I tried to make my mind memorize the sweet sounds of their sleepy voices.*

*I waited then, for what seemed an eternity before I heard Mattie go check on them one last time. When I heard her leave their room, it was then that I cried out to her. At first, I thought she was not going to respond to my cries. I began beating on the door, and that's when I heard hurried footsteps coming up the steps to the attic. I quickly, but carefully took the lid off the noxious liquid and poured it onto a piece of cloth I had torn from my nightgown. I stood behind the door and heard the key turn in the lock. When the door opened, I came quickly from behind and put the cloth over her face. She did not make a sound as she crumbled into my arms. That's when the moonlight coming in from the small attic window allowed me to see her face; it was Esther, not Mattie! I hadn't heard her come in. It frightened me so, but I was somewhat relieved as Mattie had been the only one to show me any sign of kindness in the past.*

*I knew I had to hurry before Mattie woke and came looking for*

181

*Esther. I drug her lifeless body over to the bed and quickly began taking off the dress she had altered to fit her and was thankful, once again that she was bigger than Mattie and closer to my own size. The dress fit perfectly as I slid it over my body. I then turned, and put the New Orleans white nightgown on Esther's lifeless body. I shook uncontrollably as I went out of the room; pulling the door shut behind me. I crept down the stairs, and for a brief moment, I considered going into the children's room to see them one last time before I left. I quickly reconsidered knowing Mattie could wake up and, Andrew could come home any minute. I crept to the front door and opened it as gingerly as I could and quietly pulled it shut behind me.*

*Once outside, I ran as I never have before. The night was very dark, the moon and stars suddenly gone behind clouds. Dogs barked as I ran through the shadows. I hid behind bushes when I heard a buggy coming down the road. My heart was beating so loudly in my chest; I was sure it would give me away. As the buggy drew closer I could see Andrew at the reins; I held my breath. I could see that he was once again in a drunken state. He finally passed me, but I had to wait several moments before my body would stop shaking so violently so that I could run. I knew he would go home and go straight to my room, as he always does when he has been drinking, and expect me to be his wife once more. I had to hurry now, as I knew it would only be minutes before they would all know what I had done.*

*I followed the map Grandmother had drawn on the back of the last letter. I was quite exhausted by the time I reached the Jones' house. I beat on the door, and a large black man flung the door open and jerked me inside. He stuck his head out the door and looked both ways to make sure I hadn't been followed. His wife guided me to a back room and gave me a strong drink to calm my nerves. The man came in then and moved a rug on the floor and began pulling up loose boards. There was a small room built under the floor, and I crawled down into it. He lit a candle and handed it to me, and then told me he would be back to get me in a few hours. As he put the boards back, I noticed how small the space really was, and then by the light of the candle, I could see tunnels running from the main room.*

*It seemed like an eternity before the man came back to get me, but once outside, I realized it couldn't have been long because it was still pitch-black outside. I asked him where he was taking me, and he whispered, "They's waiting on you in Jefferson ma'am. Now, get down low in the back of the wagon, and I's going to cover you up with hay so's nobody knows what we doin'."*

*I did as he instructed, but my mind was reeling. Why was he taking me to Jefferson? Once he had me covered completely with a blanket and hay,*

*I felt him board the wagon, and then, felt the horses immediately break into a run. The ride was very rough, but I was able to hang on to the hardware under the seat of the wagon. We seemed to be on the road for quite a while, but then, I finally felt the wagon begin to slow and then stop.*

*"Miss Virginia? You alright back there?" The man called out.*

*"Yes," I answered hesitantly.*

*"You can come out now."*

*I pushed the blanket and the hay aside and sat up and looked around. We were in a grove of trees beside what appeared to be a wide creek. The man offered me a tin cup with water in it and I drank it completely.*

*"Where are we?" I asked him.*

*"We's close to Jefferson, but I's afraid we gonna haf' to walk the rest of the way cause the road ain't safe for us to travel. The wagon's gettin' bogged down and the horses can't pull us."*

*It was so dark I could barely see my hand in front of my face. But I inched myself to the edge of the wagon and jumped down.*

*We began treading through the mud and the bushes that ran beside the creek. I held my keepsake box close to my chest, desperate not to lose it; I had lost enough. We went on for what seemed forever before the creek fed into what I could now tell was a river. I saw what appeared to be the lights in the distance and knew it must be Jefferson. Fear began to creep up my spine at the thought of what might happen to me here.*

*"Mr. Jones," I inquired. "Why are we going to Jefferson?"*

*"Ma'am, yo' cousin, she be waiting for you there. She gonna help me get you on one of her Daddy's steamboats, and it will take you back to New Orleans."*

*I almost cried. I knew it had to be one of my mother's nieces that was going to help me. When we got closer, another black man came to meet us.*

*"Hey Wilfred." The man addressed Mr. Jones just above a whisper.*

*"Where's Miss Virginia's cousin?"*

*"She's be up there," the man pointed towards what appeared to be a dock. "We's gonna haf to take her up to the back by the paddle wheel. There be a rope hanging down, and she gonna haf to take hold of it and they gonna pull her up so nobody sees."*

*Fear shot through me. "I don't know how to swim."*

*"Miss Virginia," Mr. Jones attempted to comfort me. "Don't you worry none. We ain't gonna let nothin' happen to you." We began to tread through thicker mud. I held my dress up the best I could. I didn't want it to get wet and weigh me down. We finally reached the back of the steamboat and I was surprised to see my Mother standing there. She reached and*

*hugged me and I suddenly recovered a memory of when she hugged me when I was a little girl, before they left me in New Orleans.*

*"Virginia, I love you. Give my love to everyone back home. Now go," she gently put her hand on my back and steered me closer to the paddle wheel.*

*I looked up and saw a young woman standing on the upper deck of the boat. I reached for the rope and began to pull myself up the best I could. I could see a man on the other end was pulling as well and I finally felt a woman's hand touch mine and I was pulled onboard. I could barely make out her face in the dark, but I saw her hold a finger to her lips, so I stayed quiet. I turned then and saw my Mother standing on the riverbank below, waving good-bye and I knew I would never see her again.*

*The woman then took me by the arm and led me to a room towards the side of the boat and we went through a door, and down a narrow set of stairs. When we reached the landing, she turned to me and whispered, "I will bring you food and something to drink once we depart." I nodded.*

*It wasn't long before I felt the rumble of the paddle wheel come to life, and I could tell we were beginning to move. A flood of relief swept through me and I cried. The woman came back some time later with a plate of food and a jug of water. She finally introduced herself as Annabelle. Once daybreak came and I could see her features, I knew we must be cousins. She and I shared some of the same facial features and our hair was the same chestnut color. She was extremely kind and told me we would be on the steamboat for several days before reaching New Orleans. She then explained how Grandmother Abby had orchestrated everything by writing to Annabelle's mother asking for them to help me.*

*Later she came and brought me a clean dress, and after I changed into it, we quietly went up onto the upper deck and I watched as the sun made the stars grow dim. I jumped when a man approached us, but Annabelle quickly put me to ease by telling me he was helping us. She turned then and handed him something and said, "William, we're taking her home."*

*I am full of gratitude knowing I will see Grandmother Abby once again, but my heart breaks to know that I will do so without my children. I will come back, once again, to this place that I loathe, but only to get them and then we shall shake the dust of this horrible place from us, once and for all.*

# Chapter 21

*Suzanne*

I pulled through the intersection and turned and pulled into the driveway of the filling station. I reached into my bag and pulled the pictures of Virginia out and found the one of her standing in front of the filling station.

"See," I said as I held it out to Gina.

She leaned over and looked at the picture and then looked back at the station. "You're right, Suzanne! This is the same place."

We got out of the car and approached three black men that were sitting on a wooden bench against the building. "Hello. Does one of you own this place?"

"No ma'am," one of them spoke up. "That would be Mr. Edgar. He's inside." He got up from the bench and Gina and I followed him and the other two men came through the door behind us. We stood by the front door with two of them, while the other man went to find the owner. An old, weathered black man came walking towards us with the other man following behind.

"I'm Mr. Edgar, I own this place. How can I help you?"

"Yes sir," I stuck my hand out to shake his. "I'm Suzanne and this is my sister Gina. How long have you owned this station?"

"Well, number one," he said with a grin, "I been here since I was fourteen. But, I bought this place when I was forty. So, I guess you could say I been here all my life, 'cause I'll be eighty-two in a few weeks."

"Does the name Virginia ring a bell with you? She was my great-grandmother."

He looked up at the ceiling and rubbed his chin for a minute. "Can't say that name rings no bells."

"I have a picture of her," I said as I held it out to him. "I think this is the filling station she is standing in front of."

He took the picture and walked into his office and we followed. He picked up a big magnifying glass from his desk and looked through it at the picture. "Ah, that's Ms. Jennie!"

"What?" I gasped. "You recognize her?"

"Course I recognize her, she used to keep Ms. Laura's little girl."

Gina grabbed my hand and squeezed it. "Who is Ms. Laura?"

"She was the owner of this place. I went to work for her when I was fourteen and then I worked real hard all them years and when she wanted to sell it when I was forty, I bought it from her."

"So," I began slowly, "*Jennie* babysat for this, *Ms. Laura?*"

"Well," he said as he handed the picture back to me. "I wouldn't say she babysat for her. She loved Ms. Laura's girl. She would walk her to school and take her to Palmer Park to play all the time."

I felt my knees go weak. "How long was she here?"

"Here in Carrollton?"

"What?" I gasped again. "What do you mean, *Carrollton?*"

"This part of New Orleans; it's called Carrollton."

I glanced over at Gina and her eyes were huge. "So, she lived here; in Carrollton?"

"Oh yes. She was a real, good woman. Everybody loved Ms. Jennie. But…"

"What is it?" I asked just above a whisper.

"There was something; I never did know just what, but something deep in her was real sad. I know Ms. Laura knew what it was. Ms. Jennie, she would just start crying, and Ms. Laura would just hug her, but never ask her what was wrong." He shook his head. "Yeah, she knew what it was. She didn't need to ask."

"I can't thank you enough," I said as I reached and shook his hand again.

"Well, I don't think I did much of nothin' just told you what I know. But, you say you are her great-granddaughter?"

"Yes sir," I said with a smile.

"Well, did you know what hurt her so bad?"

"Yes sir," I said nodding my head. "I believe we do now."

Once back in the car, I just looked over at Gina and shook my head. "Are you believing this?"

"I swear Suzanne, I've never heard of anything like this! This isn't like those kids having past life memories; you're a grown woman and you're proving every single word you've written in that journal of yours."

I pulled the car slowly back to the intersection where Palmer Park stood on the corner. I looked up at the street sign; *Carrollton Avenue.* "So, the whole time Mama thought Virginia was up close to Dallas at *that* Carrollton, she was actually mailing those letters from here."

"Yep," Gina said shaking her head. "Unbelievable."

"I knew when I drove past that park I had been there before; it was such a strong feeling."

"I think you better get ready for more of that," she said as she reached and patted my arm. "She was all over this city."

"Yeah, I'm getting that now."

"Where are we going now?" She asked as I slowly drove by the park once again.

"Georgia, the desk clerk at the hotel, said the library downtown has archive files too, so that's where we are headed as soon as I stop and get some gas."

We rode in silence as I drove back down Carrollton Avenue and turned onto St. Charles Avenue and went back the way we had come. I drove to the downtown area of the city. I found the library and we parked and got out and went inside. We took the elevator to the fourth floor where we were told they kept the archive files. We got off the elevator and spotted a man standing behind the information desk.

"Can I help you?" he asked with a smile.

"Yes, I'm trying to find information on my great-grandmother and her family that lived here in the 1800's. Their last name was Fontenot. Abbigail and Henry."

He keyed the name into his computer. "It looks like I have some sort of court documents with that name. Have a seat over there," he said pointing towards an enclosed area, "and I'll pull them for you." Moments later he brought a file over and handed it to me. I opened it and the first page was dated the very same day; a hundred years earlier. I pointed it out to Gina.

"No way," she said as she grabbed my arm."

I just shook my head and began to look over the papers. It appeared to be a court deposition; a family battle over something, but I couldn't figure out what, but I was amazed to see Grandmother Abby's words recorded on the paper before me.

Every so often, I kept seeing a reference to a five-digit number, so I called the man back over and asked what it was. He wasn't sure so he said he would try to find out while we continued to look over the document. He came back a few minutes later with a look of shock on his face.

"That five-digit number is a succession number." He put his hand to his forehead. "It's the sixty-one-page will of Henry Fontenot!"

"Oh!" I gasped. "Can I see it?"

"You'll have to come back in four days," he said nodding his head. "We have to de-humidify it; nobody has touched in 117 years!"

"You've got to be kidding me," Gina screeched.

He shook his head. "No, I'm not kidding! Please come back in four days! I can't wait to see what you've found!"

"Me either!" I said as I stood up from the table. "We'll be back; I guarantee you! In the meantime, could you make me a copy of this deposition?"

"Oh yes," he said picking up the file from the table. "I can make you a copy of the will as well so you can pick it up when you return."

"That will be fantastic," I said as I shook his hand. "Thank you."

"You know," he said as he tilted his head. "Those succession papers shouldn't even be here."

"Why do you say that?" I asked.

"Well, those files were moved here when Hurricane Katrina was going to hit. You know, so they were protected from the water. But, nobody ever came back to get them. I guess they just forgot about them."

"Like so many other things," Gina said shaking her head.

I was absolutely speechless until we reached the car. So much had happened within the hour. First Mr. Edgar and now this. I got in and cranked the car. "Wow," was all I could manage.

Gina shook her head. "You know when I read that journal entry that said Virginia was raised in wealth?" I nodded my head. "Well, I'll be honest, I had no idea how you would ever prove that. I mean you're talking about the 1870's, and they had to have a lot for him to have a sixty-one page will."

"I know! I just can't begin to think of what all is in that will. I'm just pumped now! First Mr. Edgar and Carrollton and now this! I'm so excited! Mother is going to flip!"

"That's an understatement! Did you see in the deposition it mentioned something about her grandparents being from Germany?"

"Yeah," Gina nodded, "I did. I don't remember what it said, exactly, but I do remember seeing *Germany* written. Why?"

"Well, did you notice that stand by the French doors just before you go out onto the porch at the hotel? The one that has all those pamphlets advertising places to visit while in New Orleans?"

"Yeah, but I didn't really pay any attention to them; I know you want to stick to business while we're here. I didn't think we would have time to do any sight-seeing."

"Well, we're going to be here for the next four days, at least, and I think I remember seeing something about Germany on one of them. Let's go back and look."

I drove straight to the hotel and parked and we rushed upstairs to look over the pamphlet stand, and I was right. In the center of all the others, there was one for the Gretna German Museum. I pulled it from the slot it was in. It was a single card with a few pictures and the address of the Museum. "Come on," I grabbed Gina by the arm, "let's go."

We ran back downstairs and got in the car and instinctively I somehow knew to drive across the Mississippi Bridge to reach the little town of Gretna. I drove to the downtown area and quickly found the building. We got out and went inside. We were greeted by the curator that told us we could take the tour of the displays on our own and that there were buttons on each display that would play a narrated explanation of what we were viewing.

Gina and I slowly walked into the display area and my heart began to pound at what I was seeing. There in the pictures, were the houses that *Swiss Miss,* the little restaurant, of my childhood had reminded me of. We rounded the corner and there stood two mannequins of children dressed in the customary dress of German children. The tears flowed down my face before I could stop them. I knew this stuff; inside and out. I wiped my face before we finished the tour and rejoined the curator at the front entrance.

"I have a question," I said as we reached the man that was now sitting at his desk. "Was it customary for the Germans that lived in New Orleans, back in the late 1800's, to go to Germany to visit?"

"Oh absolutely," he said with a smile. "The ones that could afford it went back and forth often. You might also be interested in the German Coast area."

"Where is that?" I asked.

"Do you know where Carrollton is?"

"I do now," I said with a smile.

"Well," He said as he picked up a piece of paper and began drawing a map. "If you go down Carrollton Avenue, you would turn here." He drew an 'X' on the paper. "Follow that street around and it will take you to River Road. Follow it all the way until you reach the German Coast. There will be signs; you can't miss it."

"Thank you," I said as I took the paper from him. We went back out to the car.

"Why did you ask that?" Gina asked as we got into the car.

"Well," I said as I cranked the car. "I've never been to a German Museum before, so I'm figuring Virginia was living with them as a young child; right?"

"Oh," she said nodding her head. "She would have gone with them."

"Exactly," I said as I pulled back onto the highway to take us back across the river.

"So, if you *were* Virginia, you would have had the memories of those trips."

"Precisely." I said as I took the ramp to cross the bridge. "Are you up for a drive down River Road?"

"Sure, why not?"

I drove back to Carrollton and turned beside the bank like the man at the museum had instructed and discovered the downtown area of the town and was once again inundated with memories; from another time when I was another woman.

"You know," Gina began. "I was thinking about something last night."

"Yeah?" I looked at her and raised my eyebrows.

"Well, you were born in December of 1958, so that means you were conceived in the spring of that same year."

"Yeah," I said with a laugh, "it usually takes nine months."

"You're missing my point," she frowned.

"Okay, so make your point." I said as I turned onto River Road.

"Virginia died in January and you were conceived in March. She came back quick. Maybe that explains all those nightmares you used to have. You would walk, or should I say run, in your sleep, and Daddy would find you and you would be screaming for him to help you."

The memory came flooding back. "You're right. After I was grown, he and I talked about that once and he said I would yell people's names that he had never heard of."

"Exactly," Gina nodded. "Maybe the memories were still so fresh in her mind when she died that you just naturally still had them when you were small."

"That would make sense, because I can still remember thinking I needed to run and hide; that people were after me."

"I know all of this has got to freak you out, but at the same time, the relief must be there too as you can begin to piece together all the strange things from your childhood."

"There is a certain level of relief in knowing that I wasn't as quirky as mother thought."

"I cannot imagine what she is going to say about all of this. You're planning on telling her everything, aren't you?"

"Might as well. She already knows what we think all of this is. So, yes, I'm going to tell her everything."

"I just wonder what's going to be in the will?" Gina asked.

"Oh look," I said pointing at a sign. "We are entering the German Coast."

I drove a little further and pulled over at a Church with a cemetery next to it. We got out and walked among tombstones. I felt like I had definitely seen the church before. "I guess being German, they would have possibly had friends that lived out here."

"Oh, I'm sure they did," Gina agreed.

We looked around a little longer and then got in the car and headed back to the hotel. I hadn't realized how tired I was until I took a hot bath and got into bed and fell into a deep sleep. Gina and I both woke up at the same time the next morning and went down to eat breakfast together. We decided to spend the next three days riding around the Garden District looking at all the houses and old buildings that seemed so familiar to me.

Thursday night finally came and I couldn't sleep in anticipation of getting a copy of the will the next morning. I went downstairs to the library and found a book titled *The Germans of New Orleans.* I brought it back upstairs with me and went out on the porch to read. I read for hours learning of the hardships most early German immigrants faced. One of the chapters covered the last names of some of the families that had settled in the German Coast. The name *Fontenot* was not among them. I took the book back downstairs and came back up and tried once again to go to sleep. Gina was sleeping soundly, so I decided to grab a throw that was at the end of the bed and took it and piled up on the sofa in the room.

I woke up, still on the couch, but the sun was trickling through the gauzy sheers that hung on the window. I rose and saw that Gina was not in bed and I saw the bathroom door was open, so I knew she had gone downstairs for breakfast. I took a quick shower and got dressed and went downstairs to join her. I hadn't realized it was already eight-thirty. I barely had time to order my food and eat before we left to go to the library downtown.

I tried to drive the speed limit as I drove towards library. I quickly found a parking space and we jumped out and ran to the building and got on the elevator. As soon as we stepped off, the man saw us and waved.

"Good Morning Ladies! I've been so anxious for y'all to get here. Come on back," he said as he motioned us to follow him back to the same enclosed area we had been in before. "Just have a seat and I'll grab the paperwork."

Gina and I got to the table and Gina sat down, but I couldn't. I paced the floor. The man finally came over and was carrying a rather large stack of papers in his hand. "Here we are," he said as he handed them to me. "One is a copy of the deposition and then I have the will clipped separate."

I finally sat down next to Gina and he laid the papers between us. "Oh, look Suzanne! The first page is dated December 13th! That's your birthday!"

"Wow," the man said with a grin. "Happy Birthday!"

"I began to read the will and by the time I hit the third page, my mouth fell open when I saw all the property he owned listed and then it continued on two more pages. I recognized some of the street names that bordered the blocks of land. I stopped reading and looked up at the man as he was still standing at the end of the table. I saw that he was smiling.

"I'm assuming you recognize some of the streets?"

"Yes," I said nodding my head.

"It's the Garden District area. He owned a very large part of it. I spoke to a historian about this when I saw it and they agreed, he must have begun buying the land when the plantations were put up for sale. Honey," he said with a big smile, "your people were some of the early pioneers of the Garden District!"

"Oh my God!" Gina gasped.

"Oh yes, I called over to the land office and they have records of him buying and selling land as early as 1846! This is quite the find, and you must be the first person to find it because like I said, nobody has touched this will in 117 years. But, I did discover something else."

"What's that?" I managed to get out.

"When Henry Fontenot died, it appears he had tried to keep his wealth a secret, although I'm not sure why."

"I bet I know," I said just above a whisper. "I'm sorry, go ahead. What did you find?"

"Well, the deposition states he left each of his children equal parts, but it didn't really touch the total sum of the estate. He was worth over a million dollars when he died. And back then that was an astronomical amount."

"Still is today," Gina said raising her eyebrows.

The man nodded. "So, anyway, the family fought over the estate and it went all the way to the Supreme Court! It was one of the earliest cases heard! So, I called over there and they have a record of it and they are going to make a copy for you. When y'all leave here, you can go on over and pick it up. But, parking is horrendous down there; the Supreme Court building is in the French Quarter, so you want to take the trolley and walk down to the building. Here," he handed me a piece of paper, "I drew you a map of where it is."

I rose slowly from the chair and took the piece of paper from him. "I can't thank you enough for all your help."

"Oh, think nothing of it. This was a sheer pleasure for me to be a part of you finding something like this!"

Gina and I gathered the papers from the table and walked in a stupor to the car. I got in and just sat there staring out the windshield and Gina sat quiet for a minute before she spoke. "I think you just solved the mystery."

"I know I did. Virginia was sold for the Grandparent's Estate!" A deep sigh escaped me. "That's why Mamaw said she was having an *Estate Sale* in the dream. She found out the truth when she died and got to the other side."

"Yes." Gina nodded. "She wanted to help Virginia; well you, to find the truth and tell it."

I cranked the car and we headed back to the hotel. I ran the papers back up to our room while Gina waited on me downstairs. I came back down and we rushed out front to the trolley stop. It was only minutes before one came along and we boarded. We rode in silence to the French Quarter and got off. I looked at the paper the man had given me. "This should be easy to find, it's by the Williams Research Center." We took off walking in the direction we had gone before, but turned on a different street as the map instructed. When we rounded the corner, Gina had to grab me before I fell to my knees on the sidewalk. "Look!" I screamed as I pointed to a statue in front of the Supreme Court Building.

"What?" Gina said looking where I was pointing.

"That's the monk from my dream," I said pointing at the huge bronze statue. "He's even carrying the book!"

Gina drug me to the base of the statue. "Oh my God, Suzanne! It's not a monk in a robe, it's a Supreme Court Justice! That's a law book he's carrying! What did you hear someone say in that dream?"

"That all my answers would be found in that book!"

# Chapter 22

*Virginia*

*It was once again night time as the boat pulled into the dock of New Orleans. The lights of the city beckoned me. I walked down the plank, arm in arm, with Annabelle and found James, Cissy's husband waiting for me. The same carriage that had taken me to the train station that day stood in wait behind him. Even though it's been four years, it feels like I have been gone a lifetime. I couldn't help myself, as I approached James, I began to cry as he took my hand and helped me on to the seat. Then he helped Annabelle and she sat down beside me. She took my hand in hers and whispered, "Everything is going to be all right now. Grandmother Abby will see to it."*

*As the carriage pulled onto St. Charles Avenue, I didn't need the light of day to recognize my surroundings. Every scent, every sound; spoke home to me. I began to cry again before we pulled onto Carondolet Street, and I could see my home still standing on the corner before me. When James pulled the carriage to a stop, I jumped down and ran. As I opened the back-iron gate and heard its familiar creak, I sobbed. Cissy came out from the servant's quarters, carrying an oil lantern. I got to my feet and she rushed to me. She sat the lantern on the ground and grabbed me and embraced me in a fashion I haven't known since I left this place. We both fell to the ground and both of us were sobbing so hard we couldn't speak. She finally raised herself up and reached down and helped me stand.*

*Annabelle had stood nearby and didn't attempt to interrupt the homecoming she was witnessing. Cissy picked up the lantern and took me*

194

*by the hand and led me to the house, with Annabelle following close behind. We went into the house and found Grandmother Abby sitting in her parlor asleep in the chair. She had her Bible draped open, across her lap. Her rosary beads were still in her hand. Clearly, she was awaiting my return. I had forgotten what it was to be loved like this. Her eyes fluttered open, and I went to her and fell on my knees and laid my head in her lap. Cissy held us both as our sobs were carried away through the large open windows, into the stillness of the night into the Garden District.*

*It was only the next day as the sun rose, that I inhaled the sanctity of the freedom this house held for me and truly realized just how much I had missed it. My dreams had not been as vivid of these people or this house as I had believed. I know now that our minds and hearts cannot hold all our memories or the ache of missing these things would surely overcome us.*

*Grandmother Abby has aged greatly since the last time I saw her. The devastation of losing Grandfather and I have clearly left its mark. I will never forgive Andrew for the things he has done to me, but especially for the grief I know he caused my beloved Grandmother.*

*The first time I climbed the staircase to my room, I held my breath. I slowly opened the door and cried once again when I saw my room was exactly as I had left it that sorrowful day. My dresses still hung in the armoire, and my books still lined the shelves. That first night I undressed and instead of putting on a nightgown, which has been my only article of clothing that Andrew allowed me to wear, I put on one of my dresses and crawled into bed. Cissy came in later and brought me a warm glass of milk. I saw her eyes tear up, but she never questioned why it was that I was sleeping completely clothed. I feel she senses my spirit has been damaged. When I awoke in the morning, I was startled at my surroundings. I cried again when I realized I was, in fact, home. It had not been a dream, like so many times before. So many things I had taken for granted when I lived here before, I knew I would never take for granted again.*

*I went downstairs to find Grandmother Abby having tea in the parlor. I stood in the doorway, unnoticed for a moment, and savored the sight of her and of the room itself. I had played here so often as she and her friends would sit and visit in the afternoons. I fought back the desire to cry again as the memories of my childhood and Grandfather flooded my mind.*

*Grandmother took notice of me standing there and motioned for me to come and sit beside her. I told her all about Elisabeth and Jonathan. I told her I feared I would forget their faces until I could be back with them once again. She patted my hand and reached inside her Bible and pulled from it the photograph she had sent the money to have made while I was still at Andrew's house. I grabbed her and hugged her, and then I came to understand that had been her reasoning for insisting on the photograph to be taken. She had known this day would come. I stared at myself and my children in the photograph, and all the pain came rushing back to me. How Andrew had made me wear the dress that had been altered to fit his sister and how it was now too small and the back had gaped open. Then I looked into the eyes of my children and sobbed uncontrollably. I did not want to leave them behind, but I knew Andrew would take my life if I had stayed. Grandmother pulled me close and begged me to forgive her for sending me to Texas. Now, Andrew has my children. I know I will not rest until I rescue them as well.*

*I have spent the last four years counting down the days until I could come back here, to be with the people I love and I know love me. Now, I will count the days until my children are here with me as well.*

# Chapter 23

*Suzanne*

By the time I drove back to Brookfield, I had more questions than answers. Henry Fontenot had left each of his children an equal share of his estate, but even I could see something was missing. Three of the grown children had fought Grandmother Abby against the other three children and the fight had indeed gone all the way to the Supreme Court. The Civil Court deposition stated the family owned so much of Napoleon Avenue that the city of New Orleans was forcing them to pay to pave it and put in sidewalks. It was all so mind boggling, but I had other things I needed to be concentrating on. I had to find a divorce attorney I could afford, and I dreaded the thought of going through all of it, but there was no turning back now. I slept all day Saturday and most of Sunday. I knew I was just dodging the inevitable, but I just couldn't think about it all yet.

When I drove into work on Monday morning, one thing was certain in my mind. The question was no longer whether I believed I had been Virginia in another lifetime; I knew it had to be true. My concern now was with this lifetime. I didn't want to waste another minute fighting, running and losing. I wanted to be free of time constraints and pressures that every job had always leveled against me; including the one I currently had.

I was straightening books on a shelf in the store when I heard the tinkling of the bell. I turned and saw a man walk towards me.

"Suzanne Peyton?" he asked with apologetic eyes.

"Yes?"

"You've been served." He held out the papers to me.

I shifted the books I had in my arms and took them from him. He turned and walked briskly back to the door. He turned, once more and looked back at me, and then opened the door and went out. I walked over to the counter and laid the books down and read the papers. Tony had filed for divorce. Since Texas is a no-fault State, the reason listed was simply *'irreconcilable differences.'* It hurt, but the pain was different somehow than what I had expected. I felt the loss, much the way I felt the loss of so many other things along the way. But, it also felt like I had been handed a clean slate; a place to begin a new life. I folded the papers and put them in my purse under the counter and walked over and continued to put the new books on the shelf.

I was working on the best sellers that had just come in when I happened to look closer at one of them before putting it on the shelf. It had a picture of an angel on the front cover. I flipped the book over and read the back jacket. I dropped the other books to the floor and ran for my office.

"What's wrong?" Tracy asked as she came back in from her lunch break.

"Watch the front," I yelled back at her as I closed my office door. I sat down at my desk and began reading the story of a man who had experienced exactly what I was with the *'4's'* showing up all over the place. I read for over an hour before I picked up the phone and called Gina.

"Gina! The *'4's'* are Angels!" I yelled into the phone.

"What are you talking about?"

"The *'4's'* are signals that the Angels are bringing all this information to me! It's really reincarnation! It's all in this new book!" I explained everything I had just read to her. How this man had been waking up at 4:44 and had been given messages. "They regressed him and they believe he was Paul; the Apostle! The book is a bestseller!"

The telephone line fell silent. I thought she had hung up. "Gina?"

"I'm here," she said slowly. "So, you just found this book today?"

"Yes, I was putting the latest best sellers on the shelf and that's when I found it. It's on the New York Times Bestseller List and no, before you ask, it's not fiction."

"I don't know how you can still shock me at this point," she laughed, "but you have. Every little piece of this puzzle is coming together."

"Yes, and the timing couldn't have been more perfect."

"Why do you say that?"

"Tony had me served with divorce papers today."

"Oh," she sighed. "I'm sorry."

"I'm not. I'm ready for that chapter of my life to be over. I'm ready to change my life for the better, I think I need to do it without a man for awhile."

"That has to be the best thing I've heard you say in a long time." I could hear the sincerity in her voice.

"I mean it." I sighed. "Well, listen, I've got to get back to work. I'll call you later."

I hung up the phone and got up and took the book to the counter to pay for it. I was definitely going to finish it at home later on tonight. There was one more thing I wanted to do concerning Virginia. I told Tracy I would be coming in late the next morning. I wanted to go to Terrell to pick up Virginia's death certificate. It was the last thing I felt I needed to be able to close the book on her story.

I spent the rest of the day at the bookstore enjoying our customers and felt a lightness my soul hadn't known in a long, long time. By the time I drove home that evening, I was no longer worried about how I would make it or what I would do now that Tony was really gone from my life. I also knew his threat *to put me away* would no longer hold up; I had too much proof that *something* had truly happened whether he considered it *reincarnation* or not. I found myself smiling when I thought of the story I was now ready to tell the world. As soon as I walked into the house the phone began to ring. I put my things down on the foyer table and rushed to answer it.

"Hello?"

"Mom?"

My breath caught in my chest. "Sam, how are you?"

"I'm going to let you adopt her," she said quickly.

*"Her?"* My free hand went to my chest. "It's a girl?"

"Yeah, I just found out today."

I took a deep breath. "Thank you, Sam. You won't regret it. Can I tell Max and Matt now?"

"Yeah," she said slowly. "The baby is due in March; you'll be ready by then?"

"Oh," I said as I felt the smile cross my face, "I'm ready now."

After we hung up, I went over and sat down on the couch. It really was going to be a fresh start in a lot of areas for me. I had never had the opportunity to be close to Sam due to the divorce. I suddenly had the thought that maybe the beliefs of some people who had experienced past lives might be right. They believed people we were close to once before would sometimes agree to come back and be a part of our lives again. If that was true, I hoped this little girl would be Grandmother Abby. I only knew her from the journal entries, but I felt love for her. I had never experienced the kind of love Virginia and Grandmother Abby had shared. It would be nice. This time we would be reversing our roles, but nonetheless, we would be together again and I would see to it that we were happy.

I got up from the couch and stopped in the foyer to retrieve my purse and book bag. I turned and saw Max coming down the stairs.

"Hey Mom," he came over and hugged me.

"Hey, where are you headed?"

"Just down the street to shoot some hoops with friends."

"Okay, just don't stay gone too long."

I went into the kitchen to find Maggie finishing dinner. "You know you don't have to cook every day now that it's just me and Max."

"Why? Have you and Max stopped eating?"

"No," I laughed. "I just meant since it's just us now, we can have a sandwich some nights."

"I'll not have you two eating junk food," she said with a scowl. "Not on my watch."

"Okay, okay, have it your way," I laughed as I sat down at the bar.

"How was work?"

"It was great, actually." I pulled my latest discovery from my book bag and laid it on the bar. "Come over here, and take a look at what I found. It's one of the books that came in today. It's on the New York Times bestseller list."

She turned the fire down under the pot on the stove, and wiped her hands on her apron and came over and sat down across from me. She picked up the book and read the title and opened it and flipped through the pages. She opened it to the table of contents and saw that there was a chapter titled '444'. She looked up at me.

"Yep, I'm not the only one seeing that number everywhere. The author believes it's a sign when Angels bring him messages, and get this; he believes he was reincarnated too. So, at least I'm not the only adult going through this."

"I'm sure you're not. But how fascinating this book came out right now; at the very time, it's all happening to you."

"I just think it's God coming to my rescue and putting my mind at ease."

"Well, you certainly couldn't have made any of this happen! Are you still working on *your* book?"

"Absolutely," I said patting my book bag. "I keep a spiral notebook and the journal with me all the time now."

"Have you had any more *diary entries?*"

I nodded my head. "Oh yeah, and they're pretty bad."

"I feel so sorry for her," Maggie said shaking her head. "What a horrible life."

I nodded in agreement. "But, guess what? Tony had me served with divorce papers today and I didn't even get upset." I got up and got a Coke from the refrigerator and popped the top and took a drink. "And," I said raising my eyebrows. "Sam called. She has decided to allow me to adopt the baby and she just found out today that it's a girl."

Maggie leaned back on the barstool and just stared at me.

"Oh, come on Maggie," I said as I went back over and sat down across from her. "Be happy for me."

She leaned forward and crossed her arms on the bar. "If this is really what you want to do, I'll stand behind you all the way. Just make sure; it's eighteen years, you know?"

"I know," I said with a smile.

"Well," she said as she stood up, "I guess we need to go shopping for baby things."

I jumped up and went around the bar and hugged her. "Yes! Let's go together. It will be fun."

We went shopping at a local baby specialty shop and bought all of the necessities and then went out to eat. When we got home she helped me bring everything inside and then I walked her out to her car so she could go home. As she pulled away, I reached down and pulled my shoes off and stood in the cool, St. Augustine grass. The night was clear, and the stars lit up the sky.

A car pulled up out front, and Max got out and came up the sidewalk. We went inside and I told him all about Sam and the baby. He surprised me by being almost as excited as I was to have a baby on the way. I went to bed that night and slept more soundly than I had in months.

I got up early the next morning and headed to Terrell, Texas to attempt to get the final papers on Virginia's life. I decided to go to the mental hospital first. I parked my car and got out and looked at the old buildings scattered all over the hospital grounds. Vines grew over the metal bars on the windows of the buildings that were no longer being used. I felt a chill run down my spine. I made my way up the steps to the front door of the main building.

I went inside and walked down a desolate hallway. Every hair on my body was now standing up. I glanced up and saw wire mesh covering the bottoms of the bell type lamps that hung from the ceiling. I was convinced not much had been done to the building since Virginia walked this same hall.

I saw a door with *Office* written on it and went inside. I was greeted by a white-haired lady at the front desk. "Can I help you?" Her voice was flat with no emotion. I instinctively knew it had to be from working in a place like this for far too long.

"Yes," I said as I put my purse on the counter. "My name is Suzanne Peyton, and I was wondering if you have archive files on patients that used to be here; back in 1957 or early '58."

"We don't have them here on the property, they are on file in Austin. You have to write to the office there and tell them what you need and why you want them. Then they will make a decision of whether or not to release them to you. Most are sealed."

"Oh," I said with a disappointed sigh. "Do you have the address?"

She didn't say a word as she jotted down the information on a piece of paper. She rose slowly from her desk and came over and without saying a word, she handed me the paper and turned to go back to her desk.

I went back out the door into the hallway and experienced another *'flashback'* as I had come to refer the unexplainable things I experienced. Suddenly, the hallway took on a different lighting; a yellow haze enveloped me. I could hear patients screaming and laughing hysterically in the distance. I felt someone's hand on my arm. I jerked around and caught a glimpse of a ghostly figure in a nurse's uniform and she was smiling at me. I felt the tenderness she extended to me as she walked me down the hallway. *'I know you,'* I whispered. As soon as the words left my mouth, I snapped back to the present time, but *'her presence'* was still there. I could feel it.

I got in my car and drove to the courthouse to get Virginia's death certificate. On the way, I passed a building that once again made me feel like I was moving in slow motion. I pulled into the parking lot, and almost, as if on automatic pilot, got out and went inside. A woman stood to greet me. I saw a sign on the counter; 'Terrell State Bank.'

"Can I help you?" The woman asked with a strange look on her face.

"What did this building used to be? Back in the fifties?"

She cocked her head slightly to the side and then turned towards the others behind the counter. "Anybody know what this building was in the fifties?"

An older man in the back stood up. "It used to be Seller's Funeral Home."

"Thank you," I heard myself say as I turned and walked back out to my car. I got in and sat for a moment and knew this had to be the place they brought Virginia's body to be held until Wright's Funeral Home in Marshall could get here to pick her up. The grief was surreal. So many lies; words spoken so many years ago had continued on without the voices that produced them. I felt the regret I knew she had left this earth with. Regret for leaving her dear grandparent's home in New Orleans. Regret for letting a man hold her captive until she had the children that would haunt her dreams in their absence. Such a damaged spirit; no wonder she wanted to come back. She had to settle it once and for all.

I cranked the car and drove to the courthouse. I found the records office and filled out the form requesting Virginia's death certificate. When I finished, an older woman rose from her desk and came and took the paper from me. She went back over to her desk and began entering the information on her computer. Suddenly, she stopped typing and looked over at me. She had the strangest look on her face as she came back to the counter. "Are you related to Virginia Avery?" She spoke so low, I almost didn't hear her.

"Yes. I'm her great-granddaughter."

She shook her head. "This is amazing."

I cocked my head and stared into her eyes. "Why would you say that?"

"I know the nurse that took care of her when she was in the State Hospital."

I felt my knees go weak. "Are you serious?"

She held her finger to her lips. "Shh." She looked around at her co-workers to make sure they weren't listening.

I nodded. "Okay," I whispered.

"I could get in trouble for telling you this, but her name is Hazel Stanbury. She was a friend of my mother's."

*"Was?"* I could feel the disappointment run through my veins.

She shook her head. "My mother passed, but Hazel is still alive."

"Does she live here? In Terrell?" I had to contain the excitement in my voice.

"Yes," she held up a finger for me to wait as she went back over to her desk and wrote something down on a piece of paper. She folded it up and walked back to the counter. "Here," she said as she handed me the piece of paper. "It's her phone number. Now wait here and I'll print out the death certificate for you."

My hands were shaking as I held the paper down where no one could see it and unfolded it and read the phone number. Could this really be happening? I stuck it in my purse when I saw the woman coming back over with the death certificate.

"I've heard Virginia's story all my life," she said as she handed me the paper. "It still haunts Hazel to this day."

"I cannot thank you enough," I said as I reached out to shake her hand."

"Just go see Hazel, that will be thanks enough. I always felt so sorry for her. She has carried all of that around with her for years."

*"Carried all of what?"* I whispered.

"Just go see her; she'll tell you."

I raced back to my car and finally looked at the death certificate. I was not surprised to see *Addison;* the youngest son had been the informant. It explained all the lines that were left blank; he hadn't known anything about her.

I cranked the car and pulled out of the courthouse parking lot in search of a pay phone. I spotted one next to the entrance of the *Piggly Wiggly* grocery store just down the street. I pulled into a parking space and jumped out. With shaking hands, I put a quarter in the payphone and dialed the number on the piece of paper.

"Hello?" An older woman answered on the third ring.

"Yes, can I speak to Ms. Hazel Stanbury, please?"

"Who this be callin'?"

"My name is Suzanne Peyton. I was given this phone number by a lady at the courthouse who said Ms. Stanbury was a nurse at Terrell State Hospital and knew my great-grandmother, Virginia Avery."

"Oh, my Lawd!" I heard the phone receiver hit the floor, then a rustling sound and finally the woman picked up the receiver again and told me to hold on. I was shaking from head to toe while I waited for what seemed like forever before a sweet voice came back on the line.

"Hello? This is Hazel; you're kin to Ms. Virginia?"

At the sound of the woman's voice, I felt a longing stir in my heart. "Yes, ma'am, this is Suzanne, her great-granddaughter."

"Sweet Jesus," the woman said as she began to cry. "Where are you calling from?"

"I'm here in Terrell," I managed.

"You're here, in town?"

"Yes ma'am," I said as I choked back tears of my own.

"Hold on just a minute and I'll get my friend, Lizzie, to give you directions. You'll come, won't you?"

"Well, of course, if you're sure you don't mind," I said as I swiped at a tear that ran down my face.

"I insist! Now hold on, here's Lizzie." She handed the phone back to the woman that had first answered and I pulled a piece of paper from my purse and jotted down the directions to her house.

I got back in my car and the shaking would not subside as I cranked it and followed the directions to Hazel's house. A few minutes later, I pulled up the driveway of a beautiful cottage style house that sat up on knoll. Flowers bloomed all along the sidewalk as I made my way up to the front porch. Just as I got to the top step, the screen door opened and a white-haired woman, stooped with age, pushed her walker through and came out onto the porch. My heart pounded with a memory I couldn't explain, but new this kind of love needed no explanation.

I walked up to her and we hugged and cried; like the long-lost friends that we were. Then I turned to see Lizzie come out the front door as well. I reached and squeezed her hand. She had barely been a teen-ager when I had seen her last, as an aide at the mental hospital.

I followed the two women into the house and Hazel pushed her walker into the living room and sat down on the sofa. She patted the space beside her and I went over and sat next to her. I glanced around the room and was instantly calmed by the soft colors and personal touches of a woman that had surely brought me comfort before.

"I've waited a lifetime for this," Hazel said, as she swiped away tears with her wrinkled hand. "Virginia was like a mother to me for the short time I knew her. She was just such a dear, sweet, woman."

"I'm so glad I found you," I said as I wiped tears of my own.

Lizzie came back in with glasses of iced tea for all of us. I reached and took two of the glasses and sat one down on a coaster on the coffee table in front of Hazel.

"Just look at us," Hazel said with a smile. "We look like a couple of crybabies." She grinned, and my mind spiraled backwards. The room took on that yellow-hazy color again; like when I was at the mental hospital and suddenly a memory surfaced. I could see Hazel's face; much younger, but she was smiling at me and handing me a present that was wrapped in paper with yellow butterflies all over it. Then, just as suddenly as it came, it was gone and I was sitting staring at the old white-haired lady before me.

"How long was Virginia at the mental hospital?"

"Not long," she said shaking her head. I could see the pain of the memory all over her face. "That boy; well that man," she said with a frown. "The one that put her there, he never knew the truth. Virginia was insistent that I didn't blame him, but it was hard," she said shaking her head. "She said he had grown up with all the lies those people had told him and he didn't know any better, but still, he should have at least listened to her." She hung her head. "He could have at least told her where Elisabeth was."

"Elisabeth was my mother's mother; she's passed away now too."

"Well," she sighed, "maybe Elisabeth knows the truth now that's she's on the other side."

"I can almost guarantee it," I said with a small smile. "You see, I had a dream, and it was Elisabeth that came to me and put me on this path to find you."

Hazel turned her watery brown eyes to me then, and I told her my story. She didn't seem the least bit surprised when I told her I believed I had, in fact, been Virginia and felt a bond with her that we had shared before. Lizzie, however, was a different story. Hazel and I just smiled when Lizzie slowly got up from her chair, with eyes as big as saucers, and excused herself as she backed out of the room; never taking her eyes off us.

I reached and took the journal from my book bag and began to read some of the *diary entries* to her. "Well," she said with wide eyes, "I can tell you this. She had me read her diary, and those are her words alright! When she died, they took her personal belongings with her. I guess *that boy* got everything."

We sat and visited a while longer before I noticed the tired look in her eyes and knew the whole ordeal of reliving everything had taken its toll on her. I rose from the couch and helped her up and we hugged one last time before I headed for the door. She followed me out to the porch. I went down the front steps and then turned to wave good-bye; for the final time. She held up a wrinkled hand. "I've missed you," I said as I got in my car and drove away.

# Chapter 24

*Suzanne*

The months that followed my trip to Hazel's house were somewhat of a blur. I continued to work on the book when I wasn't working at the bookstore. Sales were still not where Paul, Mrs. Drexel's son, wanted them to be, and the pressure was mounting.

I hired a divorce attorney, and the proceedings were moving forward, although Tony had complained they weren't moving fast enough to suit him. I was fighting him to be able to stay in the house until school was out so Max didn't have to change school districts this close to the end of the school year.

Sam was keeping me posted with letters that included pictures of sonograms. I had been tempted to call her, but decided to let her call the shots. I finally told her, in one of my return letters, that Tony and I were getting a divorce and held my breath for her response. She finally wrote back that she was glad and that he had been a concern for her as far as me adopting the baby, because she had never liked him. I had to laugh; she hadn't liked me much either, but again, I just let it go. But, Max had more than once, voiced the same opinion where Tony was concerned. Why had they, especially Sam, since she had never lived with me since I had married him, been able to see in him what I hadn't? Maggie stayed on, just as she had promised and refused to take any money from me. She even went as far as saying she would stay and help with the baby as well, so that I could still work.

I had finally finished the book, and had begun to send out query letters to agents and publishing houses. Two agents had requested the first fifty pages and I was ecstatic. I had sent both of them the requested paperwork and was now waiting for a response.

The holidays rolled around and I found myself in a slump. Without all the excitement that had surrounded me for months concerning Virginia; I didn't know what to do with myself. Unfortunately, with all the free time, my mind started playing its old familiar tricks. There were times where I actually thought my heart was going to break wide open over missing Tony. My mind knew how insane the thought was but it was my heart I was having trouble convincing.

With Maggie only coming three days a week and Max staying gone a lot visiting his first girlfriend; the house was way too quiet when I would come home from work. Kate was putting in a lot of hours at her own job, so I was at home alone; a lot. You can make some really bad decisions when left alone too long.

I was busy working on the Thanksgiving display in the bookstore when I had a feeling someone was watching me. I looked up and gasped out loud, despite my efforts to act nonchalant. Tony stood only a few feet away, and he looked really good. He had grown a beard that was shaved close to his face. There were traces of gray that stood out at his temples. He had on a tweed blazer over a sweater with jeans. He looked very distinguished. I stood up on wobbly legs.

"Hey," he said as he smiled in a way I hadn't seen in ages. "Can I talk to you for a minute? Privately?"

"Yeah, sure," I said as I headed towards my office with him following close behind. I passed Tracy at the counter. "Keep an eye on things," I whispered. "I won't be long."

"Okay," she said hesitantly as she eyed Tony.

"Come on in,' I said as I opened the door. "I stood aside as he came through and I could smell his cologne. "Have a seat," I motioned to the chair in front of my desk. I closed the door and came around and sat down. I took a deep breath. "So, what's this all about?"

He looked at me and ran his hand over his beard. "Listen," he said as he fiddled with his car keys. "I'm just going to say this, and I won't blame you if you kick me out of your office."

I tilted my head. "Maybe you just need to say whatever it is you came here to say; I'm busy."

"I know you are," he said as he got up and paced the floor of my office. "I probably should have waited and came by the house, but I've been ordered to stay away."

"Look Tony," I said as I stood up behind my desk.

"No, wait," he said holding up his hand. "Let me just get this out." He looked down at the floor and then looked back up at me. "I've made a mistake."

"What kind of mistake?" I asked slowly.

"Filing for the divorce; it was a mistake. I want to come home." He glanced up at me. "I know I've treated you terribly." He began to pace the floor again. "I take all the blame."

My legs went weak and I plopped down in my chair.

"I've had a lot of time to think about this," he said as he sat back down in the chair across from me. "Suzanne," he leaned across the desk and took my hand in his and it sent a shockwave through my body. "I've missed you more than I thought possible. Please, give me another chance and I'll make it up to you; I promise."

I honestly don't remember the rest of the conversation. All I remember is leaving the bookstore with him and going back to the house. I helped him move all his things back into the house over the Thanksgiving weekend. Maggie, Kate and Gina were shocked, but reserved their comments to each other rather than to me. With Max and Maggie gone for the holiday weekend, we had turned the phone off, determined to be undisturbed as we tried to put our broken marriage back together.

When Monday rolled around, I was walking on air when I went into the bookstore. I got everything up and running and was about to replace the Thanksgiving display with our Christmas decorations, when the phone rang. When I picked up the receiver, I had no idea my life was about to come crashing down on me; again.

"Drexel's bookstore," I said happily.

"Can I speak to Suzanne Peyton, please?"

"This is she," I said slowly, not recognizing the voice on the other end.

"Ah," the man said with a laugh. "I'm sorry to call you at your job, but I am glad to finally get ahold of you."

"I'm sorry; who is this?"

"This is Guy Martin with The Barton Agency; we requested the query of your story?"

"Oh! Yes, Mr. Martin, of course." I began to tremble.

"I called your home last week, didn't your husband tell you?"

"No, he didn't give me the message," I said as the wheels of my mind started to spin out of control.

"Oh," he acted surprised. "Well, I asked him to have you give me a call so we could discuss your work. I told him we are very interested in representing you. We all think your story is very intriguing."

I felt the blood rush to my head and felt my heart pounding in my chest. "Mr. Barton, when, exactly, did you call my house?"

"A few days before Thanksgiving," he sounded confused. "But.."

"Mr. Barton," I interrupted him. "Can I please call you back? I have your number."

"Yes, of course," he said hesitantly.

"Thank you, and I'll speak again with you soon." I hung up before he could say anything else. I turned and went into my office and picked up my purse. My eyes were pulsating with the anger that now raged through my body. "Tracy," I yelled out as I came out of the office.

She came from around the corner of the bookcases. "Yes, Suzanne? What is it?"

"I'm going to be out the rest of the day. If you need anything call me at home." I didn't wait for her response as I went out the door and ran for my car. I got inside and cranked it and tore out of the parking lot, slinging gravel behind me. *'You bastard,'* I yelled as I pulled onto the interstate.

I reached my house in record time and pulled into the driveway. I got out of the car and left the door standing open as I rushed across the street to our *nosy* neighbor's house; the woman Tony hated and accused of spying on him all the time. For once I prayed he had been right. I rang the doorbell and then banged on her door. I turned to see Maggie rushing across the street to where I was.

"What on earth are you doing?" she asked breathlessly.

About that time my neighbor, Mrs. Miller, opened the door. "Oh, Mrs. Miller," I turned to face her. "I'm so sorry to disturb you, but I need a favor."

She pulled the housecoat she had on closer to her body. "Well," she said hesitantly, "I'll try. What is it?"

I took a deep breath. "I know you pay special attention to what goes on in our neighborhood, and I'm sure you probably know that before this past weekend, my husband had moved out."

"Well," she said looking down.

"I just want to know, if by any chance, did you see him going into our house while I was recently out of town?"

"Oh, Suzanne," Maggie reached and touched my arm.

I brushed her hand away. "It's really very important, Mrs. Miller, or I wouldn't ask."

"Okay," she said as she took off her glasses. "Yes, I saw him. One day last week, I saw a blonde-headed woman bring him to the house. I've seen that black sports car before that they were in. Anyway, she pulled up and let him out and he went inside while she pulled down into the next block and waited on him. He was in there quite awhile before he came out and she pulled back up and he got in and they took off."

I felt my blood pressure go through the roof. "Thank you, Mrs. Miller; you've been very helpful." I turned and went down her front steps and stormed back across the street with Maggie running to keep up with me. "That liar!" I screamed as I slammed my car door and went into the house.

"Will you please tell me what is going on?" Maggie asked as she caught up with me in the living room of the house.

"Tony! He took a phone call from an agency that is interested in publishing my book! He never said a word to me about it though," I said as I grabbed one of the boxes from the corner that we had used when he had moved back home. I began grabbing anything that even looked like belonged to him and started throwing them in the box. At some point, I heard glass shatter and I could have cared less. "He came back for the money! Not for me!"

I saw the look on Maggie's face change and she reached and picked up a picture of me and Tony from the mantel and threw it in the box. We went through the upstairs closets and took out his clothes and fishing tackle and brought it all downstairs and put them in garbage bags. When we finished, she helped me load everything into the trunk of my car.

Thirty minutes later, I pulled into his company's parking garage and found his BMW backed into his spot. I got out and popped the trunk and ripped the garbage bags open and threw all his things on the hood of his car. I took the box with all his, now broken, racquetball trophies and took the elevator up to his office. I stormed past his secretary and barged into his office. The woman I had seen, and the same one Mrs. Miller described, was right beside him at his desk. Before either one of them could react, I stormed over and threw the box of his broken trophies on his desk. The box tilted and they all fell out; some landing on the desk and others on the floor.

"Suzanne!" Tony said jumping up from his desk. "What the hell?" The woman turned and ran from the office.

"You said I was crazy! You threatened to have me committed!" I yelled. "That is," I said in a low, cold, voice, "until you thought I would make money off Virginia's story." I saw the shock on his face. "Oh, yes, I know all about it, Tony. You're such a liar! You've been cheating with her," I motioned behind me, "for God knows how long, but you were ready to come home and still continue to see her!" I turned and walked towards the door.

"I don't know what you're talking about," he stammered.

"Let me put it in simple terms for you then," I said turning to face him. "You keep your ass away from me and don't you dare come to the house or my job ever again! The locks at the house will be changed today!"

"What about my clothes?"

I smiled. "You'll find them all over your car in the parking garage, along with everything else you own." I walked out his office and saw the *woman* he had been seeing hiding in a corner. I stopped. "Oh, and honey, you can have him! Good luck!"

I went back to the garage and got in my car and sped away. A thousand pounds of tension I didn't even know I was carrying, left my body. I drove home and told Maggie everything and then sent her home early. I just wanted to be alone.

After I calmed down, I called Mr. Barton back, only to be discouraged again. He said he would have to have the *diary* I had found. When I tried to explain to him that *I* had written the diary entries but could prove they were true, he was no longer interested. He calmly told me how much he wanted to represent me, but if I wasn't willing to give up the *real diary,* his hands were tied. I hung up the phone and screamed. Tony had come back home and put me through all this hell for nothing! I had completely forgotten that I had promised Kate that I would meet her for dinner and when I didn't show up and she couldn't reach anybody at the house, she came looking for me. By the time she found me, I was well on my way to being severely inebriated.

I didn't see her as she made her way across the backyard to where I was sitting in a lawn chair under the trees. "I've been beating on the front door forever before I found my key."

I jumped when she spoke and dropped the bottled wine cooler in the grass. "You scared the hell out of me," I said as I leaned forward to pick it up and almost fell out of my chair. I sat back up and wrapped the throw I had across my shoulders tighter around my body.

"What are you doing out here getting smashed," she reached and picked up one of the empty bottles, "on this *stuff.* I would have thought you would remember the headache these things give you."

"It's all they had at the convenience store. I broke all the bottles of liquor that was in the house."

She hesitated. "Where's Tony?"

"Long gone," I said as I polished off the bottle and reached in the carton and took out another one and opened it. "You want one?" I offered as I pulled another from the carton.

"No," she said shaking her head. "I think one drunk is enough, especially on that stuff." She pulled a lawn chair over and sat down. "Why don't you tell me what's going on?"

"Oh, nothing really, I just busted Tony's ass."

"So, I heard," she said making a face.

"Who told you?"

"Well, when you didn't show up and I couldn't get anybody to answer the phone, I called Maggie and she filled me in. She thought you might be home and just not answering the phone. Remind me when we go inside to call her and let her know you're okay; or rather will be." She said with a faint smile. "Look, I wish I could say I'm sorry, but I'm not. I'm only sorry you gave him another chance to hurt you."

"Oh, Kate," I said leaning back into the chair. "My life is such a train wreck. I don't know what I'm going to do." I took another drink from the bottle. "Another marriage has officially ended. That makes three if you're counting. My daughter is pregnant and," I laughed, "I offered to adopt her baby! Me! Can you imagine?"

"Now, you listen to me," she said as she leaned forward in her chair. "Failed marriages have nothing to do with you being a great mother and you are! This baby will be lucky to get you!"

"Yeah, right," I said as I lit a cigarette and blew out the smoke. "I'm not sure Sam would agree with you." I took another drag from the cigarette. "Did Maggie tell you an agent called and wanted to represent my book?"

"What? No, she didn't tell me! That's great!"

I sighed. "No, it's not. The man that called thought I had really found an ancient hundred-year-old diary. He didn't believe I had written it."

"What *diary?*"

"Oh, that's right. You don't know because I never showed you because I was afraid you would *really* think I was crazy!" I crushed the cigarette out in the ashtray and put my hands over my face and cried.

"Okay," Kate said as she got up from her chair and pulled me up by the arm. "We're going inside now; it's freezing out here."

I figured she wanted to hurry up and get me inside before I started talking about being reincarnated again and the neighbors might hear. She pulled me by the arm all the way into the house and closed and locked the French doors behind us. She led me upstairs and pulled a pair of pjs out and put them on me and laid me in the bed and covered me up. I was sound asleep in minutes.

The next morning, I woke with a pounding headache. I stumbled into the bathroom and pulled the aspirin bottle from the medicine cabinet and put two in my mouth. I cupped my hands under the faucet to get enough water in me to swallow them. I slowly made my way downstairs and found Kate sitting at the bar reading the newspaper.

"Oh, hey," I said when I saw her. "You stayed."

"You didn't think I was going to leave you alone in the shape you were in last night, did you?" She folded the newspaper and laid it on the bar.

"Sorry about that," I said as I eased onto a barstool. I leaned forward and put my elbows on the bar and propped my head in my hands. "How the hell does this keep happening to me?"

"Bad choice of poison, I'd say." She got up and went over to the cabinet and pulled down a bottle of vodka from above the sink.

"I forgot that was up there," I moaned.

"Well, it's just what you need right now. I'm going to fix you a Bloody Mary."

"Oh Kate, no," I protested.

"It's the only thing that's going to get you over the hump." She fixed the drink and brought it over and sat it in front of me. "Drink up."

"I need a cigarette."

She slid a package and lighter over to me and got up and got an ashtray from the counter and brought it over to the bar. "Now, tell me what you were talking about last night."

I looked up at her. "You don't honestly expect me to remember what I said last night, do you?"

"The part about the *diary*," she said raising her eyebrows.

I ran my hands through my hair and winced at the pain of anything touching my head. "The journal is in my purse; it's in the den."

She got up and went and got my purse and brought it to me. I pulled out the journal and handed it to her. I sighed. "You might as well read it."

She took the journal and I watched her face as she read the entries. More than once I could see the shock on her face. She finally looked up at me. "This doesn't sound anything like you."

"That's because it wasn't me writing them. Please don't ask me to go into details right now, because I can't. But, I've proven every one of the diary entries are true; even the part that she was raised in wealth. We found a sixty-one page will. Plus, you may have seen some of the words, like *attestation,* I had to look it up. I had never heard of the word before, much less used it."

"Oh wow," she said as she handed the journal back to me. "I know I was hard on you when you told me what you thought was really happening, and I'm sorry, it was just all so weird."

"No kidding," I said as I picked up the glass and took a drink. "Oh," I made a face. "I'm not sure I can get this down."

"Well, you're going to even if I have to pour it down you. You'll feel better; trust me. So, where is this book you've written?"

"It's in my bag in the den. You can read it if you want to."

"I intend to," she said with a smile.

Max came in the back door into the kitchen. "Hey everybody," he said with a smile. "Wow, Mom, you look bad."

"She's just sick…." Kate started to make excuses.

"No," I said as I straightened myself on the barstool. "I promised him I wouldn't lie again. The truth is Max, I caught Tony in a lie, we had it out and I kicked him out for good. And then," I said looking down, "I got drunk. I have a really bad hangover."

Max laughed. "Okay, I'm sorry you're hungover, but I'm really glad he's gone for good." He came over and hugged me and I winced. I felt like a truck had hit me. "Okay, the confessional is now over. I've got to go back to bed." I got up and climbed the staircase back to my room and curled up in the covers of the bed and went back to sleep. Sometime later, the ringing of the phone woke me up. I rolled over and pulled the pillow over my head. But, a few minutes later, Kate came in and lightly touched my arm. I pulled the pillow back and looked up at her. She had the cordless phone from downstairs in her hand. "It's Paul, Mrs. Drexel's son." I took the phone from her and she left the room, closing the door behind her. After I hung up the phone, I went downstairs and found Kate and Max in the den watching a movie.

"What did Paul want?" Kate asked when she saw me come into the room.

I put the phone back on its base and went over to the couch and motioned for Max to scoot over, and sat down. "He wants to meet with me tomorrow at *his house.*" I sighed.

"What for?" Kate asked as she leaned forward, past Max, to face me.

"I'm sure it's to go over some scheme he wants to implement after the first of the year. He's always trying to come up with a way to make more money without spending any."

# Chapter 25

*Suzanne*

I arrived at Paul's house and he escorted me into his living room. I was surprised to see Mrs. Drexel sitting in a chair in the corner. I knew she had been released from the hospital, but I wasn't aware she was living with them. I sat down in a chair next to her. I reached and took her hand and she attempted to smile. She said something, but it was hard to understand, so I just smiled back at her.

Paul didn't waste any time dropping the bombshell. He sat across from us on the sofa and looked directly into my eyes and told me they had decided to sell the bookstore. I gasped out loud. My body went numb as he promised they were going to give me a substantial severance package. The room grew quiet. I glanced over at Carol and she dropped her head.

"When are you planning on doing this?" I asked as I turned to face Paul again.

"The first of the year. We think we have a prospective buyer in place. We'll know more around the middle of January."

"I'm sorry," Mrs. Drexel struggled, but pushed the words out.

"Oh, no Mrs. Drexel," I said as I squeezed her hand. "I understand." I lied through my teeth; I didn't understand any of it. My world was spinning out of control and down some dark black hole.

I barely remember leaving their house. I drove in complete silence and knew I needed to go home and not to the bookstore; not at that moment. I pulled in the driveway and was relieved to see Maggie's car sitting there. I parked in the garage and went in through the door to the kitchen. She turned to face me and when she did I broke down and sobbed. She rushed to me and wrapped her arms around me. "What's happened?"

"They're selling the bookstore," I managed to get out between the racking sobs. She knew what this meant. I wasn't just out of a job; I was now without a way to pay the mortgage payments on the house until school was out; the agreement I made in the divorce. Maggie led me to the den and sat me down.

"Sit here and I'm going to get you some hot tea."

When she left the room I aimlessly went over and pulled the curtain back and just stared out the window. I felt hollowed out; empty. Maggie came back in a few minutes later and handed me a mug of hot tea.

"I called Kate; she's on her way," she said as I took the mug from her hand.

"What am I going to do?" I went back over to the couch and sat down and put the mug on the coffee table. I ran my hands through my hair. "They're going to give me a severance package, but I know Paul well enough to know it won't be *that* big." I got up and paced the floor. I can't take anymore! I just can't!"

Kate came in the front door and when she saw me, she rushed over and hugged me. "Oh, Suzanne, I'm so sorry."

"Aren't you supposed to be at work?" I asked as I pulled back from her.

"I told them I had an emergency," She said as she reached and brushed my hair out of my face.

I sighed. "I don't know what I'm going to do."

"We'll think of something; we always do," she said as she smiled and reached and took my hand.

The phone rang and Maggie answered it. "It's Gina," she said as she handed me the cordless.

I took the phone and started crying all over again as I told my sister the latest news. She immediately told me to pack everything up and come stay with her. The thought of moving back to the very place I had run from when I was eighteen made me ill. I didn't hate the town; I hated going backwards. I had worked hard to make a life for myself and my kids, but my options were narrowing by the minute.

I hung the phone up and turned to face Maggie and Kate. "Gina wants me to pack everything up and put it in storage and come stay with her for a while."

Maggie got up from the couch and walked over and rubbed my back. "You know, right now, I think that might be a God send for you. You could go there and just live off your severance package for a while. I know Gina's not going to charge you anything for staying, so you wouldn't be under any pressure."

"Plus," Kate piped in, "all the good companies won't start hiring again until after the first quarter."

"I wanted to start over; fresh, but not like this. I feel like the rug has been jerked from under my feet. And the worst part is, Tony won!"

"Why do you think Tony won?"

"He still has his job and once I move out, he will move right back in and he will have our house all to himself and I'm sure he will waste no time moving *that woman* in."

"Okay," Kate said as she put her hands on her hips. "You have got to get Tony out of your mind now! He's only holding you back from picking up the pieces of your life and moving on! I know it seems hard right now, but you need to concentrate on you and Max."

"Oh my God! I hadn't even thought about Max! I can't pull him out of his school! He's just started dating; and he has his friends!" I went over to the couch and sat down and covered my face with my hands."

"I bet Terry's parents would let him stay with them until school is out," Maggie said.

I looked up at her and slowly nodded. "They might."

"Great idea Maggie," Kate smiled at her. "You can go to Gina's and regroup and Maggie and I will keep an eye on Max. It will work, Suzanne, you'll see."

The following weeks found me packing my belongings and taking inventory for Paul at the bookstore. I was working non-stop in an attempt to keep my mind off the fact that my entire life was changing right before my eyes; whether I liked it or not. I had talked to Max's friend's parents and explained my dilemma to them and they had been more than willing to help by letting Max stay with them until school was out. I think both the boys loved the idea of bunking together for the next six months.

Paul agreed to allow me to leave as soon as the inventory was finished and I must admit, the severance package was much bigger than I thought. I was relieved knowing it would easily last until school was out and I could come back to Dallas and find a new job and a new place to live. But, in the meantime, I would stay at Gina's and give myself a chance to heal. At least that's what I told myself as I pulled onto the freeway headed back to Marshall. I cried all the way.

Gina and Doug met me at the storage unit and helped me unload the U-Haul, and then followed me to drop it off. I was beyond exhausted when I pulled into their driveway that afternoon. I felt totally defeated as I climbed their staircase back to my childhood bedroom; once again. I closed the door behind me and remembered what I had *wished* for the last time I was here. I had wished I could live here again, but not like this. It wasn't so much the loss of my beloved bookstore, my house, my son or my husband. I felt like my life had come untethered from whatever had kept it tied together. I was lost; period.

I had survived so many things in my life, I didn't know how to accept the defeat that was growing inside of me. I was back where I started; alone, just like Virginia. My kids were gone too. I laid across the bed. I didn't have the energy or the fortitude to begin to unpack my bags or the small box of books I had brought. I closed my eyes and so desperately just wanted the world to stop spinning and let me off. Gina knocked on the door. I closed my eyes tighter; I wasn't ready for *anybody,* not even her, but I was in her house. "Come in," I managed.

She opened the door and came in and closed it behind her. I opened my eyes to see her standing there staring at me. I raised up on my elbows and sighed. "So, here I am, back where I started."

She had a glass of Coke in her hand and sat it on the table beside the bed and sat down next to me. "You *know* everything is going to be okay. It may not look like it right now, but you know it will."

I let her words soak in. "Really?" I sat up on the bed and stared at her. "When? How many times Gina? How many times do I have to do this?"

"You'll beat this, you always do, and you'll get right back up on your feet."

"Why should I get back up again? Just so somebody can knock me down again?"

"Look," she said as she reached and put her hand on my knee. "I wouldn't dream of robbing you of this pity party. Hell, I don't know how you've made it through most of the things that have happened to you, but you have." She stood up then. "Suzanne, there is a little girl coming in March that is counting on you to be the strong and loving woman that you have always been."

I fell back on the bed and closed my eyes and grimaced at the thought of the offer I had made to Sam. Would she even let me adopt the baby if she thought I couldn't even take care of myself and her little brother? And wouldn't she be right? Then it hit me.

"Who told you about the baby?" I sat up and faced her.

"Max did. I talked to him the other day when I called the house. Don't be mad at him, he thought you had already told me, and I'm wondering why you haven't."

"Oh, Gina. What am I going to do? I can't even take care of me and Max right now, how am I going to be able to take on a baby?"

"Look! I will allow you to wallow in this self-pity, but I will not stand here and let you beat yourself up! You will find your way out of this!" She walked to the door. "Why don't you run you a hot bath and rest. That's what you need now. Come downstairs when you're ready." She went out and closed the door behind her.

I took her advice and filled the claw-foot tub with hot water and climbed in. I began to cry and this time I let it all out. I allowed myself to cry over everything I had lost. By the time I was finished I was so sleepy, I barely got into my pjs and crawled into bed before sleep took me. I didn't wake up until the next morning as sunlight trickled through the curtains. I couldn't remember the last time I had woke up and not had a single, solitary, thing that demanded my attention. Maybe Kate and Maggie were right; maybe this was exactly what I needed; at least for now.

I got dressed and put my hair up in a ponytail. I went downstairs to find Gina, but found a note instead. *'Ran to the store – make yourself at home – EAT!* I smiled and it felt good. I opened the refrigerator and pulled the stuff out for a sandwich and grabbed a can of Coke. I was busy fixing the sandwich when the phone rang. I thought it might be her, so I answered it. It wasn't my sister, but Deidre, my counselor. I had skipped a lot of appointments lately. She said she had called my emergency contact, Maggie, and she had given her Gina's number. I brought her up to speed on the train wreck that was currently my life.

"I'm really sorry to hear you are going through so much right now," she said with genuine sympathy. "I wish you would have called me."

I sighed. "I no longer have insurance; it was through the bookstore. And besides," I said as I leaned against the kitchen counter, "I'm not sure anybody can really help right now. It's just going to take me some time to get it together again."

"Well," she said slowly, "I like the fact that you sound hopeful."

"Just be glad you didn't call me yesterday," I said with a laugh.

"Bad, huh?"

"Very," I said as I took my plate over to the table and sat down.

"Well, listen, insurance or not, please call me if you need to talk. Okay?"

"I will, and thanks Deidre."

"Now listen, if you run into any of those *Virginia haters,* and they try anything with you, you just call and I'll come get you."

Her words made me smile. "I'm really glad I found you."

"Well, I'm still here if you need me. I mean it, if things get too tough, just call me."

I hung up the phone and was so grateful to have people like Deidre in my corner. A blessing, no doubt. I had only taken a few bites of my sandwich when I looked out the window and saw my mother pull up out front. I shook my head. I wasn't ready to face her alone without Gina with me. I took a deep breath just as she came in the front door.

"Suzanne?"

"Back here," I yelled.

She came into the kitchen and sat down across from me at the table. "Where's Gina?"

"She's running some errands," I said as I took another bite of my sandwich. "You want one?" I asked pointing to the plate.

"No, I've already eaten. I'm really sorry you lost your job. Gina told me."

I nodded my head. "I figured she did." I noticed she had a brown envelope in her hand. "What's that?"

"I found some more pictures of Virginia," she said as she pulled them from the envelope.

I wiped my hands and mouth on a napkin and picked up one of the pictures. It was Virginia when she appeared to be in her sixties. She had on a fur and really nice jewelry as well. Her hair was coifed close to her head; very stylish. "Where did you get these from?"

"I hadn't gone through all of the things I got when your grandmother died. I just figured it was a lot of junk; she never threw anything away and you know we were never close. I had just pushed the box to the back of my closet." She looked me straight in the eye and for once I could see the regret there for our situation being so similar. "I think I know what the symbolism was of the four boxes in your dream."

"Oh yeah?" I asked looking up at her.

"I think it's the four generations of women; mothers and daughters that have had real problems between them that wasn't really of their own making."

I nodded. "That's the same conclusion Maggie came up with." I looked up at her then and saw that she was misty eyed. This was the closest thing to an apology as I was ever going to get for the way she had treated me for as long as I could remember. "Well," I dropped my head. "You know my relationship is no better with my own daughter. Maybe it's time for all of this to just stop. Maybe we need to forget everything that has happened in the past and start over." I looked back up at her.

She nodded her head. "You know my mother always treated me differently than she did my brother and sister. Nothing I ever did was good enough."

I knew then she was trying to offer an explanation of why she had treated me the way she had and suddenly, I did understand. I knew deep down that any resentment I had towards her had just floated away. We might never be close in a way that either of us wanted, but I knew we would never again be the way we had to each other. And that was enough.

She got up to leave and stopped in the doorway and turned to face me once again. "You know, I really do believe you were her; Virginia, I mean." She turned then and quietly left the house and I watched out the window as she drove away.

For the next month, I stayed holed up in my childhood bedroom and finished writing mine and Virginia's story. I never dreamed it would run so parallel. As each chapter was finished, my mood began to lift and in the Spring, I stood beside my daughter in the delivery room and welcomed a sweet baby girl into the world. A true gift from God to sooth my broken heart.

# Chapter 26

*Virginia*

*It has been years since I have seen my children. Grandmother Abby made every attempt to find a way to get them away from Andrew, all to no avail. She continued to write letters addressed to me to Andrew's house so that he wouldn't suspect I was here. Grandmother sold Grandfather's business to be able to continue to send money so Andrew wouldn't be tempted to mistreat the children. She passed away never seeing my children's faces other than in the one photograph she had paid to have taken and is now the only photograph I have of them as well. They are frozen in time at an age they have long since passed. I dare to say I fear I might not recognize them now, especially young Jonathan. I grieved for many months after losing Grandmother, but then, I had to concentrate on trying to get the children from Andrew, it was her dying wish.*

*I took the money she left me and bought a small bungalow in Carrollton, a small town outside New Orleans. No one knows me here, and I have been attending the Catholic Church under the pretense of being a widow. I saved every penny I could earn, from sitting with children to cleaning houses, to hire an attorney to represent me in my petition for divorce.*

*I disguised myself and traveled by train once again to Texas, but this time I did not sleep at all during the trip. I stayed once again in the hotel by the train station. I met with my attorney in the restaurant of the hotel and told him everything that had happened when I still lived at Andrew's house. He seemed a very compassionate man and assured me we would, in fact, win and I would be able to take my children back home with me to Louisiana. I left without making any attempts to see the children at the advice of the attorney. I came back to Carrollton to await my court date. Two months later, my attorney wired me that the date had been set.*

*I walked into the courtroom and saw Andrew sitting at a table next to his attorney. He was clean shaven and dressed in a nice, but conservative suit. My chest grew tight with anxiety at the sight of him. As the trial began, witness after witness took the stand to testify against me. The men and women that had been at the hotel the night that Andrew had lied and said Grandmother Abby was waiting for me, were there to testify as well. They stated they had seen me there dressed quite fashionably when Andrew and the children came in dressed no better than the poorest of people. Then, the doctor took the stand to say that he had in fact treated Elisabeth after an apparent beating from me on the same night. The doctor further testified that he had been summoned to treat me on at least two other occasions when I had harmed myself in such a way as to lose the children I carried in my womb at the time.*

*I sat aghast as I listened to the brutal lies they told about me, even though they had sworn on the Bible to tell the truth. Then, it occurred to me that it was truth to them. It was exactly what they had observed, all planned and plotted by Andrew himself. Although, none of their testimonies would deal the blow that Andrew did in the end. I had asked for custody of Elisabeth and Jonathan in my petition for divorce and the judge inquired of me as to why I was not also seeking the custody of the youngest child, a boy by the name of Addison. When I told the judge, I was not familiar with the child in question, the onlookers in the courtroom hissed and yelled their objections. Andrew then took the stand and testified that I had been with child when I had abandoned him and our children. He then added that shortly before I had filed the petition for divorce that I had sent the child, now three-years old, back on a train by himself. He said I had pinned a note to him that read, 'Andrew, if you don't want him, put him in a home.' Once again, the crowd in the courtroom shouted and yelled horrific things.*

*When Andrew testified that the child was three years old, the truth of the matter slowly crept up my spine. I remembered once more the night that I poured the noxious liquid into the torn material and held it over Esther's face and then switched clothes with her. It was then that the full knowledge of what had happened that fateful night came to me. I was not the woman in the New Orleans nightgown that he found when he made his way up the stairs into the makeshift bedroom in the attic. In his drunken state, he did not realize, until it was too late, what he had done. I knew at that very moment, in that courtroom, I would never again be with my children, and Andrew would chase me the rest of his life and mine. I ran that night to keep Andrew from taking my life. I realized now, even though I had escaped, he had surely taken my life by taking my children, forever, away from me.*

# Chapter 27

*Suzanne*

Six months later, as I packed my bags and got ready to move back into the real world, with a baby in tow, Gina wanted one last day together. She wanted me to go with her to an art show that was being held in downtown Marshall. So, with a baby on my hip, we strolled through the gallery looking at all the work from talented local artists. Both of us stopped dead in our tracks when we saw a shadow box hanging on the wall. The wooden box, we quickly discovered, had once been the lid from a keepsake box. We spotted the keyhole on the side. The word 'Dream' was carved in wood and attached to the top. Inside the mirrored lid, there was a Mardi Gras court jester dressed in purple and gold, sitting atop a four-inch ruler that had *'Forget Me Not'* flowers growing up the side of it. On the mirror, these words were written: *Dreams Really Do Come True.*

I gasped out loud and the artist came up behind us and claimed the work as her own. She just shook her head as she told me she didn't know why she had done this particular piece; as it was not her normal medium of art. I told her the story about Virginia. When I had finished, she had tears in her eyes. She reached and took the shadow box from the wall and handed it to me. "I just know you're supposed to have this."

We took the box back to Gina's house and sat it on the table. There was a piece of paper covering the back of the box telling about the artist and her work. I pulled the paper loose and there in the center was the letter *'B'*. Virginia's maiden name was *Barrister*. There were swirls in each of the four corners; just like on the mirror I had seen in my dream. I knew I had just been reunited, with at least the lid, of Virginia's keepsake box. But wasn't the lid the most important part in the dream? By opening that box, my grandmother, Virginia's only daughter, had made it possible to bury all the lies once and for all.

A year later I would find myself back at Drexel's bookstore. It no longer carried my friends name and I wasn't there to manage the store. I stood at a podium in the back of the store telling a large group of customers all about my book, *Virginia's Diary.*

Later, as I signed books, I glanced over at Gina, who stood holding my beautiful baby girl; who I had named Abby. Just at that moment, a smile crossed Abby's face and the world seemed to stop turning for a moment. I suddenly caught sight of something familiar in her beautiful eyes; a look I could swear I had seen before, in another time and another place.

Later that night after tucking Abby into bed, I too fell into a blissful sleep. I dreamed I was riding in what appeared to be a brand-new trolley car. The wood was so pristine and beautiful. In my peripheral vision, I saw an old white-haired woman sitting next to me and knew it was Virginia. The trolley car stopped in front of the arch of Palmer Park on Carrollton Avenue in New Orleans. I watched as the old woman slowly made her way down the aisle and got off. I looked out the window of the trolley and saw her go through the archway of the park and disappear into a beautiful mist of color. Virginia was finally free, and so was I.

CPSIA information can be obtained
at www.ICGtesting.com
Printed in the USA
LVHW010423160120
643424LV00004B/61

9 780578 493411